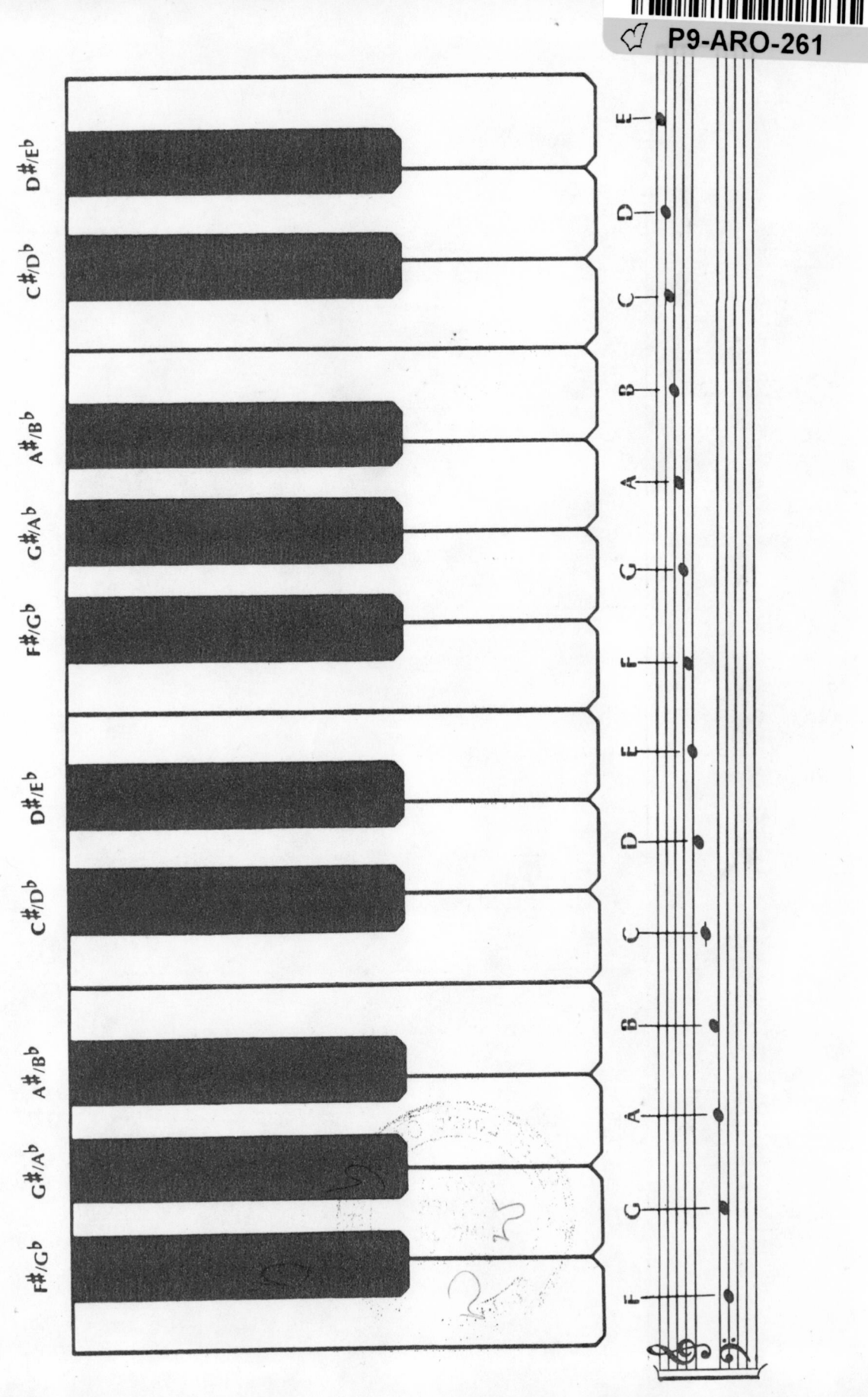

Silver Burdett
music
Centennial Edition

Elizabeth Crook

Bennett Reimer

David S. Walker

SILVER BURDETT COMPANY MORRISTOWN, NEW JERSEY

ATLANTA, GA · CINCINNATI, OH · DALLAS, TX · NORTHFIELD, IL · SAN CARLOS, CA · AGINCOURT, ONTARIO

Contents

Using What You Know About Tone Color

Music is made of sounds and silences. There are many different kinds of sounds (tone colors) and many different ways to combine them. Because of this, we will probably never run out of interesting ways to create music with a variety of tone colors.

Some of the tone colors suggested by the photographs on these pages are familiar. Others may be less familiar. In this section you will review some things you know about how tone colors are used in music. You will also learn a few new things about tone color.

NATURAL SOUNDS

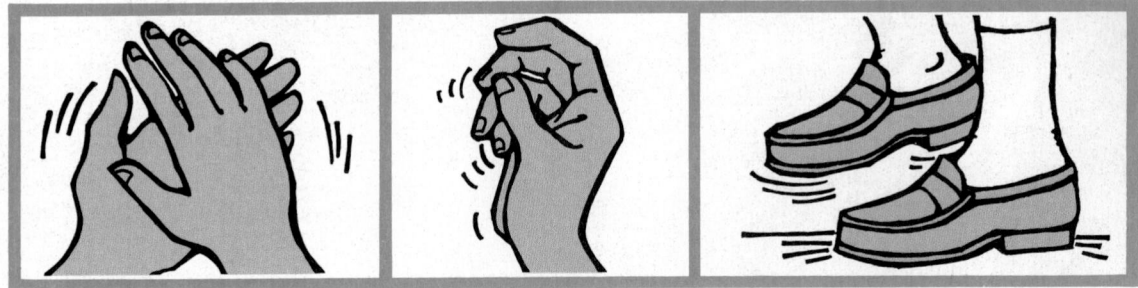

What is your favorite record? Have you ever wondered why it is your favorite? One of the reasons might be the sound, or the tone color, of the instruments or voices that are used.

Bring in your favorite record from home. Share it with your friends and ask them what tone colors they hear in the music.

As you listen to *Porcupine Rock,* think about the tone colors that give this piece its own special sound.

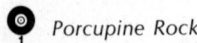 *Porcupine Rock*

When you listen to *Porcupine Rock* again, keep time to the music by clapping, snapping, or tapping the steady beat. Think of the claps, snaps, and taps as *natural sounds.*

Think of a natural sound to use and keep time to the steady beat as you listen to "Joy to the World."

Joy to the World WORDS AND MUSIC BY HOYT AXTON

1. Jer - e - mi - ah was a bull - frog, was a good__ friend of

mine. Nev - er un - der - stood a sin - gle word he said,__ but we

al-ways had a might-y fine time._   Yes we al-ways had a might-y fine

COUNTERMELODY

Sing-ing, joy   to the world.   Joy   to the world;

time.   Sing-ing, joy   to the world.   All _____ the boys and girls_ now.

Joy,   joy,   joy,   joy,

Joy   to the fish - es   in   the deep blue   sea.____

Joy   to___ you and   me.___

Joy   to___ you and   me.___

2. If I were the king of the world, tell you what I'd do,
Throw away the fears and the tears and the jeers,
And have a good time with you.
Yes, I'll have a good time with you. *Refrain*

📖 For percussion parts, see p. 223.

5

HAND JIVE

You can "play" a hand-jive pattern using natural sounds. Keep the beat with this one as you listen to "Cum-ma-la Be-stay."

L   R   L   R

snap   clap   clap

Cum-ma-la Be-stay

WORDS AND MUSIC BY DONNY BURKE, JERRY VANCE, AND TERRY PHILIPS

© 1972 BY POPDRAW MUSIC CORP., NEW YORK. NEW YORK

SOLO

Bam - a - lam - a-cum-ma-la, Cum-ma-la be-stay.

CHORUS

Bam - a - lam - a-cum-ma-la,

Cum-ma-la be - stay.

SOLO

Bam-a-lam-a-cum-ma-la, Cum-ma-la be - stay.

CHORUS

Bam - a - lam - a - cum-ma - la, Cum - ma - la be - stay.

SOLO

In the sum-mer - time__ when the sun goes down And the heat starts ris - ing

off the ground,__ My friends and I we gath-er round,__ We

dance and sing to the cum-ma - la sound.

CHORUS

Cum-ma-la sound,

SOLO

Cum-ma-la sound.

ALL

Ev - 'ry - bod - y forms a cir - cle;__

6

Now some-bod-y jumps in-side.___ *(Solo singer jumps inside circle.)* You

clap your hands, You stamp your feet,___

You do the jerk To the cum-ma-la beat.___

SOLO Bam-a-lam-a-cum-ma-la, Cum-ma-la be-stay. *CHORUS* Bam-a-lam-a-cum-ma-la,

Cum-ma-la be-stay. *SOLO* Bam-a-lam-a-cum-ma-la, Cum-ma-la be-stay.

ALL Bam-a-lam-a-cum-ma-la, Cum-ma-la be-stay.

Try these hand jives with the recording. The second one will be a real challenge.

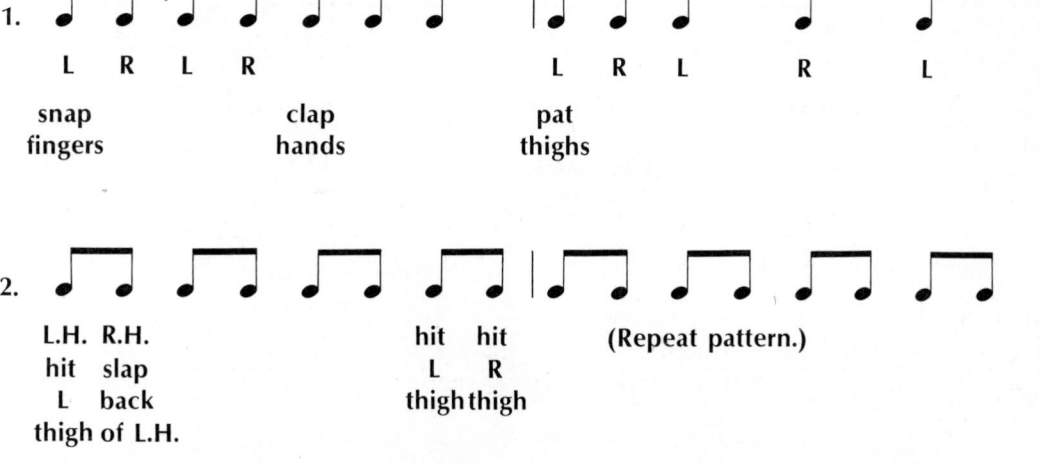

1.

L R L R   L R L R L

snap
fingers

clap
hands

pat
thighs

2.

L.H. R.H.   hit hit   (Repeat pattern.)
hit slap   L R
 L back   thigh thigh
thigh of L.H.

NATURAL SOUNDS IN SONG ACCOMPANIMENTS

In this arrangement of "Shoeflies," natural sounds are used as part of the instrumental accompaniment. Can you hear what they are? In what part of the song do you hear the natural sounds?

Shoeflies

WORDS AND MUSIC BY BOB SAKAYAMA

Shoe-flies fast-er than me,___ I got-ta run, run, run,___ or

I won't see it. And when the man says, "Fit my foot,"___

Shoe-flies.___ Dom-i-noes___

more than I do,___ and there's a chance that he may real-ly ev-en

know more than you,___ And when the man says,

"I don't know what to do," Dom-i-noes.___

But-ter-flies___ ov-er the hill,___ If

you can't find___ her then no - bod - y will.___

And when the man says, "Bake my bread,"___ But - ter - flies.___

Bob Sakayama, the composer of "Shoeflies," uses natural sounds in his performance of the song. Listen for the stamps and tongue clicks used in the introduction and interludes.

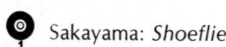 Sakayama: *Shoeflies*

LINE DANCE

R means right foot; L means left foot.

Pattern A

Step backward R, L, R. Touch L next to R (4 beats).

Step forward L, R, L. Touch R next to L (4 beats).

Repeat backward and forward pattern (8 beats).

Pattern B

Step sideways R, L, R. Touch L next to R (4 beats).

Step sideways L, R, L. Touch R next to L (4 beats).

Repeat R and L sideways pattern (8 beats).

Pattern C

Jump forward and hold for one beat (2 beats).

Jump backward and hold for one beat (2 beats).

Jump forward, then backward (2 beats).

Click heels twice and turn to face in another direction.

Repeat the dance.

HEEL-TAPPING ACCOMPANIMENTS

Heel-tapping is a natural sound to use as a rhythm accompaniment
for this Newfoundland dance tune. Try tapping heels, one after
the other, to keep the steady beat as you listen to "I'se the B'y."

I'se the B'y

FOLK SONG FROM NEWFOUNDLAND   NEW WORDS AND NEW MUSIC ADAPTATION BY OSCAR BRAND

TRO—© COPYRIGHT 1957 HOLLIS MUSIC, INC., NEW YORK, N.Y. USED BY PERMISSION.

1. I'se the b'y that builds the boat, I'se the b'y that sails her.
2. I took Li - za to the dance; Faith, but she could trav - el.
3. Su - san White is out of sight, Hid - ing like Jack Hor - ner.

I'se the b'y that catch-es the fish And brings them home to Li - za.
Ev - 'ry step that Li - za took ___ Covered an acre of grav - el.
Choose a lad and take ___ him back, ___ Kiss him in the cor - ner.

REFRAIN

Swing your part - ner, Sal - ly Tib - ble, Swing your part - ner, Sal - ly Brown.

Swing your part - ner, ev - 'ry - one, All a - round ___ the cir - cle.

Now try heel-tapping one of these rhythm patterns in 6/8 meter
to accompany the song.

1.
2.

For percussion parts, see p. 226.

10

IDENTIFYING
NATURAL SOUNDS

Listen for the different ways that natural sounds are used in this music. Can you identify each sound?

 Collage of Natural Sounds

THE SOUND OF PERCUSSION

On the recording of this song you will hear an accompaniment played on guitar and bass. You will also hear a percussion instrument. As you listen to the recording, look at the photographs on pages 2 and 3 in your book. Pick out the photograph of the percussion instrument you hear.

When you sing the song, fill in the long sounds (shown in the color boxes) with a pattern of your own.

Gingele WORDS AND MUSIC BY ASTRUD GILBERTO

© 1972 BY POPDRAW MUSIC CORP. & GREGMAR MUSIC, NEW YORK, NEW YORK

Gin-ge-le, ye-le,_____ Gin-ge-le, ye-la._____

Gin-ge-le, ye-le,_____ Gin-ge-le, ye-la._____

If you give me Gin-ge-le, I will give you Gin-ge-le.

If you give me Gin-ge-la, I will give you Gin-ge-

la. Gin-ge-le, ye-le,_____ Gin-ge-le, ye-la._____

Gin-ge-le, ye-le,_____ Gin-ge-le, ye-la._____

ONE INSTRUMENT—TWO DIFFERENT SOUNDS

Practice one of these percussion parts to play as an accompaniment for "Gingele." Notice how you can change the tone color by playing the same instrument in different ways. For notes with down stems, hold the cowbell with cupped hand. For notes with up stems, hold the cowbell with open hand.

cowbell hit with a clave

guiro

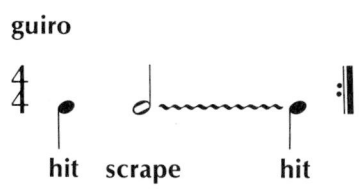

hit   scrape   hit

bongo

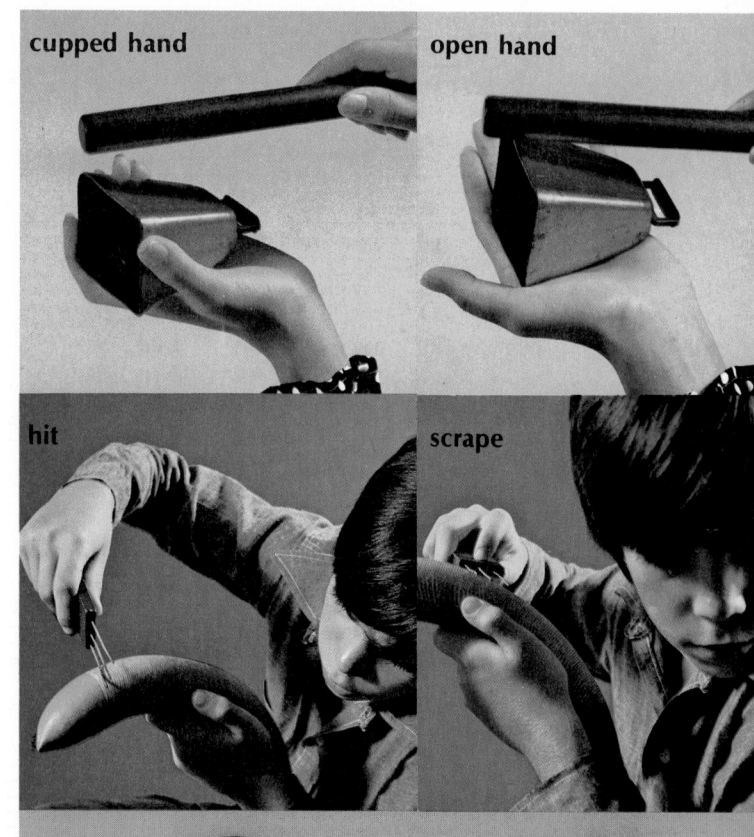

cupped hand

open hand

hit

scrape

one hand on each drumhead

both hands on one drumhead

The John B. Sails

FOLK SONG FROM THE BAHAMA ISLANDS

You will hear a variety of percussion sounds on the recording of
this song. But listen especially for the tone color of the maracas.
They play two sounds for each beat.

1. Oh, we come on____ the sloop *John B.* My
2. The____ first mate_____ he got sad,
3. The____ poor cook_____ he got fits, And

grand - fa - ther and me, A - round Nas - sau____
Feel - in' aw - f'ly bad, Captain come a -
throw way all____ the grits, Then he took and____

Town we____ did roam._____ Walk - in' all
board, took him a - way._____ Please let me a -
eat up all of the corn._____ Please let me go

night Just see - in' the sights, Well, I
lone And let____ me go home, Well, I
home, I want____ to go home, Well, this

feel so break____ up,____ I want____ to go home.
feel so break____ up,____ I want____ to go home.
is the worst____ trip____ Since I____ was born.

14

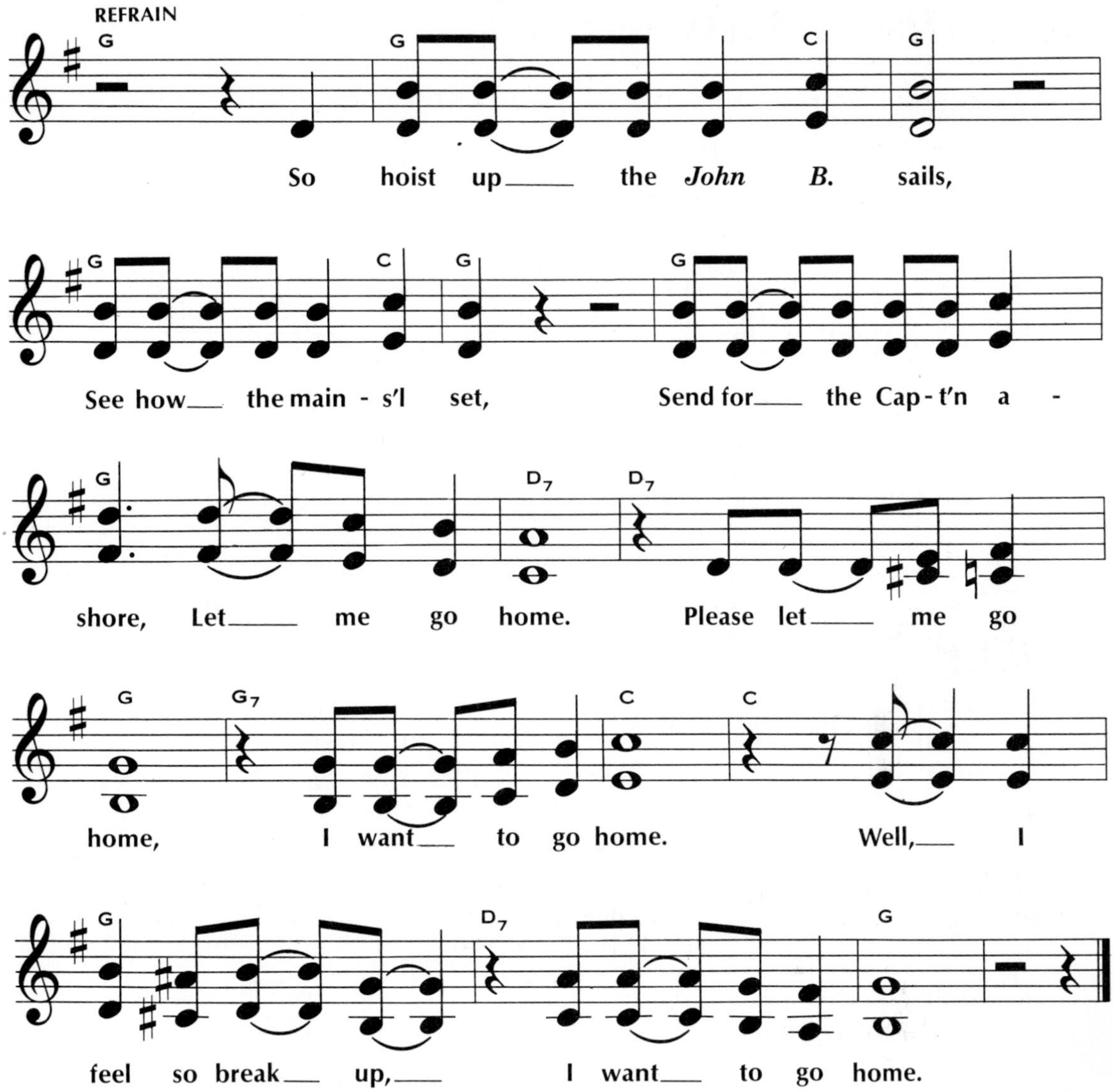
REFRAIN
G G C G
So hoist up___ the *John B.* sails,
G C G G
See how___ the main - s'l set, Send for___ the Cap - t'n a -
G D7 D7
shore, Let___ me go home. Please let___ me go
G G7 C C
home, I want___ to go home. Well,___ I
G D7 G
feel so break___ up,___ I want___ to go home.

For a percussion ensemble, see p. 232.

Now play one of these parts to accompany the song.

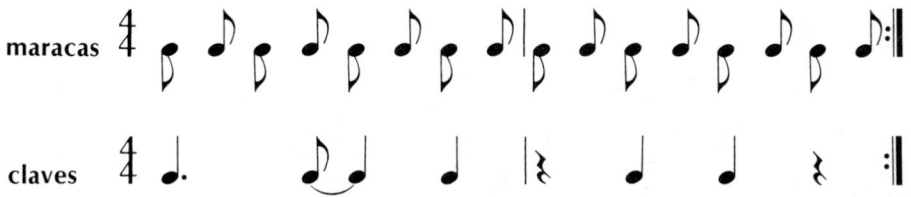

maracas
claves

You can add the tone color of bongo drum, cowbell, and guiro by playing one of the parts on page 13 in your book.

COMBO FOR PERCUSSION

When percussion instruments, such as claves, bongos, maracas, cowbell, and guiro are used to accompany a song, they give the music a special Latin-American flavor.

Use the percussion parts on pages 13 and 15 to accompany this song from the West Indies. Practice one of the parts, then plan a percussion combo with others in your class.

Limbo
SONG FROM THE WEST INDIES

FROM SONGS FROM TRINIDAD (EDRIC CONNOR)   COPYRIGHT 1958 BY THE OXFORD UNIVERSITY PRESS

SOLO / CHORUS
I want some-bod-y to lim-bo like me, Lim-bo,____ to lim-bo like me.

SOLO / CHORUS / SOLO
Lim-bo, lim-bo, to lim-bo like me, Lim-bo,____ to lim-bo like me. I

CHORUS
want a girl to lim-bo like this boy, Lim-bo,____ to lim-bo like me.

SOLO / CHORUS / SOLO
Lim-bo, lim-bo, to lim-bo like this boy, Lim-bo, lim-bo like me. I

CHORUS / SOLO
want some-bod-y to lim-bo like me, Lim-bo,____ to lim-bo like me. The

CHORUS
girl must be good to lim-bo like this boy, Lim-bo,____ to lim-bo like me,

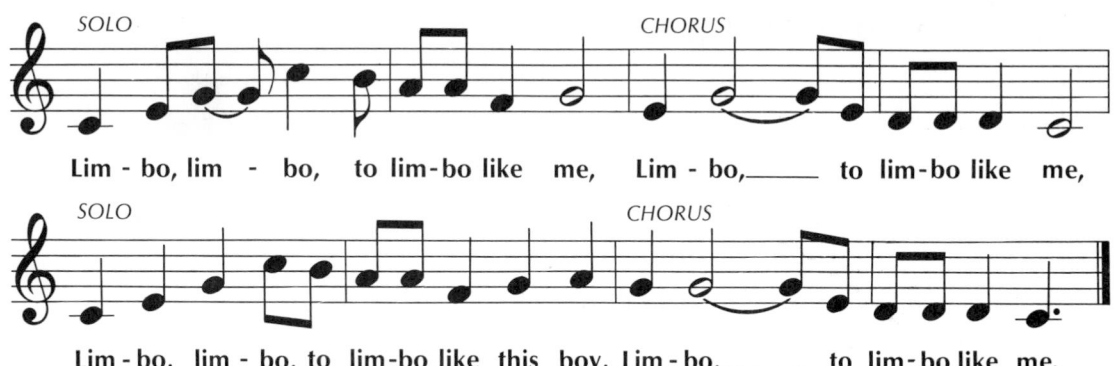

SOLO

Lim - bo, lim - bo, to lim-bo like me, Lim - bo,_____ to lim-bo like me,

CHORUS

SOLO

Lim - bo, lim - bo, to lim-bo like this boy, Lim - bo,_____ to lim-bo like me.

CHORUS

THE LIMBO CHALLENGE

Try to do the limbo. Each dancer struts under a pole that is held by two people. After everyone has had a turn, the pole is lowered. Every time the pole is lowered, each dancer must bend further backward to avoid touching the pole. The trick is to strut under the pole without falling.

People in Trinidad do the limbo to music played by a steel band. Listen to this recording of a steel band.

Highlife

CALL CHART 1: Percussion ⌾

You will hear a variety of tone colors made on a snare drum in this recording. Follow each chart as you listen. It will help you hear what is going on in the music.

Benson: "Cretan Dance"

Benson: "Fandango"

1 With snares off, drumhead is hit in center for low sound; near edge for higher sound.

1 Drum is played with snares on.

2 Tone color of sticks struck together in air is added to low and high sounds made on drumhead.

2 Right stick hits left stick, which rests loosely on drumhead, causing it to rebound.

3 Sticks struck together in air, first held tightly and then held loosely to create different tone colors.

3 Sticks struck together in air, first held tightly and then held loosely to create different tone colors.

THE VOICE

Your voice has a special tone color that makes it "you" whether you use it to whisper, speak, shout, or sing.

Try reading this poem aloud. How will you use the tone color of your voice to help express what the words mean?

Now listen to how the reader on the recording uses his voice to help express the meaning of the poem.

 Sandburg: *Snatch of Sliphorn Jazz*

SNATCH OF SLIPHORN JAZZ

Are you happy? It's the only
way to be, kid.
Yes, be happy, it's a good nice
way to be.
But not happy-happy, kid, don't
be too doubled-up doggone happy.
It's the doubled-up doggone happy-
happy people . . . bust hard . . . they
do bust hard . . . when they bust.
Be happy, kid, go to it, but not too
doggone happy.

Carl Sandburg

The pictures on this page are of Carl Sandburg, a great poet and a great American. One of the photographs shows him reading from a book of his own poems. He could have been reading *Snatch of Sliphorn Jazz*.

A COMBINATION OF VOICES

Using a variety of vocal tone colors will make a performance of "Gonna Sing" more interesting. Before you listen to the recording, decide how *you* would use voices in a performance of this song. The form might give you a clue.

Gonna Sing BLACK SPIRITUAL

Oh, I'm a - gon - na sing, gon - na sing, gon - na

sing all a - long___ the way. Oh, I'm a - gon - na sing, gon - na

sing gon - na sing all a - long the way. way.

1. One day you'll hear the trum - pet sound,
   gon-na sing all a-long the
2. Oh, Jor - dan's stream is wide and cold,

way. The trum - pet sound the world a - round, gon - na
   It chills the body but not the soul,

D.C. al Fine

sing all a - long the way.

Use a percussion instrument and play this rhythm echo during every dotted half note (𝅗𝅥.) in section A of "Gonna Sing."

Now sing or play on the bells a melody echo during the dotted half notes. Use the following patterns.

gon - na sing   gon - na sing

It's Not That Nina's Naughty

WORDS AND MUSIC BY LUIGI ZANINELLI

Two different vocal groups are used on the recording of "It's Not That Nina's Naughty." Can you tell how they are different? Also, notice that the voices sing faster and faster as the music goes along. This is called *accelerando.*

It's not that Ni - na's naugh - ty,   It's not that Ni - na's bad,   It's

just that trou - ble finds her,   No mat - ter where we hides her.

Sing this part until all parts of the round are finished.

No mat - ter where we hides her.

SOUND PIECE 1: Whistle Whatever, Hum However   BETH CROOK

You have a speaking voice, a singing voice, a shouting voice, a whispering voice. How many other sounds can you make with your voice? Here are some suggestions.

(Lip buzz)   (Animal sound)   (Gurgle)

(Hiss)   (Cough)   (Cheek or lip pop)

(Tongue clicks)   (Swoops)   (Whisper)

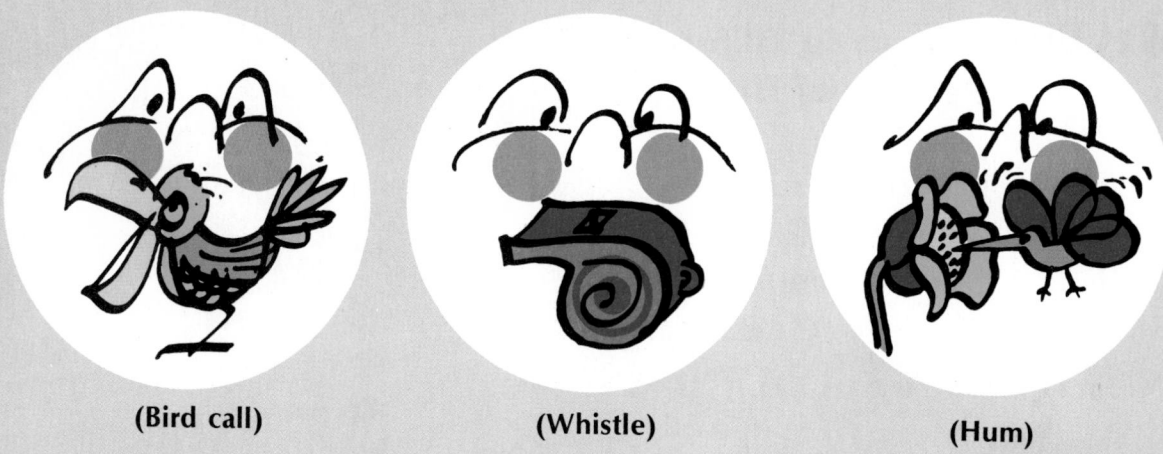

(Bird call)　　　(Whistle)　　　(Hum)

Choose three or more sounds you like best.

Start to create a sound piece by inventing a notation for each sound. Then make a score by arranging the sounds to make a line of different tone colors.

Plan the length of each sound so that the line is about fifteen seconds long. Here is an example.

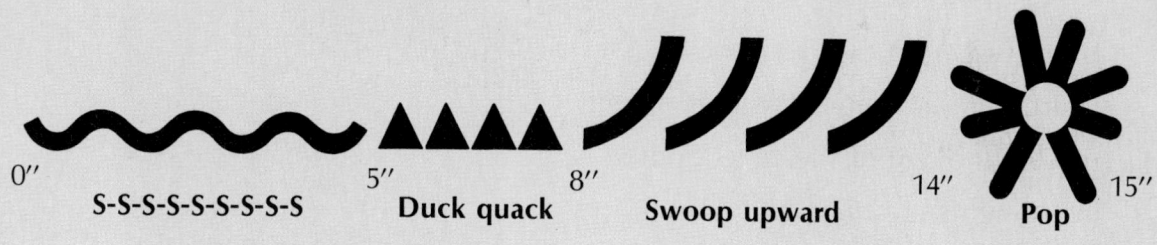

0″　　S-S-S-S-S-S-S-S-S　　5″　　Duck quack　　8″　　Swoop upward　　14″　　Pop　　15″

When you can feel the length of the line without timing it, perform the piece as a two- or three-part round. When will each part enter?

📖 For another experience with vocal tone color, see p. 242.

After performing your Sound Piece, listen to the recording of "Love for Two Cats" to discover what sounds are used.

🎙 Ravel: "Love for Two Cats"

Style: Sounds in Different Periods of History

Music is made of sounds. Throughout history, people have searched for tools (instruments) that make sounds in expressive ways.

Look at the pictures as you listen to the recording. Match the sound with its picture. Each instrument is an important part of the music of its time.

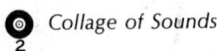 *Collage of Sounds*

In every period of history new instruments are invented that reflect the technology of the time. Some instruments continue to be used, while others are popular for shorter periods of time.

What sound-producing instruments do you think technology will inspire next?

More About Tone Color

THE AUTOHARP

The sound of the Autoharp will add its own special color to a performance of "La Raspa." You need only two chords to accompany the song—G and D$_7$. Strum on every beat.

For percussion parts, see p. 222.

La Raspa
FOLK SONG FROM MEXICO   ENGLISH VERSION BY ROSEMARY JACQUES

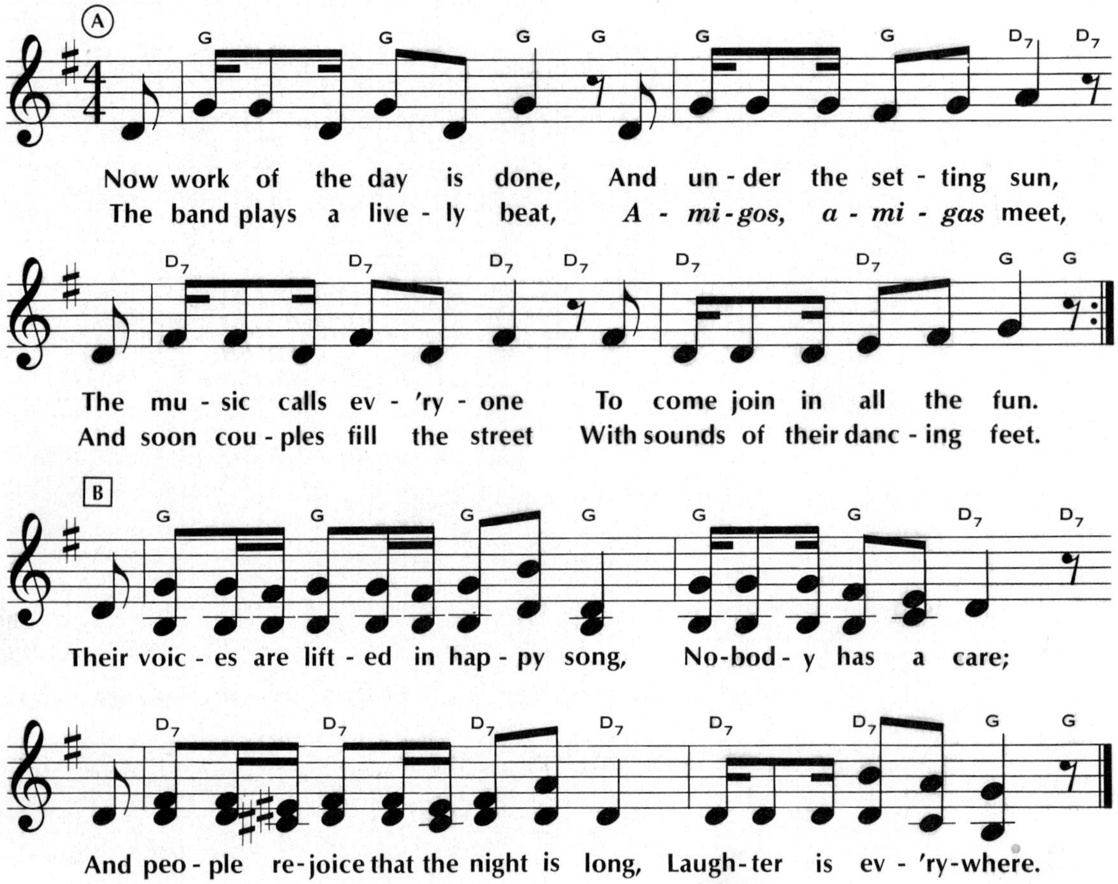

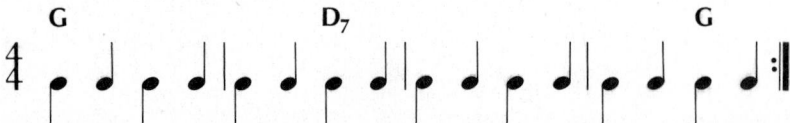

(A)

Now work of the day is done, And un - der the set - ting sun,
The band plays a live - ly beat, A - mi - gos, a - mi - gas meet,

The mu - sic calls ev - 'ry - one To come join in all the fun.
And soon cou - ples fill the street With sounds of their danc - ing feet.

(B)

Their voic - es are lift - ed in hap - py song, No - bod - y has a care;

And peo - ple re - joice that the night is long, Laugh - ter is ev - 'ry - where.

For a special Autoharp strum, play short strokes with your thumb on the lowest strings for the notes with stems down. For notes with stems up, brush the strings in the opposite direction with your fingers.

ANOTHER TWO-CHORD SONG

There's a Fiesta   FOLK SONG FROM SPAIN   ENGLISH VERSION BY ROSEMARY JACQUES

"MORENA MIA" (JOTA) FROM FOLK MUSIC AND POETRY OF SPAIN AND PORTUGAL, COLLECTED BY KURT SCHINDLER, © 1941 HISPANIC INSTITUTE IN THE UNITED STATES. USED BY PERMISSION OF COLUMBIA UNIVERSITY, DEPARTMENT OF SPANISH AND PORTUGUESE.

There's a fi - es - ta to - day, tra la la la,____

Gui - tars are be - gin - ning to play, tra la la la,____

Sweet - ly their mu - sic rings out, tra la la la,____

As ev - 'ry - one gath - ers a - bout, tra la la la.

Cas - ta - nets start keep-ing the beat, Danc - ers be - gin mov-ing their feet,

Whirl - ing a - way while ev - 'ry - one cries out "O - lé!"

For percussion parts, see p. 225.

Section A

DIFFERENT STRUMS, DIFFERENT SOUNDS

In this song, sections A and B use three Autoharp chords—G, D₇, and C. A new chord is added in section C. Can you find it?

Try these strums.

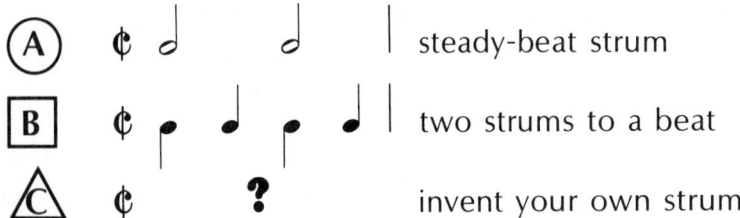

(A) ¢   steady-beat strum

[B] ¢   two strums to a beat

△C ¢ ?   invent your own strum

Take Me Home, Country Roads

WORDS AND MUSIC BY BILL DANOFF, TAFFY NIVERT, AND JOHN DENVER

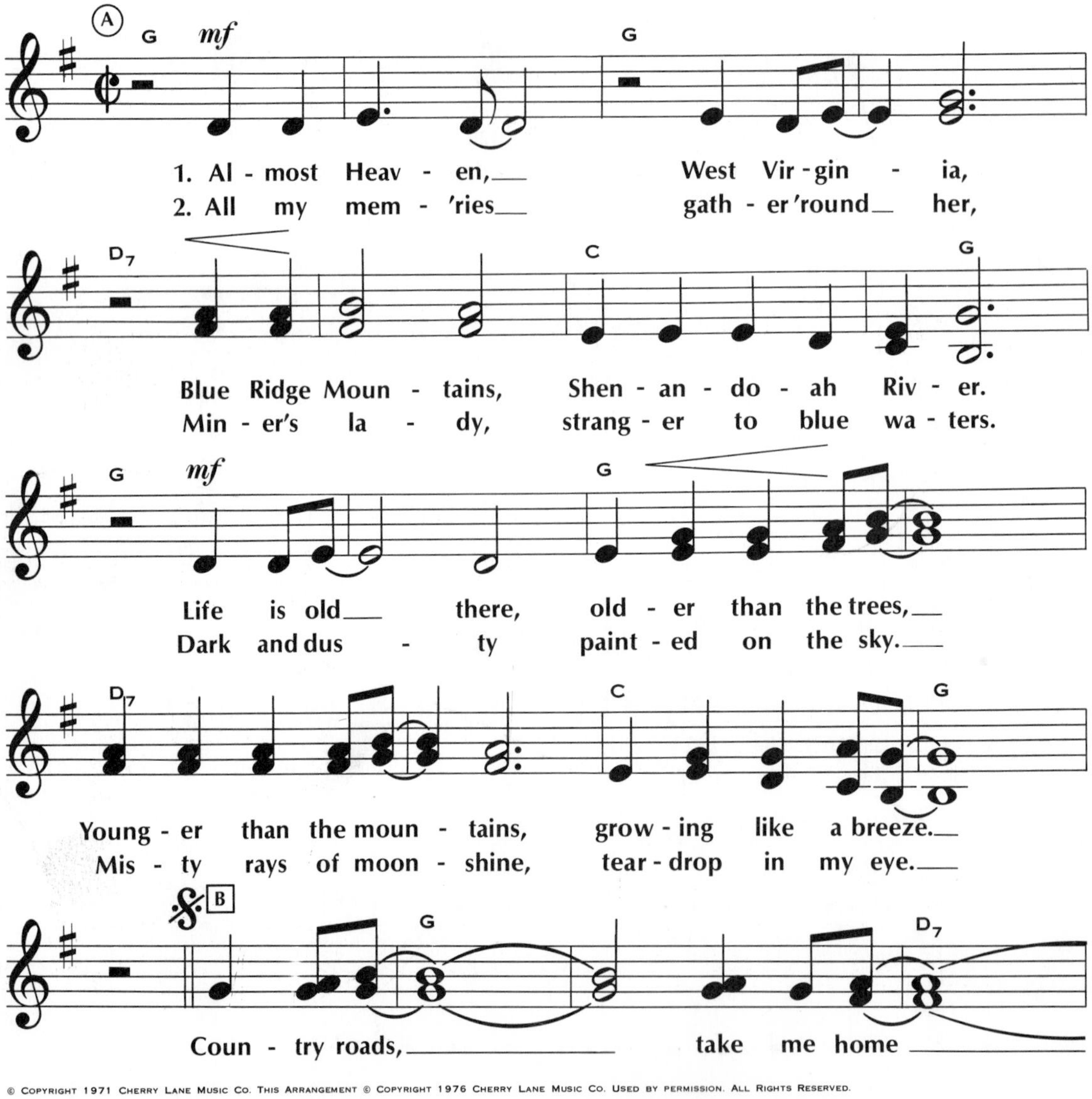

1. Al - most Heav - en,___ West Vir - gin - ia,
2. All my mem - 'ries___ gath - er 'round___ her,

Blue Ridge Moun - tains, Shen - an - do - ah Riv - er.
Min - er's la - dy, strang - er to blue wa - ters.

Life is old___ there, old - er than the trees,___
Dark and dus - ty paint - ed on the sky.___

Young - er than the moun - tains, grow - ing like a breeze.___
Mis - ty rays of moon - shine, tear - drop in my eye.___

Coun - try roads,_____ take me home _____

to the place _____ I be-long:_____

West Vir-gin - ia,_____ Moun-tain ma - ma,_____

Take me home,_____ coun - try roads._____

Last time D.S. al Fine   Fine

I hear her voice; in the

morn - ing hours she calls____ me; The ra - di - o ____ re -

minds me of my home far a-way.____ Driv-ing down the road____

____ I get a feel - ing that I should____ have been home

D.S.

yes - ter - day,_____ yes - ter - day._____

29

THE RECORDER

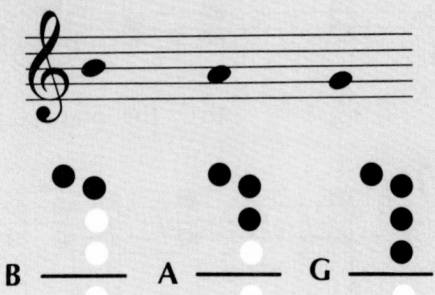

When you can play the notes B, A, and G on the soprano recorder, you will be able to play a countermelody for each song on pages 30 and 31.

B —— A —— G

My Dame Hath a Lame, Tame Crane ROUND

My dame hath a lame,____ tame____ crane,

My dame hath a crane____ that is lame.

Pray, gen - tle Jane, let my dame's lame, tame____

crane____ Feed and come home a - gain.

RECORDER COUNTERMELODIES

Soprano recorder

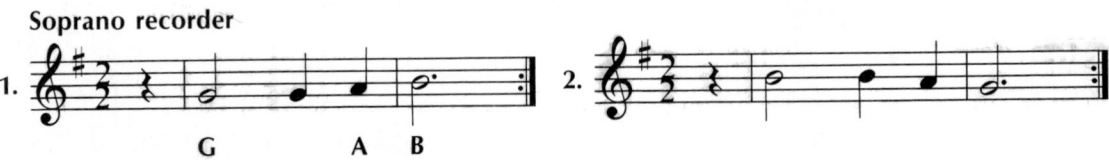

1.   G   A   B   2.

30

COMBINING TONE COLORS

You can add the sound of Autoharp, percussion, and recorder to the singing of this Liberian folk song.

Take Time in Life

FOLK SONG FROM LIBERIA

1. 2. I was pass - ing by, my broth-er / sis - ter called me in, And he / she said to

me, "You bet - ter take time in life." Peo - ple, take time in life, Peo - ple,

take time in life, Peo - ple, take time in life, 'cause you got far way to go.

Percussion

Soprano recorder

THE GUITAR

The guitar has never been more popular nor used more widely than it is today.

This page introduces you to an easy way to play the C and G_7 chords on the guitar. The photographs and diagrams will help you learn how to play each chord.

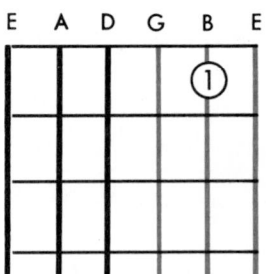

To play the C chord, put finger 1 (your index finger) on the B string. Strum the strings shown in red.

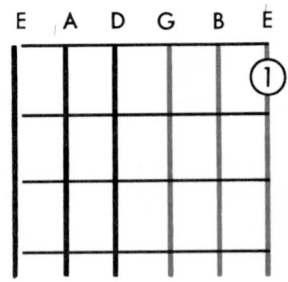

To play the G_7 chord, move finger 1 to the high-E string and strum the strings shown in red.

TWO-CHORD ACCOMPANIMENTS

When you can change from the C chord to the G₇ chord easily, you will be able to play a guitar accompaniment for the next three songs. The diagrams and letter names will tell you when to change from one chord to the other.

Chumbara

FRENCH-CANADIAN FOLK SONG

Chum - ba - ra, _____ chum - ba - ra chum - ba - ra, _____ chum - ba - ra

chum - ba - ra, _____ chum - ba - ra chum, chum, chum, chum, chum, chum, chum, chum,

Chum - ba - ra, _____ chum - ba - ra chum - ba - ra, _____ chum - ba - ra

chum - ba - ra, _____ chum - ba - ra chum, chum!

2. Fy-do-lee   5. Say-too-mee

3. Chow-ber-ski   6. Boom-ta-da

4. Chug-ah-lee   7. Zow-lee-ski

📖 For further experience with playing the guitar, see p. 189.

Puttin' on the Style

AMERICAN FOLK SONG   NEW WORDS AND NEW MUSIC ADAPTATION BY NORMAN CAZDEN

A C

Put - tin' on the ag - o - ny, put - tin' on the style, (G7)

That's what all the young folks are do - in' all the while. And (C)

as I look a - round me, I'm ver - y apt to smile To (G7)

see so man - y peo - ple put - tin' on the style. C *Fine*

B
1. Young man in a car - riage,____ driv - in' like____ he's mad, (G7)
2. Sweet six - teen____ goes to school just____ to see the boys,
3. Young man home from col - lege____ makes____ a great dis - play,

With a pair of hors - es____ he bor-rowed from his dad; He (C)
Turns and laughs and gig - gles____ at ev - 'ry lit - tle noise; She
With a fan - cy ad - jec - tive that he can hard - ly say; It

cracks his whip so live - ly just to watch his la - dy smile,____ (G7)
turns this way a lit - tle, then____ turns that way a - while, But
can't be found in Web - ster's, and it won't be for a - while, But

34

But she knows he's on - ly put - tin' on the style.
we know that she's on - ly put - tin' on the style.
ev - 'ry - bod - y knows___ he's put - tin' on the style.

La Sinda

FOLK SONG FROM SPAIN   COLLECTED BY J. DE JUAN   ENGLISH VERSION BY AURA KONTRA

COPYRIGHT © 1960 BY UNION MUSICAL ESPANOLA, MADRID. USED BY PERMISSION.

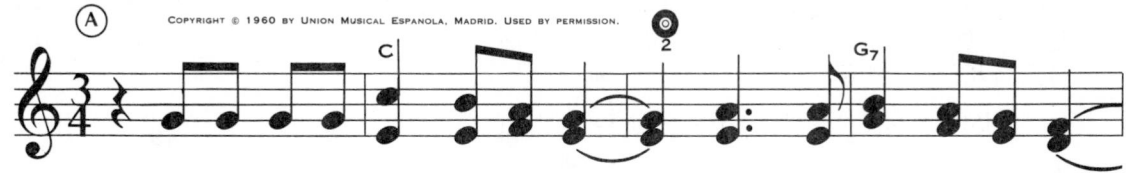

Here she comes with eyes beam-ing bright - ly, a rose in her hair,___
Spread the news to friends and com-pan - ions, for now is our chance,___

___ Here she comes with long skirts a - fly - ing, a scarf in her hand.
___ Hur-ry, we will meet in the vil - lage, she's read - y to dance.

Oh, la Sin - da___ claps her hands to the beat,

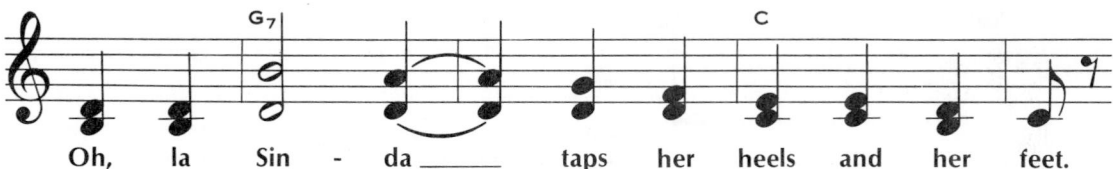

Oh, la Sin - da ___ taps her heels and her feet.
Sin - da,___

Oh, la Sin - da,___ danc - ing Sin - da, see her

danc - ing___ in the street.

For percussion parts, see p. 224.

German Dance

ATTRIBUTED TO LUDWIG VAN BEETHOVEN

SECONDO
(LOW PART)

German Dance

ATTRIBUTED TO LUDWIG VAN BEETHOVEN

PRIMO
(HIGH PART)

FAMILIES OF INSTRUMENTS

Which family members do you hear on the recording of
"Laughter Makes the World Go Round"?

WOODWINDS	BRASS	STRINGS
flute	trumpet	violin
oboe	French horn	viola
clarinet	trombone	cello
bassoon	tuba	string bass

Laughter Makes the World Go Round

WORDS AND MUSIC BY JOHN WILSON

Laugh-ter makes the world go round, so the wise men say.

Laugh-ter is the rec-i-pe to make us all feel gay:

Ha, ha, ha, ha, ha, ha, ha, ha, ho, ho, ho, ho, ho, ho, ho.

Here is the melody written for instruments of the string,
woodwind, and brass families. If you play one of these
instruments, practice the round to play with the recording.

Cello and Trombone

Clarinet and Trumpet

PLAN A PERFORMANCE

Organize an ensemble to sing and play "Laughter Makes the
World Go Round." Will you perform the piece in unison? As a
two- or three-part round? Will the instruments, or voices, begin?
Will the voices and instruments perform together? Think of
other ways to combine tone colors.

CALL CHART 2: Orchestral Instruments

Follow the call chart to help you hear how three families of
instruments are used in a piece for orchestra.

Handel: *Water Music Suite*, "Allegro deciso"

1 *CONTRAST OF STRINGS AND BRASS*

2 *STRINGS AND WOODWINDS TOGETHER*

3 *STRINGS ALONE*

4 *CONTRAST OF STRINGS AND BRASS*

STRING INSTRUMENTS

◉ Eddleman: *Shuffling Strings*

Violin

Cello

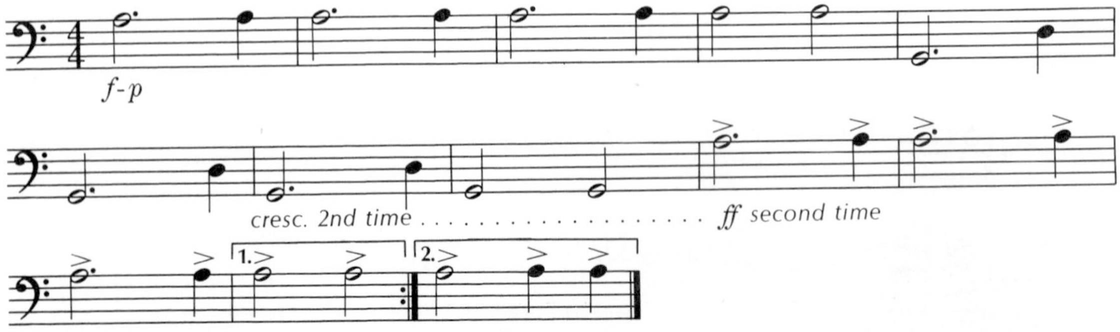

BRASS INSTRUMENTS

2 Eddleman: *Swingin' on the Levee*

Trumpet

Trombone

WOODWIND INSTRUMENTS

Eddleman: *Latin Woods*

Flute

Clarinet

Water Music

(Conductor's Score)

G. F. HANDEL
1685–1759

THE ORCHESTRA

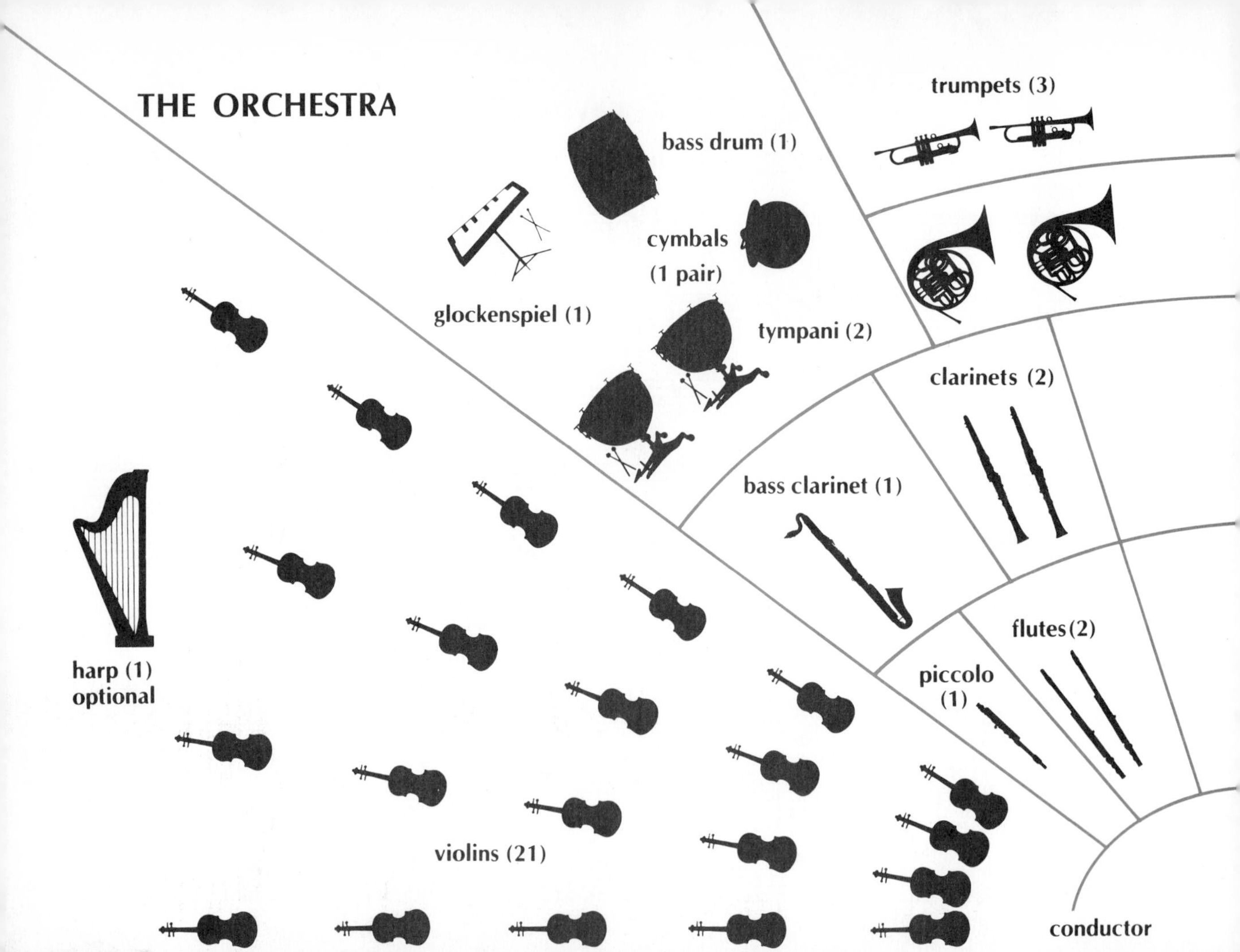

bass drum (1)

trumpets (3)

cymbals (1 pair)

glockenspiel (1)

tympani (2)

clarinets (2)

bass clarinet (1)

flutes (2)

harp (1) optional

piccolo (1)

violins (21)

conductor

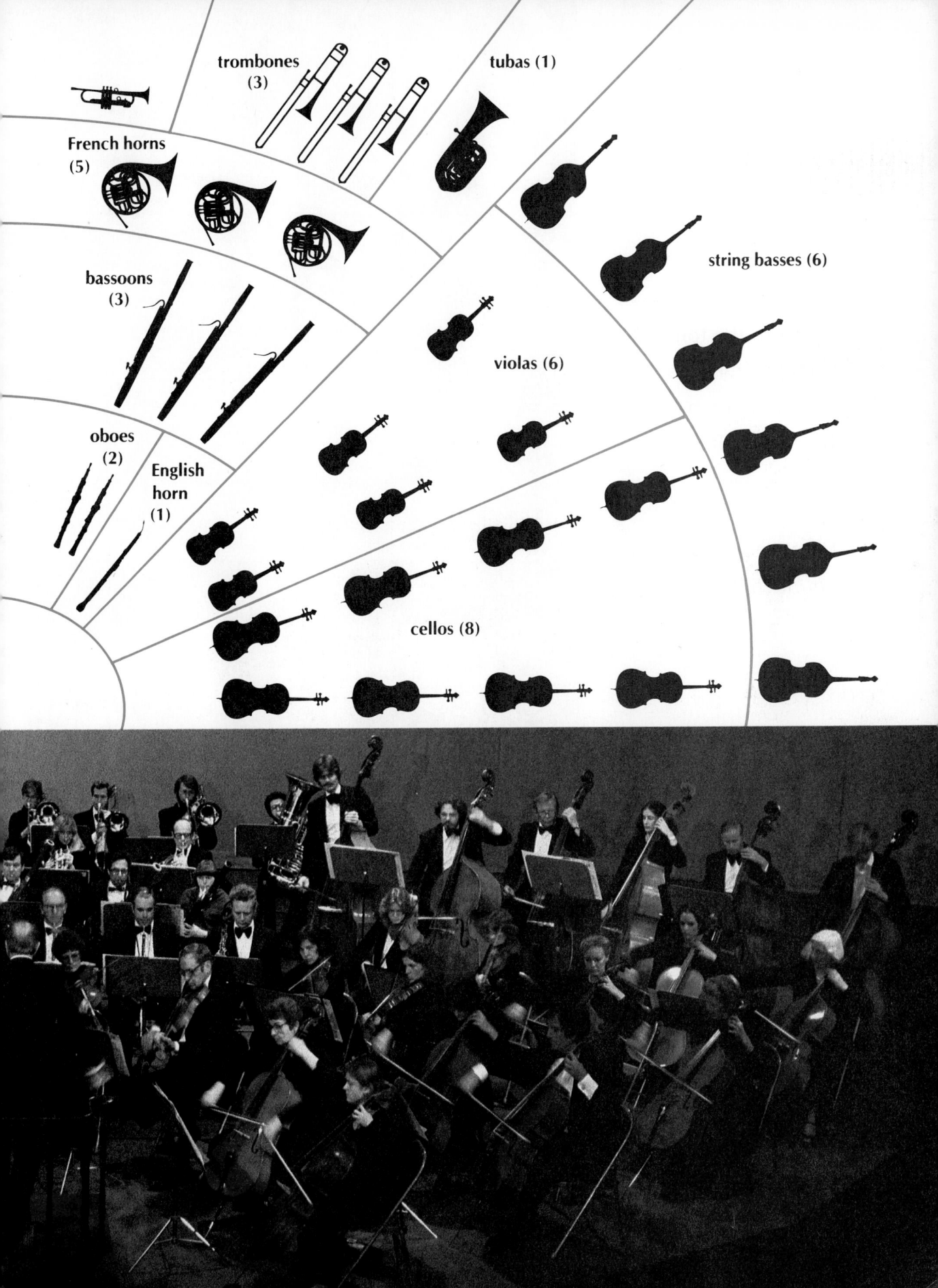

trombones
(3)

tubas (1)

French horns
(5)

string basses (6)

bassoons
(3)

violas (6)

oboes
(2)

English
horn
(1)

cellos (8)

DIFFERENT INSTRUMENTS FROM DIFFERENT CULTURES

Listen to the tone of some instruments used by people from different cultures.

 Folk Instrument Collage

How many sounds can you identify?

Steel drums from Trinidad

Koto from Japan

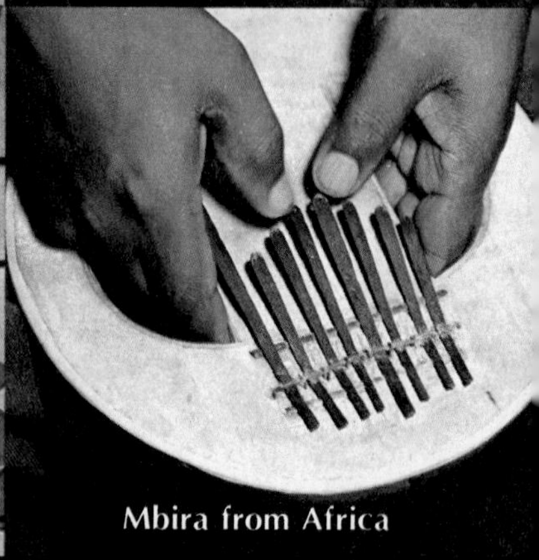

Mbira from Africa

Ipu from Hawaii

Pipe from China

Dulcimer from the United States

Drums from Haiti

Sitar from India

47

WHAT DO YOU HEAR? 1: Various Tone Colors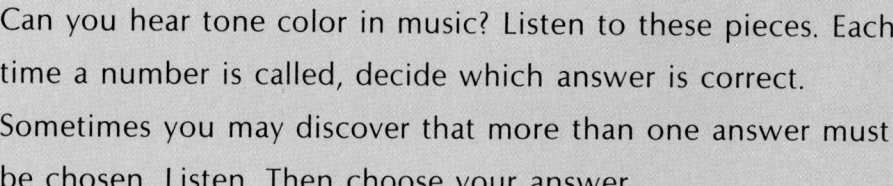

Can you hear tone color in music? Listen to these pieces. Each
time a number is called, decide which answer is correct.
Sometimes you may discover that more than one answer must
be chosen. Listen. Then choose your answer.

1	2	3
keyboard	keyboard	keyboard
electronic sound	electronic sound	electronic sound
folk instrument	folk instrument	folk instrument
voice	voice	voice
natural sound	natural sound	natural sound
recorder	recorder	recorder

4	5	6
keyboard	keyboard	keyboard
electronic sound	electronic sound	electronic sound
folk instrument	folk instrument	folk instrument
voice	voice	voice
natural sound	natural sound	natural sound
recorder	recorder	recorder

WHAT DO YOU HEAR? 2: Instruments of the Orchestra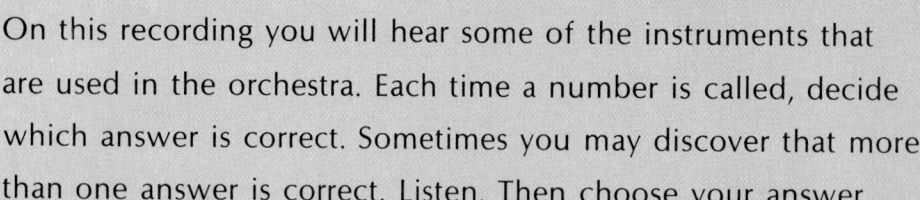

On this recording you will hear some of the instruments that
are used in the orchestra. Each time a number is called, decide
which answer is correct. Sometimes you may discover that more
than one answer is correct. Listen. Then choose your answer.

1	2	3
strings	strings	strings
woodwinds	woodwinds	woodwinds
brass	brass	brass
percussion	percussion	percussion

4	5	6
strings	strings	strings
woodwinds	woodwinds	woodwinds
brass	brass	brass
percussion	percussion	percussion

Carol from an Irish Cabin

MUSIC BY DALE WOOD WORDS ANONYMOUS

Pictured below are two of the instruments heard on the recording of "Carol from an Irish Cabin."

1. The cold wind blows o - ver the heath - er_____ The
2. The clean snow falls soft - ly, falls soft - ly,_____ The
3. So let there be no fear of dark - ness,_____ And

salt wind blows o - ver the sea,_____ The____
snow crys - tals cov - er the moor._____ Let____
let there be no fear of sea;_____ Let the

harsh wind blows down from the moun - tains,_____ And
wan - der - ers lost and grown wea - ry_____ Find
star guide the lost and for - sak - en_____ Safe

blows a white Christ - mas to me.
wel - come at my cab - in door.
o - ver the moor - lands to me.

Alto metallaphone

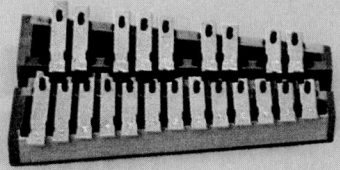

Glockenspiel

49

CHOOSING THE RIGHT INSTRUMENTS

Percussion Strings Woodwinds Brasses

When you think of march music, you probably think of brass instruments. When you think of lullabies or love songs, you might think of soft strings. What group of instruments do you think would be right to accompany this rhythmic song from Trinidad?

The Baby Boy

CHRISTMAS SONG FROM TRINIDAD

THE VIRGIN MARY HAD A BABY BOY FROM THE EDRIC CONNOR COLLECTION OF WEST INDIAN SPIRITUALS. COPYRIGHT 1945 BY BOOSEY & CO. LTD. RENEWED 1973.

1. The Vir - gin Mar - y had a ba - by boy, The
2. The an - gels sang____ for the ba - by boy, The
3. The Wise Men came to see the ba - by boy, The

Vir - gin Mar - y had a ba - by boy, The Vir - gin Mar - y had a
an - gels sang____ for the ba - by boy, The an - gels sang for the
Wise Men came to see the ba - by boy, The Wise Men came____ to see the

ba - by boy,____
ba - by boy,____ And they say that His name was Je - sus.
ba - by boy,____

He came____ from the glo - ry, He came____ from the

Choose a percussion part to play throughout one of the sections of the song. Notice the accent marks (>) in the bongo part.

Maracas

Bongo

Claves

Careers in Music: Perform

Syoko Aki is a professional violinist. She began studying the violin when she was six years old. In her early teens, Syoko went to school in Tokyo. It was there that she had her first experience playing in an orchestra. When she was eighteen, Syoko came to the United States to study violin at Yale University. She is still at Yale, where she plays in the orchestra and teaches violin. She also plays in an orchestra in New York City and gives solo concerts in this country and in Japan.

Many professional violinists own two, and sometimes three instruments. But there is always one that is a favorite. In the photographs below you see close-up shots of Syoko's favorite instrument. The photograph on page 53 shows her in a rehearsal room practicing for her next concert.

On the recording, Syoko Aki tells about her career as a performer and how she feels about the music she plays.

An Interview with Syoko Aki

Using What You Know About Melody

When you think of music, you are likely to think of melody—a series
of tones related to each other that forms a line of sounds we *hear*.

In dance, line is *seen*. Sometimes when a dancer's body is still,
your eyes see the line made by its position—from tip of toes to
tip of fingers.

At other times, you see a moving line as the dancers' bodies
move in space.

In poems, words are arranged into lines we *read*—a set of words followed by another, then another. Some poems have long lines, some very short lines. Other poems have a combination of long and short lines.

THE NIGHT WILL NEVER STAY

The night will never stay,
The night will still go by,
Though with a million stars
You pin it to the sky;

Though you bind it with the blowing wind
And buckle it with the moon,
The night will slip away
Like sorrow or a tune.

Eleanor Farjeon

NIGHT

Stars over snow,
  And in the west a planet
Swinging below a star—
  Look for a lovely thing and
    you will find it,
It is not far—
It never will be far.

Sara Teasdale

PIET MONDRIAN: OPPOSITION OF LINES: RED AND YELLOW. PHILADELPHIA MUSEUM OF ART: THE A. E. GALLATIN COLLECTION.

In paintings, sometimes only straight lines are used, carefully placed to work against each other and with each other, giving a feeling of movement and stillness together. Nothing really moves, but our eyes and our *minds* make us feel movement.

55

FOLLOW THE PHRASE LINES

The letters A and B, marked in the music, tell you that this song
has two sections. The diagram below will help you hear how the
melody phrases are put together in each section. Trace each phrase
line with your finger as you listen to the recording.

Ⓐ

Ⓑ

Anthony Mayberry

WORDS AND MUSIC BY PATRICK P. ADAMS

© 1972 BY POPDRAW MUSIC CORP., NEW YORK, NEW YORK

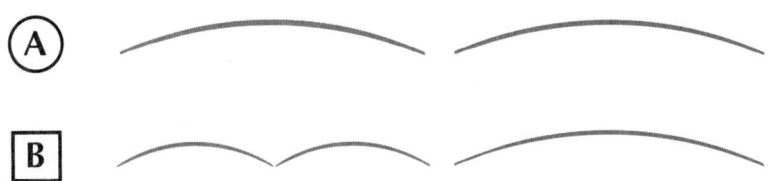

1. An - tho - ny May - ber - ry ran a - way quite ear - ly
2. An - tho - ny May - ber - ry seemed ver - y sad as he

yes - ter - day____ af - ter - noon.   With a dime in his hand,
turned to look back one last time.   With a tear in his eye,

want - ed to be a man, car - ried his clothes on a broom.____
An - tho - ny said good-by, head - ed toward Ma - ple and Vine.____

B
REFRAIN

1 2

But, An - tho - ny,____ tell me where will you sleep?____ And,

3

But, An - th'ny, where will you sleep?

56

An - tho - ny, ___ tell me what will you eat? ___ Re -

An - th'ny, what will you eat?

mem - ber ___ where the shoes on your feet come from. ___

And where will your shoes come from? ___

The Windows of the World

WORDS AND MUSIC BY BURT BACHARACH AND HAL DAVID

The win - dows of the world are cov - ered with rain.

Where is the sun - shine we once knew? ___ Ev - 'ry - bod - y

knows when lit - tle chil - dren play They need a sun - ny day to

grow straight and tall. ___ Let the sun shine ___ through.

STEPS, LEAPS, REPEATS

Look at the first two measures of this song. Notice that the notes do one of three things: move up, move down, or stay on the same pitch. As you listen to the recording, follow the outline that the melody makes from the beginning of the song to the end.

Everybody's Got a Song

WORDS AND MUSIC BY BARBERI PAULL

© 1979 Barberi Paull. Used by permission.

It was just a ___ sim - ple lit - tle mel - o - dy, ___ I used to ___ lis -

- ten to it sing to ___ me. ___ It al - ways ___ came ___ to keep me com - pa - ny, ___

___ And it would help me through when ___ ev - 'ry - thing was go - ing ___ wrong.
All those times when noth - ing seems to go my ___ way,

___ Some - times I ___ e - ven got to sing a - long. ___ I came to ___ rec -
___ No - bod - y ___ cares ___ a - bout a thing I ___ say, ___ I set - tle ___ back

REFRAIN

- og - nize it as my ___ own, ___ my own ___ song. ___ Ev - 'ry - bod - y, ___
___ and lis - ten. Come on, ___ song, ___ sing a - way. ___

ev - 'ry - bod - y, ___ ev - 'ry - bod - y, ev - 'ry - bod - y's got his/her own song.

58

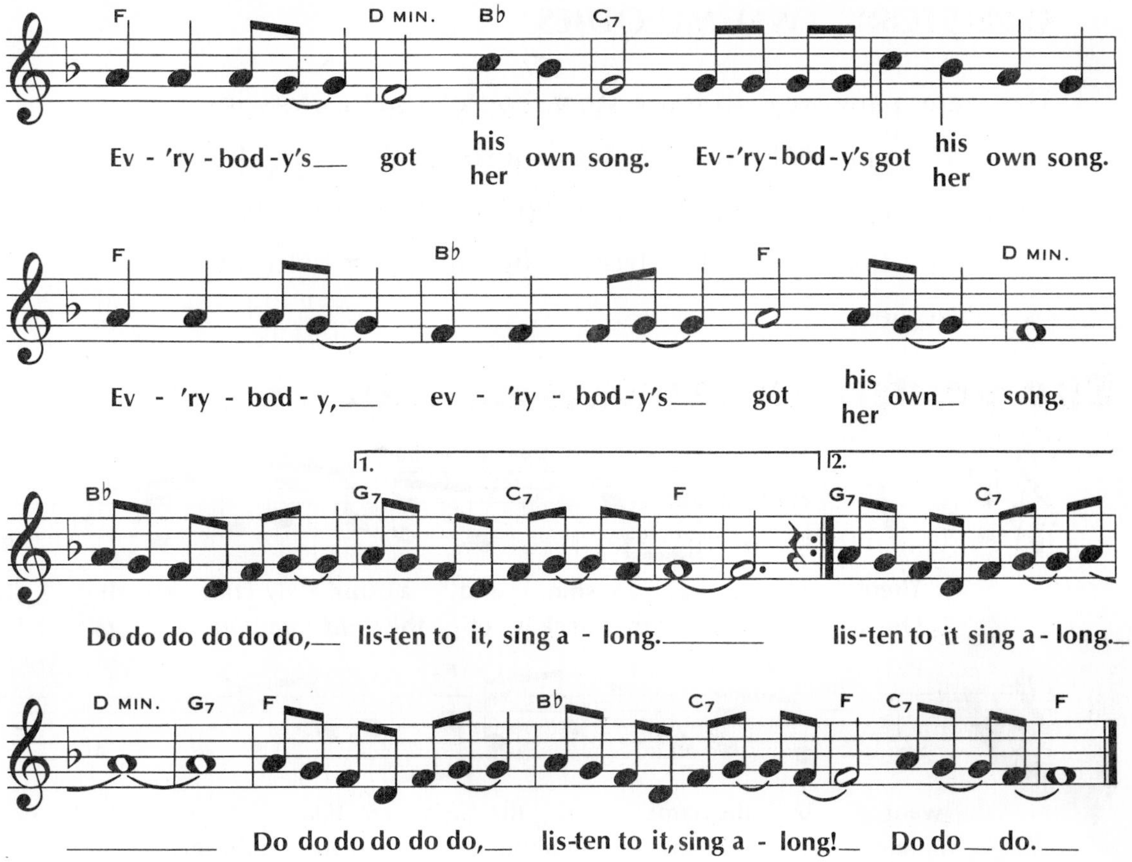

F D MIN. B♭ C7
Ev - 'ry - bod - y's got his/her own song. Ev - 'ry - bod - y's got his/her own song.
F B♭ F D MIN.
Ev - 'ry - bod - y, ev - 'ry - bod - y's got his/her own song.
1. 2.
B♭ G7 C7 F G7 C7
Do do do do do do, lis-ten to it, sing a - long. lis-ten to it sing a - long.
D MIN. G7 F B♭ C7 F C7 F
Do do do do do do, lis-ten to it, sing a - long! Do do do.

Lonesome Valley

FOLK HYMN 3

As you follow the outline, or contour, of this melody, notice where tones repeat and where they move up or down by step and by leap.

For a recorder countermelody, see p. 211.

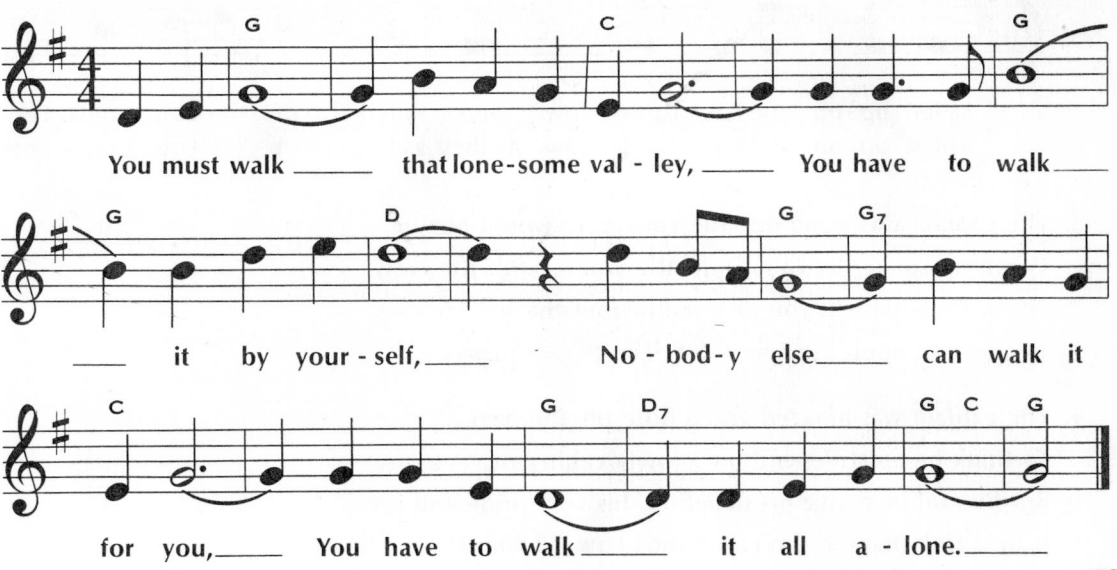

G C G
You must walk that lone-some val - ley, You have to walk
G D G G7
it by your - self, No - bod - y else can walk it
C G D7 G C G
for you, You have to walk it all a - lone.

ONE STORY, TWO MELODIES

There are many ways to tell a story. You can tell a story in poetry or in prose. Even the lyrics of a song tell a story. In music a song that tells a story is called a *ballad*. Listen to two versions of the same ballad. Notice the difference between the two melodies.

The Golden Vanity

FOLK SONG FROM ENGLAND

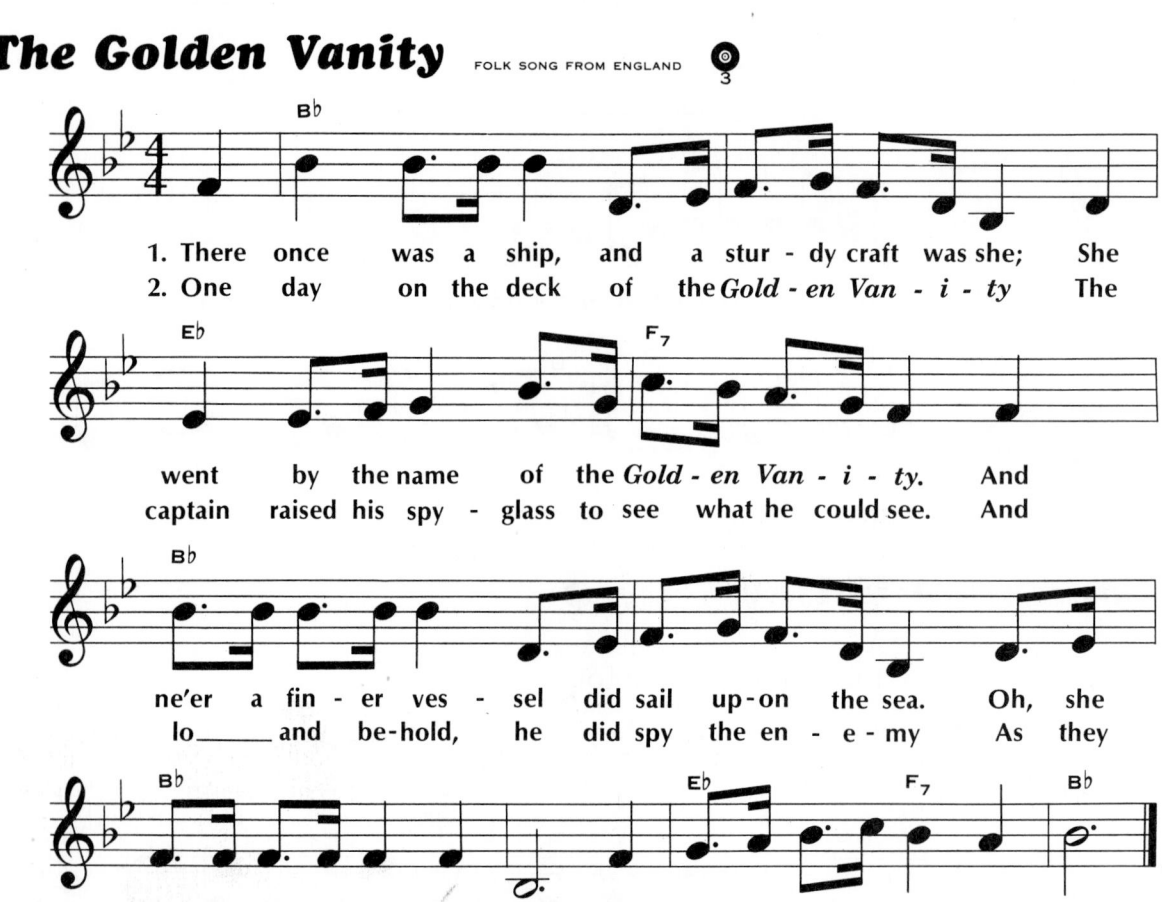

1. There once was a ship, and a stur-dy craft was she; She
2. One day on the deck of the *Gold - en Van - i - ty* The

went by the name of the *Gold - en Van - i - ty.* And
captain raised his spy - glass to see what he could see. And

ne'er a fin - er ves - sel did sail up-on the sea. Oh, she
lo____ and be-hold, he did spy the en - e - my As they

sailed up-on the Low Lands Low. She sailed up-on the Low Lands Low.
sailed up-on the Low Lands Low. As they sailed up-on the Low Lands Low.

3. The captain was pond'ring the course he would pursue,
   When up spoke the cabin boy, the youngest of the crew.
   "Pray, sir, what will you give me to rout the foe for you
   As they sail upon the Low Lands Low?" (*2 times*)

4. The captain was amazed and a little bit annoyed
   To think he must depend on a lowly cabin boy,
   But he said he'd give his daughter, his very pride and joy,
   If he'd sink them in the Low Lands Low. (*2 times*)

60

5. The boy spread his arms and into the sea he dived.
   He swam and he swam, it's a wonder he survived!
   He bored some tiny holes in the other vessel's side
   And he sank it in the Low Lands Low. (*2 times*)

6. Then back once again to the *Vanity* he sped.
   He thought as he swam of the pretty girl he'd wed,
   For, "You shall have my daughter," the captain'd plainly said,
   "And you'll sail upon the Low Lands Low." (*2 times*)

7. And when he reached the ship and was safely at her side,
   "Good captain, help me come aboard!" the cabin boy did cry.
   The captain, though, ignored him, and merely breathed a sigh
   As he sailed upon the Low Lands Low." (*2 times*)

8. "Good captain, help me up," cried the cabin boy once more,
   "Or else I'll bore your ship and send it to the ocean floor."
   The captain then moved quickly and pulled the lad aboard
   And they sailed upon the Low Lands Low." (*2 times*)

The Turkish Revery   AMERICAN FOLK SONG

To find out how this story ends, turn the page.

1. "Cap-tain, cap-tain,___ What will you give me   If
2. "Gold and sil-ver___ Shin - ing so bright,   And my

I   do sink the___*Turk-ish Rev-er-y,*   If I sink her   in the   low-down,
fair-est daugh-ter shall wed___ you to-night,   If you sink her   in the   low-down,

low - down,___ low - down,   If I sink her in the low-down lone-some low?"
low - down,___ low - down,   If you sink her in the low-down lone-some low!"

3. Then he bared his breast
   And he swam in the tide,
   And he bored three holes in the old ship's side,
   And he sank her in the low-down, low-down, low-down,
   And he sank her in the low-down lonesome low.

4. Then he bared his breast
   And he swam in the tide,
   He swam till he came to his own ship's side
   As she rolled in the low-down, . . .

5. "Captain, captain,
   Take me on board!
   If you don't, you'll have to forfeit your word,
   For you promised in the low-down, . . ."

6. "Sailor boy, sailor boy,
   Don't appeal to me,
   For you drowned sixty souls when you sank the *Revery*,
   When you sank her in the low-down, . . ."

7. "If it weren't for the love
   That I bear for your men,
   I'd sink you the same as I sank them!
   I'd sink you in the low-down, . . ."

8. Then he bared his breast
   And down swam he.
   He swam till he came to the bottom of the sea,
   And he drowned in the low-down, . . .

Now compare the two versions by answering some of these questions.

1. In which melody are all the phrases the same length? In which melody do you find both long and short phrases?

2. In which melody do you find two phrases that are similar?

3. Find the lowest and highest note in each melody. Which version has the wider range?

4. In which melody do you find an octave leap?

5. Which melody is major? Which is minor?

NAME THAT TUNE

Here are the beginnings of three patriotic songs that you know.
Can you name each song by looking at the melody contour
(general shape) of the first phrase?

CALL CHART 3: Steps and Leaps

Listen to a melody that is used in a piece by Bach. Can you
hear when the tones move mostly by step and when they move
mostly by leap?

Bach: *Two-Part Invention, No. 6, Version 1*

1 *Mostly by step*		**5** *Mostly by step*	
2 *Mostly by leap*		**6** *Mostly by leap*	
3 *Mostly by step*		**7** *Mostly by step*	
4 *Mostly by leap*		**8** *Mostly by leap*	

Follow the chart again as you listen to this melody and a
countermelody working together. Notice how the melody and
countermelody move in opposite directions.

Bach: *Two-Part Invention, No. 6, Version 2*

FOLLOW THE CONTOUR

People, Take Care

TRADITIONAL WORDS   MUSIC BY ANTHONY DONATO

FROM MODERN CANONS, EDITED BY HERMAN REICHENBACH. COPYRIGHT 1948 MERCURY MUSIC, INC. USED BY PERMISSION.

Peo-ple who live, peo-ple who live, peo-ple who live   in   glass hous-es,

Peo - ple   liv - ing   in   glass hous - es should not   throw, should not   throw,

Peo - ple   liv - ing   in   glass hous - es should not, should not   throw stones.

SEQUENCES: SAME CONTOUR, DIFFERENT LEVELS

By the Waters of Babylon

MUSIC BY PHILIP HAYES

By _____   the wa - ters, the wa - ters of Bab - y - lon

We   sat down and wept, ___   yea wept, ___   yea wept _____ When

we   re - mem-bered thee, re - mem-bered thee _____ O ___ Zi - on.

There   we hang our harps,   hang our harps,   hang our harps on the wil - lows.

Listen to hear how sequences are used in a piece by Handel.

Handel: *Royal Fireworks Suite,* "Minuetto"

CALL CHART 4: Melody Contour 🔘₃

Listen to these pieces to hear how steps, leaps, repeated tones, and sequences are used to create melody contours.

Hill: *The Bird Fancyer's Delight* (excerpts)

1	*Repeats, leaps, sequences*	*Tune for Woodlark*
2	*Steps, repeats, leaps, sequences*	*Tune for Bullfinch*
3	*Mostly leaps, sequences*	*Tune for Canary, 1*
4	*Mostly steps, no sequences*	*Tune for Woodlark*
5	*Steps, repeats, leaps, sequences*	*Tune for Parrot*

WHAT DO YOU HEAR? 3: Sequences 🔘₃

Listen for sequences or no sequences in these pieces. Each time a number is called, decide which answer is correct.

1	*SEQUENCES*	*NO SEQUENCES*	**Handel:** *Minuetto*
2	*SEQUENCES*	*NO SEQUENCES*	**Hahvah nahgeelah**
3	*SEQUENCES*	*NO SEQUENCES*	**Eddleman:** *Latin Woods*
4	*SEQUENCES*	*NO SEQUENCES*	**Strauss:** *Also sprach Zarathustra*
5	*SEQUENCES*	*NO SEQUENCES*	**Hill:** *Tune for Bullfinch*

Experiencing the Arts: *The Use of Space*

VISUAL ARTS

A mobile is a special kind of visual art. What makes it different from painting, or sculpture, or architecture?

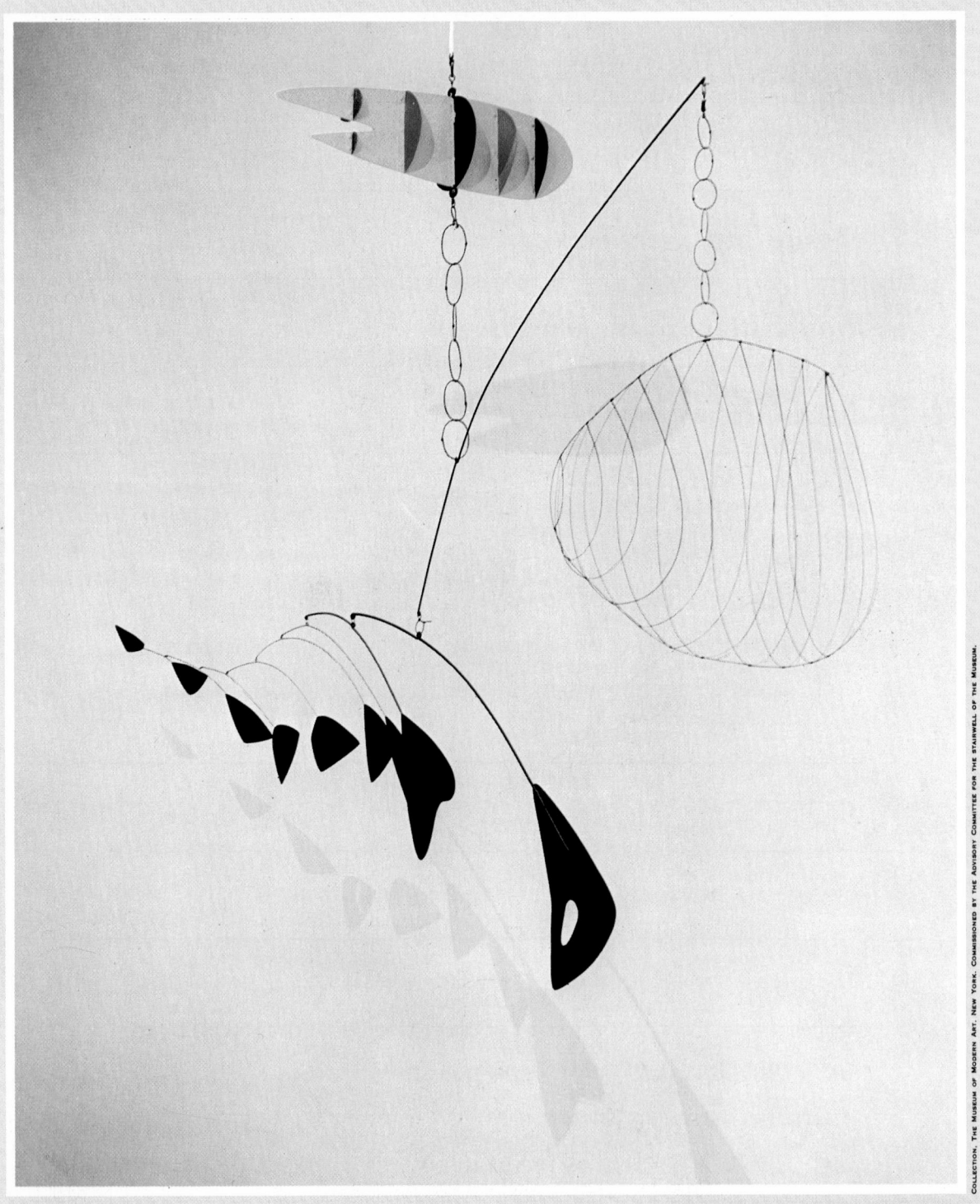

Lobster Trap and Fish Tail: Calder

JULES BRETON. THE SONG OF THE LARK. COLLECTION OF THE ART INSTITUTE OF CHICAGO.

The Song of the Lark: Breton

A painting, such as this very famous one, is on a flat canvas. How does it give us a feeling of space?

Casa Mila Apartment House: Gaudi

How does architecture use space differently from a mobile or a painting?

67

THE USE OF SPACE IN DANCE

In dance, space is used in a special
way. What makes dance something
like a mobile? In what way is dance
different from a mobile? Different
from a painting? Different from
architecture?

68

THE USE OF "SPACE" IN MUSIC

Music can give a sense of space, but it does it differently from any art you see with your eyes.

A melody has a "shape" that is heard. It can be played at different levels—high, medium, or low registers. This gives a feeling of space, using *musical* space.

Follow this chart as you listen to melodies played in different registers, using musical space.

CALL CHART 5: Register ⦿₃

Britten: *Simple Symphony*, Movement 2

---

1 *Melody 1 repeated in same and different registers—use of sequence*

---

2 *Melody 2 in medium register; accompaniment in low register*

---

3 *Melody 2 in low register, then in high register*

---

4 *Melody 1 repeated in same and different registers—use of sequence*

---

5 *Melody 2 in medium register; accompaniment in low register*

In music, space is not something you see, as in the visual arts and dance. It is something felt, as you hear sounds at different levels of high and low. There is no real space among the sounds, but it can feel as if there is.

Each of these arts uses space in its own way, and each way has something different about it. Every art has its special way to add to your experience.

What People Do with Music: Listen

As you sing this song with the recording, think about this question: Where are the sounds coming from?

Orion
WORDS AND MUSIC BY JAMES ZIMMERMAN

© 1972 JAMES ZIMMERMAN

1. O - ri - on is a - ris - ing, You can see his stars a - blaz-
2. The day is get - ting cold - er, And I real - ly start to won-

- ing in the mid - dle of a clear - eyed coun - try sky.
- der why we're cloud - ing all the coun - try skies to gray.

And it's nev - er too sur - pris - ing that the sky is still a - maz-
The__ world is get - ting old - er, You can hear it in the thun-

- ing way out here where noth - ing hides it from my eyes.
- der and the rain might come and chase us all a - way.

And sleep - ing out - side in a bag as a

kid, It seems like the best thing that I ev - er did; And

chas - ing the shad - ows and the tracks in the snow, don't you

know. _____ know. _____ The

moon is on the wane, And it looks like it might

rain, or may-be snow. ____ And how are we to stay

____ here if there's no room left to play ____ here or to

grow, don't you know, don't you know? _____

📖 For a percussion ensemble, see p. 228.

This time, listen to the recording without singing. Get your *mind* involved in hearing what the music does. For each of the five elements listed below, choose the qualities you hear.

1. TONE COLOR: man's voice—clarinet—children's voices—guitar—piano

2. RHYTHM: meter in 3—meter in 4—change in meter—little syncopation—much syncopation

3. MELODY: all long phrases—all short phrases—both long and short phrases.

4. HARMONY (TEXTURE): melody alone—melody with chords—melody with countermelody

5. FORM: ABCD—ABAB with coda (ending section)

71

WHAT HAPPENS WHEN YOU LISTEN TO MUSIC?

Sounds
come from your own
performance, records,
tapes, radio, television,
concerts or ANYWHERE.

Are received
by eardrum that is sensitive
to sound vibrations

Mind perceives
qualities of sound movement
created by melody, rhythm,
harmony, tone color, form.

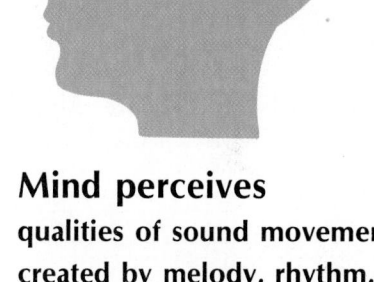

Feelings react
to all things the music is doing.
Each person reacts to the same
music, but in different ways
because of differences in
the way each person feels.

Judgment is made
about how musical qualities
are used, and how the whole
piece makes you feel.

More About Melody

OUTLINING A CHORD

The way the tones move gives a melody its shape, or contour. Sometimes the tones of a melody outline a chord. These patterns outline the C chord. Play them on the bells, then find the patterns in the melody of "Morning Has Broken."

C   E   G

Morning Has Broken

TRADITIONAL GAELIC MELODY   WORDS BY ELEANOR FARJEON

WORDS REPRINTED BY PERMISSION OF HAROLD OBER ASSOCIATES, INC. COPYRIGHT © 1957 ELEANOR FARJEON.

1. Morn-ing has bro - ken   Like the first morn - ing,   Black-bird has
2. Sweet the rain's new   fall   Sun - lit from heav - en,   Like the first

spo - ken   Like the first bird._____   Praise for the
dew - fall   on the first grass._____   Praise for the

sing - ing!   Praise for the morn - ing!   Praise for them,
sweet - ness   of the wet gar - den,   Sprung in com-

spring - ing   Fresh from the Word!_____
plete - ness.   Where His feet pass. _____

The countermelody for "Morning Has Broken" on page 75 has a contour, or shape, that is different from that of the melody.

74

COUNTERMELODY (SING WITH 2ND VERSE ONLY.)

Sweet the rain's new____ fall   Sun - lit from heav - en,

like the first dew - fall____ on   grass.____

Praise for the wet   gar - den____ where____

____ His____ feet____ pass. ____

You can sing these words with the melody of "Morning Has Broken."

BREAD FOR THE WORLD

1. Praise and thanksgiving,
   Father, we offer,
   for all things living
   thou madest good;
   harvest of sown fields,
   fruits of the orchard,
   hay from the mown fields,
   blossom and wood.

2. Bless thou the labor
   we bring to serve thee,
   that with our neighbor
   we may be fed.
   Sowing or tilling,
   we would work with thee;
   harvesting, milling,
   for daily bread.

3. Father, providing
   food for thy children,
   thy wisdom guiding
   teaches us share
   one with another,
   so that rejoicing
   with us, our brother
   may know thy care.

4. Then will thy blessing
   reach every people;
   all men confessing
   thy gracious hand.
   Where thy will reigneth
   no man will hunger;
   thy love sustaineth;
   fruitful the land.

Albert F. Bayly
Copyright Albert F. Bayly. Reprinted by permission.

OUTLINING THE F CHORD

Find the places in the B section of this song where the melody
outlines the tones of the F chord—F A C.

Upside Down-Inside Out

WORDS AND MUSIC BY PHIL NAMANWORTH AND JOEY LEVINE

© COPYRIGHT 1977 CRUSHING MUSIC (BMI) AND SHIRDI MUSIC (ASCAP) USED BY PERMISSION.

1. Ev - 'ry - bod - y knows   a friend can be___ good
   face,   more than an - y -

com - pa - ny,___   No - bod - y's clos - er to me___
bod - y else,___   I can al - ways see___ my - self___

than you.   'Cause you're the kind of friend   who's
in you.   It makes me wan - na smile   to

al - ways there___ on rain - y days,___   Think - in' up so
know that I___ was all a - lone,___   Now I have a

ma - ny ways___   To help me through. __
chap - er - one,___   Guess who?___

B When I'm feel - ing up - side down,   in - side out,

Stars   fall - in' from my skies.   You can turn my

76

seams   a - round,   Put my toes   back   on the ground, __

with   just   the love __   in   your   eyes. __   2. Hey there, fun - ny

__   in   your eyes. __

SCALES

The tones of a melody can be organized in several ways. You can use the piano keyboard or the bells to discover one way tones can be organized.

- Start anywhere on the piano keyboard and play half steps (don't skip any black or white keys) in a downward direction, then in an upward direction.
- Arrange the bells in half steps from the lowest C to the C above and play them one after the other upward and downward.

What you have played and heard is called a *chromatic scale*—a scale that uses only half steps.

Listen for places in this music where the tones move downward by half steps. Mozart: *String Quartet in D Minor,* Movement 4

How do you think a scale will sound if the tones are organized in whole steps? To find out, try this:

- Arrange the bells in this order—C-D-E-F#-G#-A#-C, and play them one after the other from low C to the C above. You will be playing a *whole-tone scale*.

Listen for the special sound of a whole-tone scale in this recording of a familiar tune. *America in Whole Tone*

THE MAJOR SCALE

Whole steps and half steps can be arranged to form different scales. Many of the songs you sing are based on a *major scale.*

Here is a major scale starting on G. Arrange the bells to match the diagram and notice the pattern of whole steps and half steps. Play this major scale upward and downward to hear its special sound.

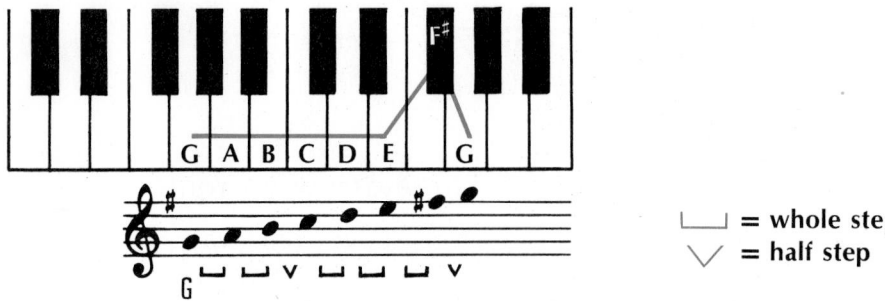

= whole step
= half step

Now listen to "Gonna Build a Mountain." The song is based on the G-major scale you just played.

For percussion parts, see p. 227.

Gonna Build a Mountain

WORDS AND MUSIC BY LESLIE BRICUSSE AND ANTHONY NEWLEY

Gon - na build   a   moun - tain   From a   lit - tle   hill.

Gon - na   build   a   moun - tain,   Least I   hope   I   will.

Gon - na   build   a   moun - tain,   Gon - na   build   it   high.

I   don't know how I'm gon - na do it,   On - ly know I'm gon - na   try.

THE MINOR SCALE

Here is another scale that starts on G. It will sound different from the G-major scale because the pattern of whole steps and half steps is different.

Arrange the bells to match the diagram and play the G-minor scale upward and downward. Then listen to "Go Down, Moses" to hear the special sound of a song based on the G-minor scale.

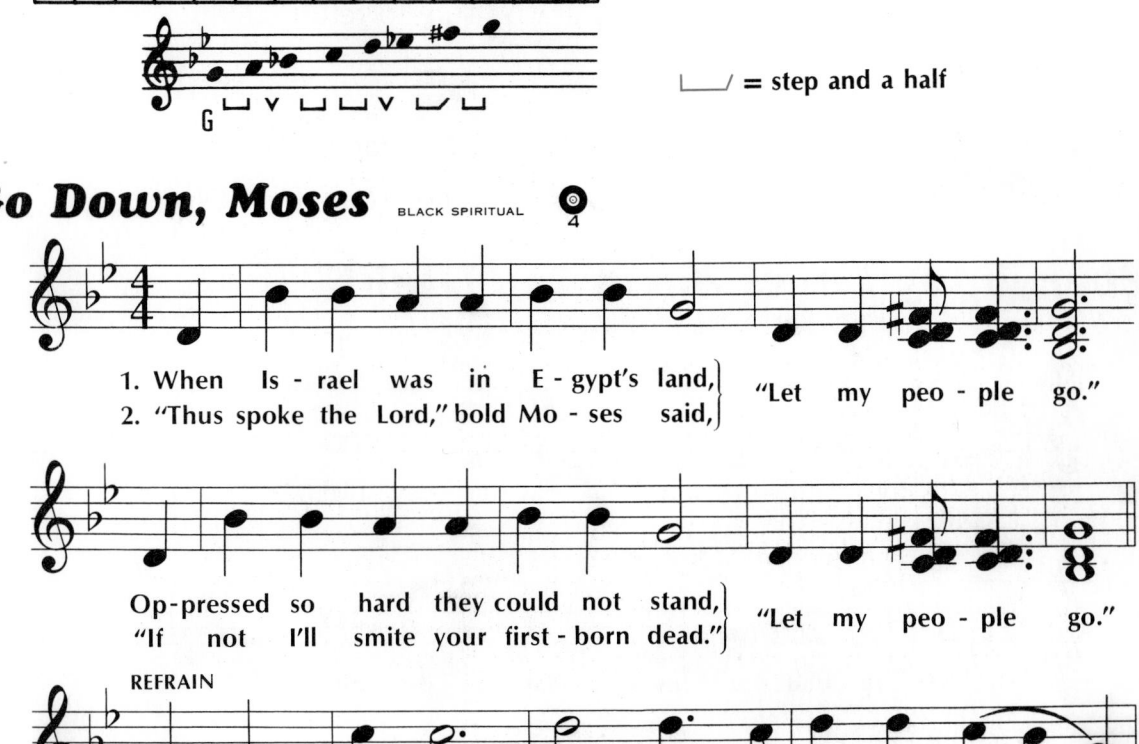

= step and a half

Go Down, Moses BLACK SPIRITUAL

1. When Is - rael was in E - gypt's land, "Let my peo - ple go."
2. "Thus spoke the Lord," bold Mo - ses said, "Let my peo - ple go."

Op-pressed so hard they could not stand, "Let my peo - ple go."
"If not I'll smite your first - born dead." "Let my peo - ple go."

REFRAIN

Go down, Mo - ses, 'Way down in E - gypt land, _____

Tell _____ old Phar - aoh, "Let my peo - ple go."

Songs in Major or Minor
4

THE HOME TONE

Look at the diagram below. The arrangement of whole steps
and half steps is the same as it is in the G-major scale shown
on page 78. But this arrangement starts on D.

Of all the tones in a scale, the first tone (the key tone or the
home tone) is the most important. Songs very often start and
end on the key tone. No matter how far a melody may wander
from this most important tone, it is always sure to return
"home."

Listen to "Everybody Loves Saturday Night." The song is based
on the D-major scale. It begins and ends on the home tone D.

Everybody Loves Saturday Night
FOLK SONG FROM GHANA

MORE ABOUT HOME TONES

"Artsa alinu" is based on a D-minor scale. Listen to the recording and notice how often the melody comes back to the home tone.

D E F G A B♭ C D

Artsa alinu FOLK SONG FROM ISRAEL

VOICES AND INSTRUMENTS

D MIN.   A MIN. D MIN.

La la la la la, la la la la la, La la la la la la.

D MIN.   A MIN. D MIN.

La la la la la, la la la la la, La la la la la la.

D MIN.

La la la la, la la la la la la, La la la la,

D MIN.

la la la la la la, La la la la la la la;

D MIN.   A MIN.   D MIN. A MIN. D MIN.

La la la la la la la. La la la la la la la;

A MIN.   D MIN. A MIN. A MIN. A MIN.

La la la la la la la.

For percussion parts, see p. 234.

Listen to *Tutú Maramba*. The piece is written in two sections. One section is based on a G-major scale, the other on a G-minor scale. Can you hear which is which?

Tutú Maramba

EXPERIENCES WITH WORLD MUSICS: INDIA

When you listened to the recording of *Folk Instrument Collage*,
listed on page 46 in your book, you heard some music from India
that sounded different from the music you hear every day. One of
the reasons that it sounded different is that the music of India is
based on organizations of tones that are different from our scales.

In the classical music of India, melodies are based on *ragas*. A raga, like a scale, is a series of tones on which a musical composition is based. There are hundreds of ragas and each one has a particular name and structure. Over a period of years, an Indian musician practices many ragas and gets to know each one of them as a friend.

On this recording you will hear a familiar melody as it is written based on a major scale. Then you will hear the same melody as it is written based on two Indian ragas—first, Raga Bhairavi, then Raga Purvi. As you listen, notice how each organization of tones gives the melody a special feeling.

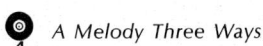

A Melody Three Ways

1. Melody based on the major scale

2. Melody based on Raga Bhairavi

3. Melody based on Raga Purvi

A FIVE-TONE SCALE

Folk music from many cultures is often based on a 5-tone scale called *pentatonic*. To hear the special sound of music that is based on a pentatonic scale, make up a melody on the black keys of the piano or on the upper row of the bells.

Before you begin, think about these questions. What meter will you use—$\frac{2}{4}$, $\frac{3}{4}$, $\frac{4}{4}$, or $\frac{6}{8}$? Will your melody move by steps, by leaps, by repeated tones, or by a combination of all three?

To add texture to your melody, choose someone to play (on the bells) one of the ostinato parts notated below. The meter of the bell part must match the meter of your melody.

With a mallet held in the left hand, play G♭ on notes with stems down. Play D♭ on notes with stems up.

THE SOUND OF PENTATONIC

The song on page 85 is based on a pentatonic scale starting on F. Play the scale, upward and downward, to hear the general sound of "There's No Hidin' Place."

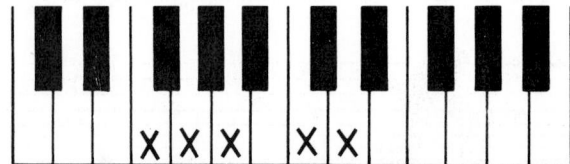

84

There's No Hidin' Place

BLACK SPIRITUAL

There's no hid - in' place down there, There's no hid - in' place down there. Oh, I went to the rock to hide my face, The rock cried out, "No hid - in' place," There's no hid - in' place down there.

1. Oh, the rock cried, "I'm burn - in', too," Oh, the rock cried, "I'm burn - in', too"; Oh, the rock cried out, "I'm burn - in', too, I want to go to heav-en as well as you." There's no hid - in' place down there. 2. Oh, the

fox got a hole in the ground, Oh, the fox got a hole in the ground; Oh, the fox got a hole, the bird got a nest, But us___ poor___ sin-ners got no hidin' place. There's no hid - in' place down there.

there. There's no hid - in' place down there, There's no hid - in' place down there. Oh, I went to the rock to hide my face, The rock cried out, "No hid - in' place," There's no hid - in' place down there.

TONAL MUSIC, ONE KEY TONE

You have sung and played melodies based on a variety of scales—each scale focusing on one tone, the key tone.

Music that uses one scale at a time, each with its key tone, or home tone, is called *tonal* music.

Using the four fingers of each hand, place your fingers on the keys that show the C scale in the diagram at the bottom of the page. Practice "playing" the C scale on the diagram, then try playing the C scale on the piano keyboard.

Look at the diagram at the bottom of page 87. It shows you how to play the D scale. Practice "playing" the D scale on the diagram, then try playing the D scale on the piano keyboard.

When you can play both scales, try playing the melody of "Chumbara" (page 33 in your book) in the key of C, then in the key of D.

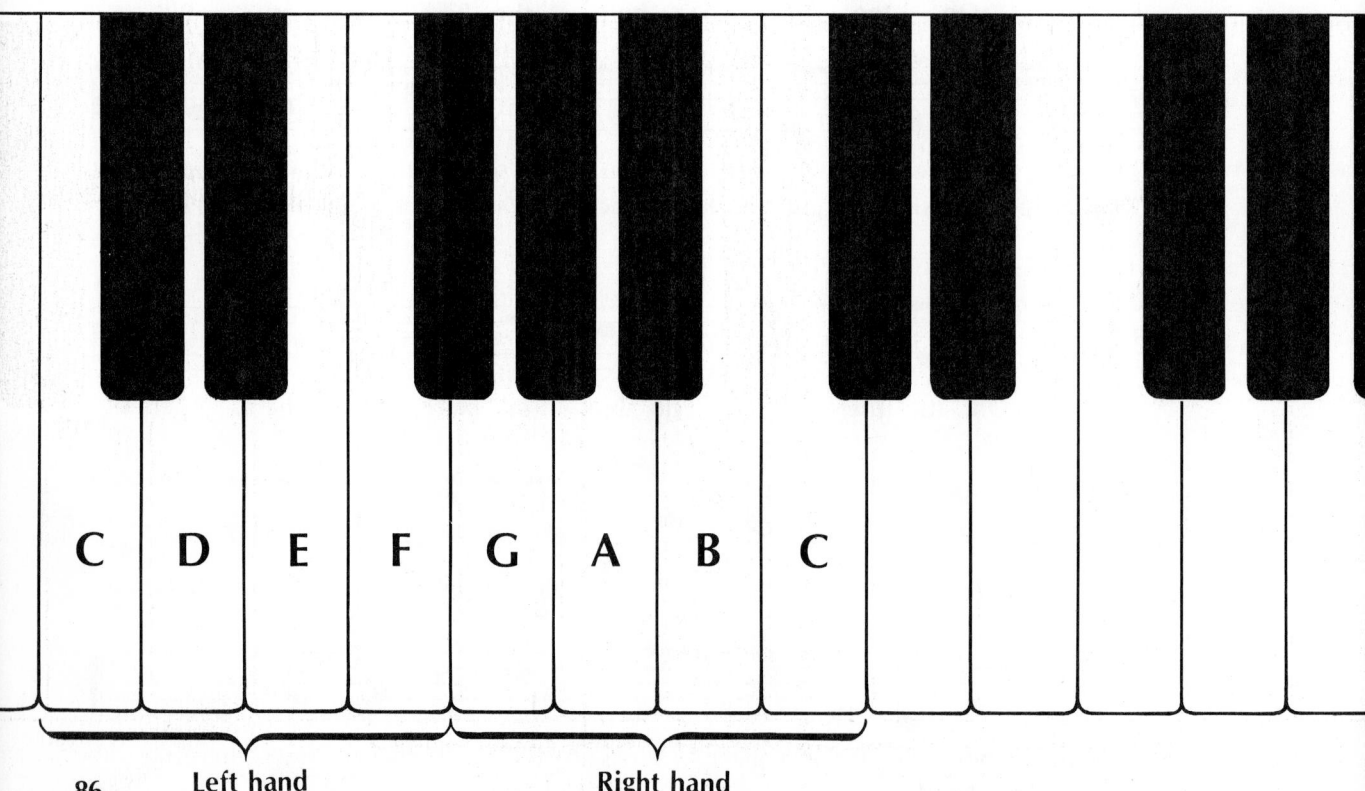

C D E F G A B C

Left hand   Right hand

POLYTONAL MUSIC, MANY KEY TONES

Most of the music you hear every day is tonal music. It is based on one scale and moves around one important tone. In some music, however, more than one scale is used at the same time. When music uses several scales together, it is called *polytonal* (*poly* means "many").

To hear the general sound of polytonal music, try this:
• Play "Chumbara" using the tones of the C scale.
• At the same time, have someone else play the same tune using the tones of the D scale.

Now listen to a piano piece that is polytonal. In this piece the left hand plays music based on one scale. At the same time, the right hand plays music based on a different scale. Notice the special sound when two scales are used together.

Can you think of a reason why *Black and White* is a good title for this polytonal music? ⊚ Starer: *Black and White*

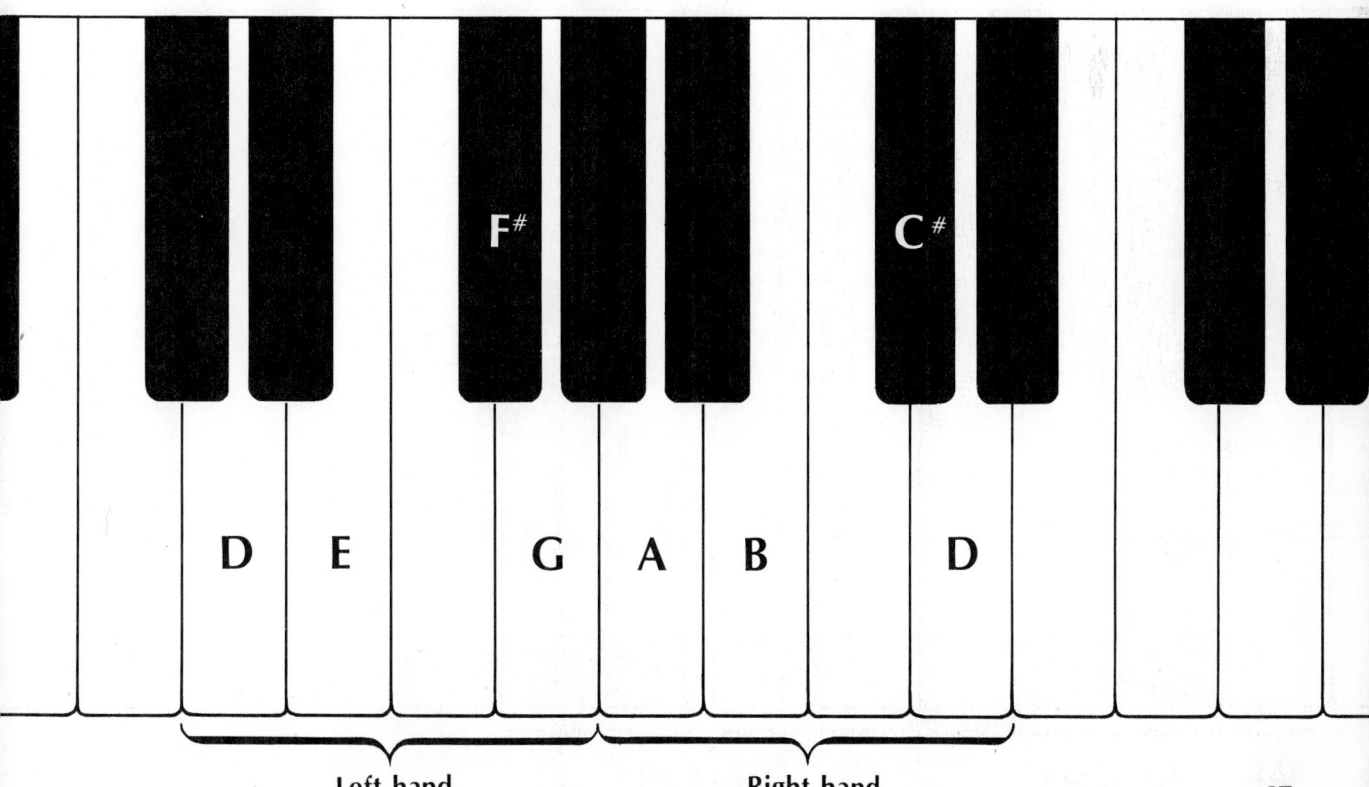

Left hand   Right hand   87

ATONAL MUSIC, NO KEY TONE

Some music uses an organization of tones in which there is no one focus sound—no key tone. All the tones are of equal importance. This music is called *atonal*.

Many composers use all the tones within the octave as a basis for their music. The twelve tones are arranged in a certain order, called a *tone row*.

Listen to this atonal piece played by a woodwind quintet.

 Eddleman: *Dualisms No. 2*

To play a tone row, arrange twelve bells in four sets of three bells as shown in the diagram at the bottom of pages 88 and 89.

After you have arranged the tone row, experiment to find ways of playing it.

1. Play the tones from left to right—the *original*. (You may repeat a tone several times when you get to it, but don't go back to it once you go on.)

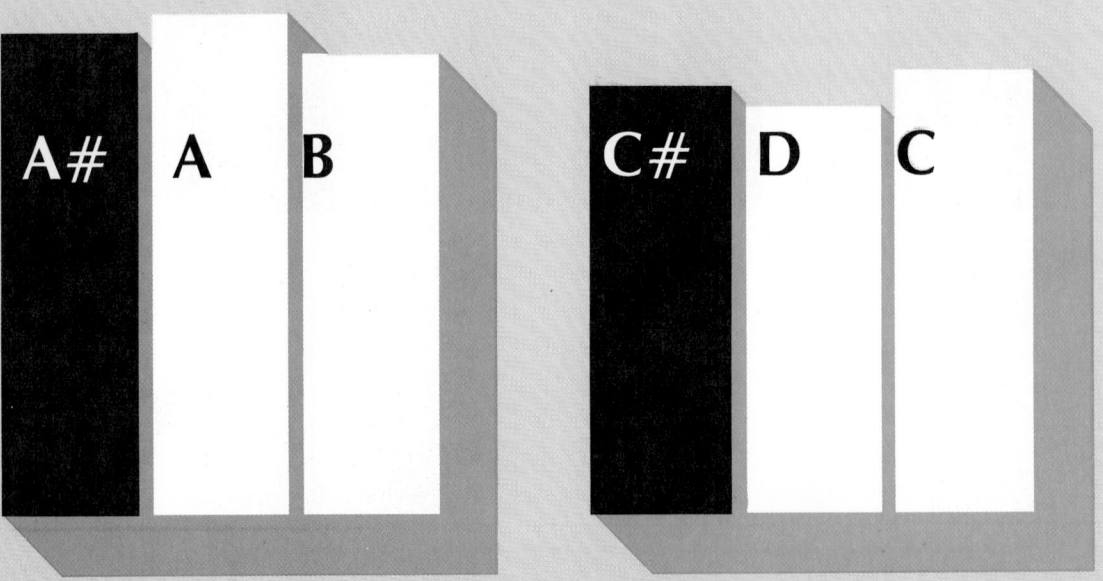

2. Play the row from right to left—the *retrograde*.

3. Play the tones in each set at the same time. Use three mallets, or strike them with the edge of a ruler or comb. Play the retrograde in the same way.

4. Going from left to right, play the tones in each set separately, then all three together. Play the retrograde in the same way.

After you have experimented with ways of playing the tone row, you can play along with the recording of *Dualisms 2*.

There are four places in the music where the instruments play a long sustained sound. Fill in one of the sustained sounds by playing the bells in one box of the tone row. During the next sustained sound, play the bells in a different box. Play another set of bells during the third sustained sound and the last set of bells during the fourth sustained sound.

Another time, play your part in a different way.

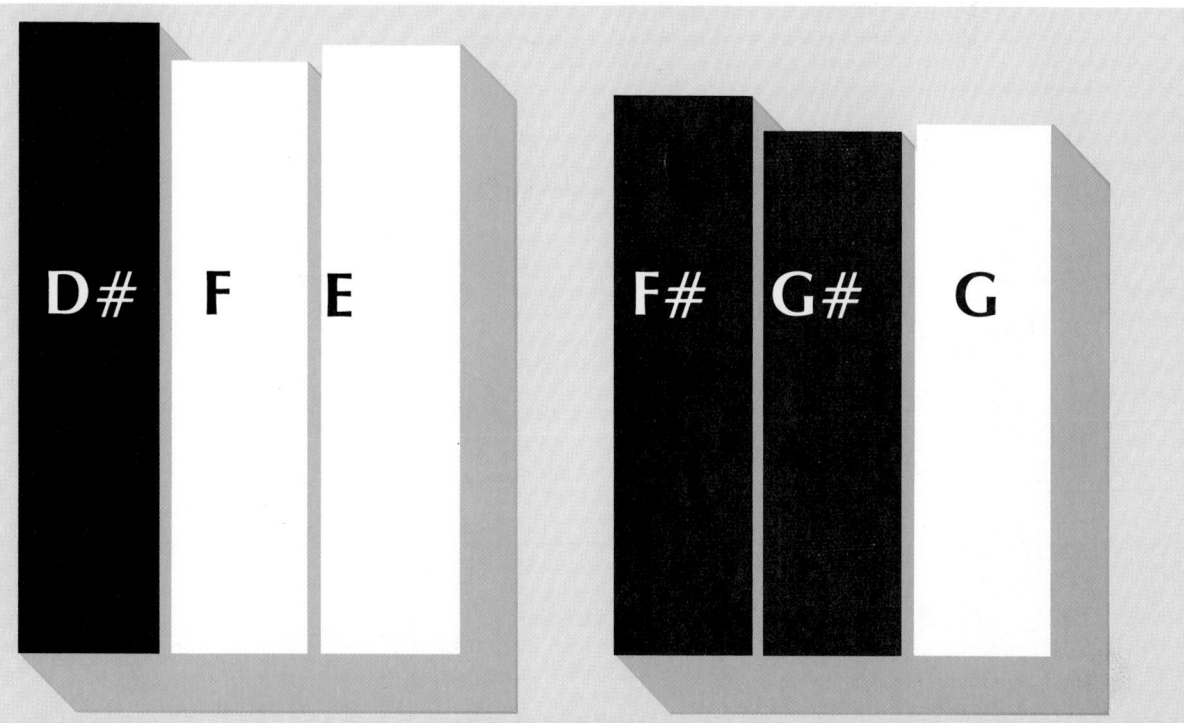

Listen to these pieces. Each time a number is called, choose the word that describes the tonality (the organization of whole and half steps). Is it major, or minor?

1	*MAJOR*	*MINOR*	**Bach: *Two-Part* Invention, No. 6**
2	*MAJOR*	*MINOR*	**Mi Caballo Blanco**
3	*MAJOR*	*MINOR*	**Raindrops Keep Falling on My Head**
4	*MAJOR*	*MINOR*	**Ez Jahia Ez Dantza**

This piece for orchestra has three sections. Each time a number is called, choose the word that describes the tonality.

1	*MAJOR*	*MINOR*
2	*MAJOR*	*MINOR*
3	*MAJOR*	*MINOR*

Tchaikovsky: *Dance of the Reed Flutes*

Listen to the recording. Each time a number is called, choose the word that describes the tonality. Is the music tonal, or atonal? If it is tonal, decide whether the melody is built on a major or a minor scale.

---

1   *TONAL*   *ATONAL*

major   minor

---

2   *TONAL*   *ATONAL*

major   minor

---

3   *TONAL*   *ATONAL*

major   minor

---

4   *TONAL*   *ATONAL*

major   minor

---

5   *TONAL*   *ATONAL*

major   minor

---

6   *TONAL*   *ATONAL*

major   minor

Balkan Hills Schottische
Joshua Fought the Battle of Jericho
Hill: *Tune for Canary, 1*

Eddleman: *Dualisms, No. 2*
Starer: *Variants for Violin and Piano*
Mozart: *String Quartet in D Minor*, Movement 4

DRESSING UP A MELODY

As you listen to the recording of this carol from Spain, decide
whether the tonality is major or minor. Also, follow the notes to
find two places where the melody is "dressed up," or decorated.
The color boxes will give you a clue.

Carol of the Birds

TRADITIONAL CAROL FROM SPAIN   ENGLISH WORDS BY ROSEMARY JACQUES

1. The night the Child was born,_____ The skies were bright as morn, The
2. The crea-tures proud and tall,_____ The low-liest ones of all, Did
3. And birds from ev-'ry-where_____ Flew gent-ly through the air And

heav'ns were filled with won - ders;_____ There shone a ra - diant star;_____
jour - ney forth to Beth - le-hem;_____ And round the man - ger bed_____
hov - ered o'er the sta - ble;_____ The ea - gle and the quail_____

_____ It beck oned near and far, "Come_ ye, oh come and praise_____
_____ They hum - bly bowed their heads, For_ they had come to praise_____
_____ The wren, the night - in - gale With_ one sweet voice did praise_____

Him."_____ There shone a ra - diant_ star;_____ It
Him._____ And round the man - ger_ bed_____ They
Him._____ The ea - gle and_ the_ quail,_____ The

beck-oned near and far, "Come_ ye, oh come and praise Him."_____
hum - bly bowed their heads, For_ they had come to praise Him._____
wren, the night - in - gale With_ one sweet voice did praise Him._____

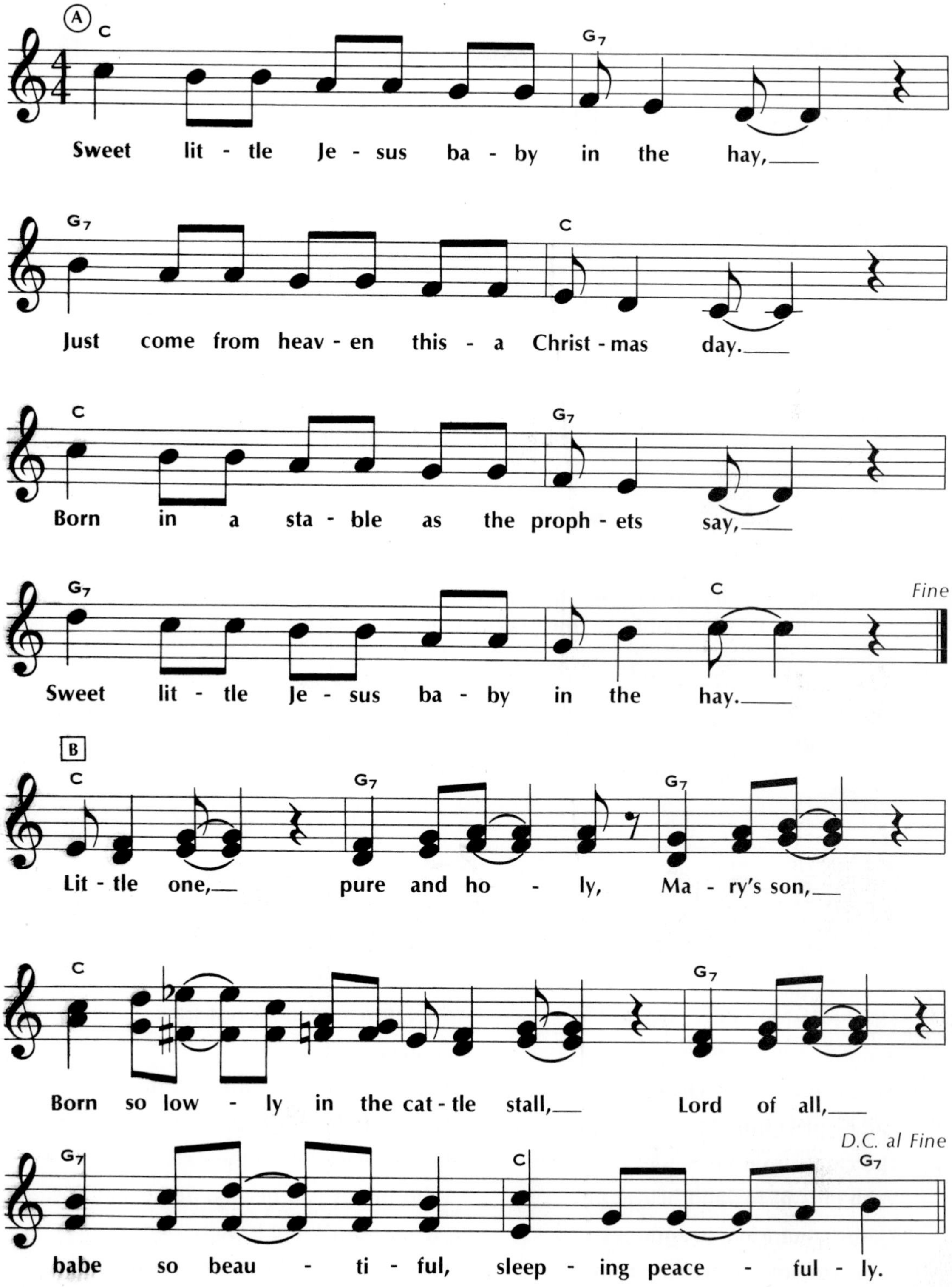

Sweet Little Jesus Baby

CHRISTMAS SPIRITUAL ENGLISH TEXT BY WALTER EHRET 5

What's going on in this melody? Is it major or minor? Are there sequences? To find out, use your eyes as well as your ears.

A
C G7
Sweet lit - tle Je - sus ba - by in the hay,
G7 C
Just come from heav - en this - a Christ - mas day.
C G7
Born in a sta - ble as the proph - ets say,
G7 C Fine
Sweet lit - tle Je - sus ba - by in the hay.
B
C G7 G7
Lit - tle one, pure and ho - ly, Ma - ry's son,
C G7
Born so low - ly in the cat - tle stall, Lord of all,
D.C. al Fine
G7 C G7
babe so beau - ti - ful, sleep - ing peace - ful - ly.

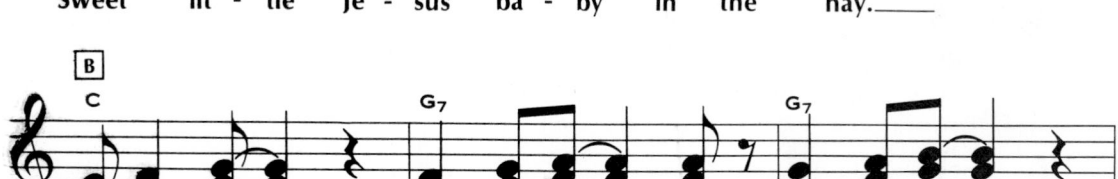

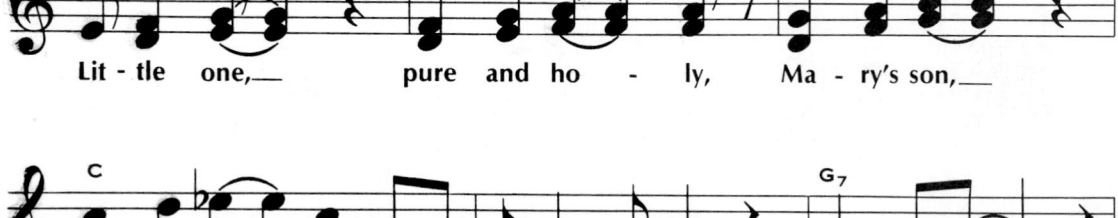

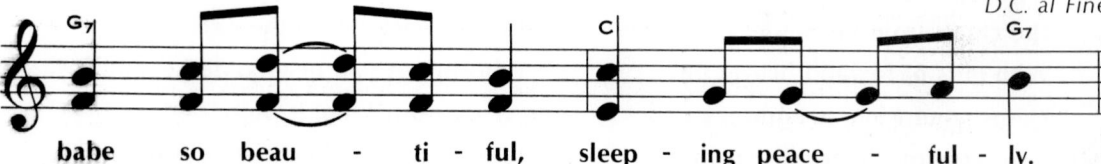

YOU'RE ON YOUR OWN

Think about all you have learned about melody. Then, using the
piano or bells, try playing this song from the notation.

The Huron Carol

CHRISTMAS CAROL FROM CANADA   ENGLISH WORDS BY J. E. MIDDLETON

TEXT BY PERMISSION OF THE FREDERICK HARRIS MUSIC CO., LTD.

1. 'Twas in the moon of win-ter-time When all the birds had fled,
2. With-in a lodge of bro-ken bark The ten-der babe was found,

That might-y Git-chi Man-i-tou Sent an-gel choirs in-stead.
A rag-ged robe of rab-bit skin En-wrapped his beau-ty 'round;

Be-fore their light the stars grew dim, And won-d'ring hunt-ers heard the hymn:___
And as the hunt-er braves drew nigh The an-gel song rang loud and high:___

"Je-sus, your King, is born. Je-sus is born.

In ex-cel-sis glo-ri-a!"

3. The earliest moon of wintertime
   Is not so round and fair
   As was the ring of glory on
   The helpless infant there.
   The chiefs from far before him knelt
   With gifts of fox and beaver pelt.
   "Jesus, your King, is born.
   Jesus is born. *In excelsis gloria!*"

4. O children of the forest free,
   O sons of Manitou,
   The holy child of earth and heav'n
   Is born today for you.
   Come kneel before the radiant boy
   Who brings you beauty, peace, and joy.
   "Jesus, your King, is born.
   Jesus is born. *In excelsis gloria!*"

Styles: *Performance*

A melody can be performed in a variety of ways by changing the tonality, rhythm, tempo, dynamics, tone color, and texture. For some melodies, there is no one right way—no one "proper style." Each different style of performance has a musical flavor of its own.

"Amazing Grace" has been sung and played by many people since the early days of America. In this sound collage, you will hear the melody performed in different styles. The chart will help you hear what is going on in each performance.

CALL CHART 6: Styles of Performance

1 *Melody alone—played on a dulcimer*

2 *Melody ornamented—played on a dulcimer*

3 *Melody with a drone accompaniment—played on a dulcimer*

4 *Melody ornamented—sung by a woman with vocal accompaniment*

5 *Melody ornamented—played on a bagpipe with drone accompaniment*

6 *Melody sung by children with Autoharp and recorder accompaniment*

7 *Music performed by adult voices*

8 *Melody ornamented—sung by a woman with piano and organ accompaniment*

A STYLE OF YOUR OWN

Use *Call Chart 6* (page 95) as a guide and create your own style of performance. Combine the melody of "Amazing Grace" with some of the added parts on the next page. You can use

- different vocal tone colors,
- different instrumental tone colors,
- different textures—combination of parts,
- different tempos and dynamics.

Amazing Grace

EARLY AMERICAN MELODY   WORDS BY JOHN NEWTON

1. A - maz - ing ___ grace how sweet the sound That
2. 'Twas grace that ___ taught my heart to fear, And

saved a ___ wretch like me! ___ I once ___ was
grace my ___ fears re - lieved; ___ How pre - cious ___

lost, but now ___ am ___ found, Was blind, but ___
did that grace ___ ap - pear The hour I ___

now I see. ___
first be - lieved! ___

3. Through many dangers, toils, and snares,
   I have already come;
   'Tis grace has brought me safe thus far,
   And grace will lead me home.

4. The Lord has promised good to me,
   His word my hope secures;
   He will my shield and portion be
   As long as life endures.

ADDED PARTS FOR "AMAZING GRACE"

Sing this vocal countermelody with the melody of "Amazing Grace."

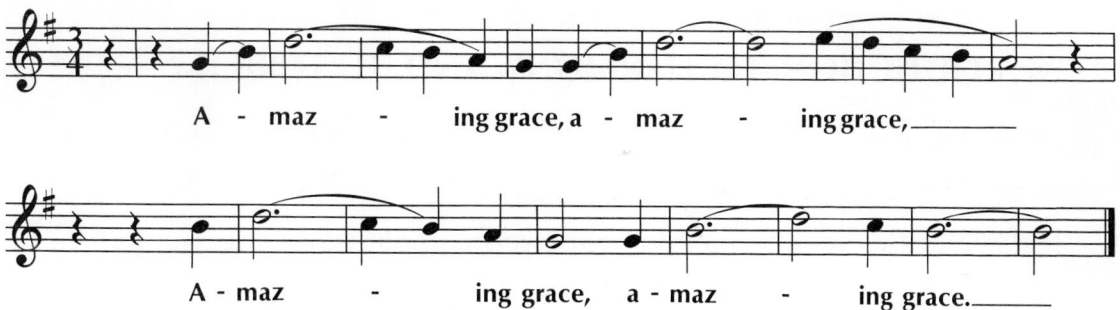

A - maz - ing grace, a - maz - ing grace,____

A - maz - ing grace, a - maz - ing grace.____

Play a drone on the bells or on the Autoharp throughout the song.

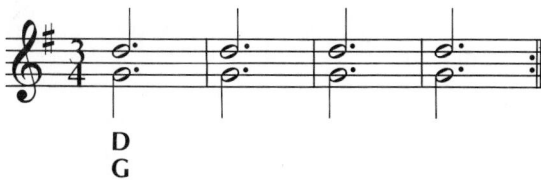

D
G

Which instrumental countermelody will you play—the one that uses mostly low tones, or the one that uses mostly high tones?

COUNTERMELODY 1

COUNTERMELODY 2

Using What You Know About Harmony and Texture

INTRODUCTION TO HARMONY AND TEXTURE

Music has melody and harmony. They can be put together in a variety of ways. The way they are used, separately or together, is called *texture*. In this section you will learn more about musical texture.

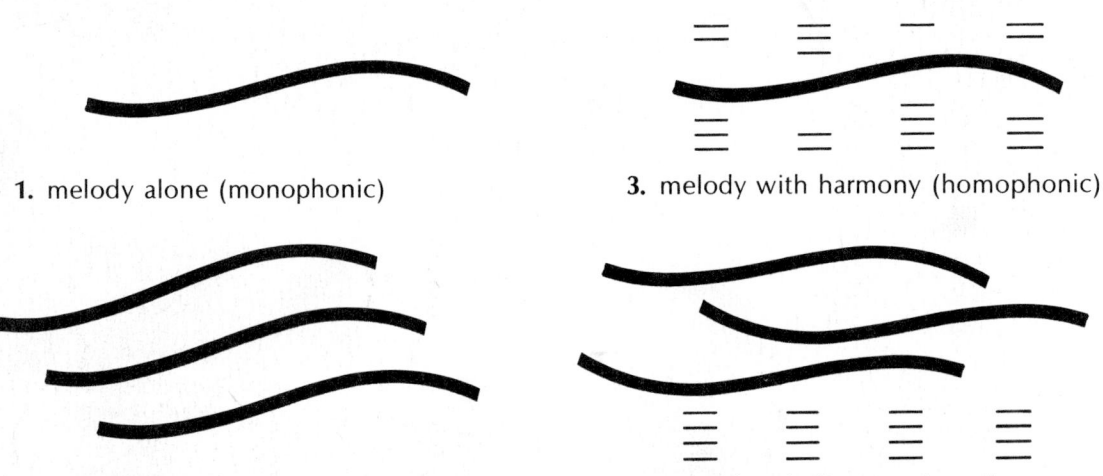

1. melody alone (monophonic)

3. melody with harmony (homophonic)

2. several melodies together (polyphonic)

4. several melodies together plus harmony (mixed texture)

Fabrics have texture. The kind of material used, the colors, the thickness and thinness of yarn, the amount of space between the strands, the repetitions and contrasts, all add up to something we can almost feel, even if we do not touch it.

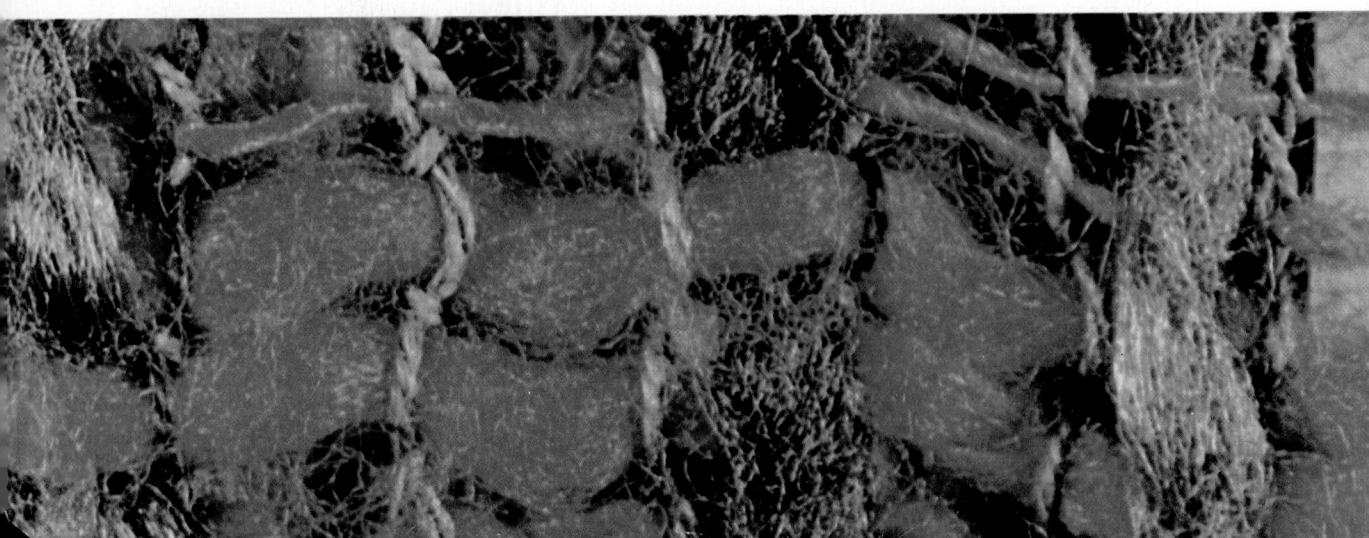

The Starry Night: Van Gogh

We don't usually feel paintings with our fingers. Yet our eyes tell us that they have a "feel." This visual feel—texture—is an important part of the experience we get from many paintings.

Many things we see give us a sense of texture—of a "feel" they have—whether we touch them or not. Our eyes tell us what our hands would feel if we touched them.

In music, there is nothing for our hands to feel—only sounds. Our ears hear how the sounds go together in melodies and harmonies. We can't see it. We can't touch it. But somehow we can feel it.

99

A MELODY LINE ALONE

Turn back to page 98 and look at the photograph of the woolen fabric. Trace one of the red strands of wool that goes horizontally from left to right.

With the tip of your finger, trace the melody line in the song "Let Us Rejoice."

Let Us Rejoice   MUSIC BY CHRISTOPH PRAETORIUS   ENGLISH WORDS BY RICHARD MORRIS

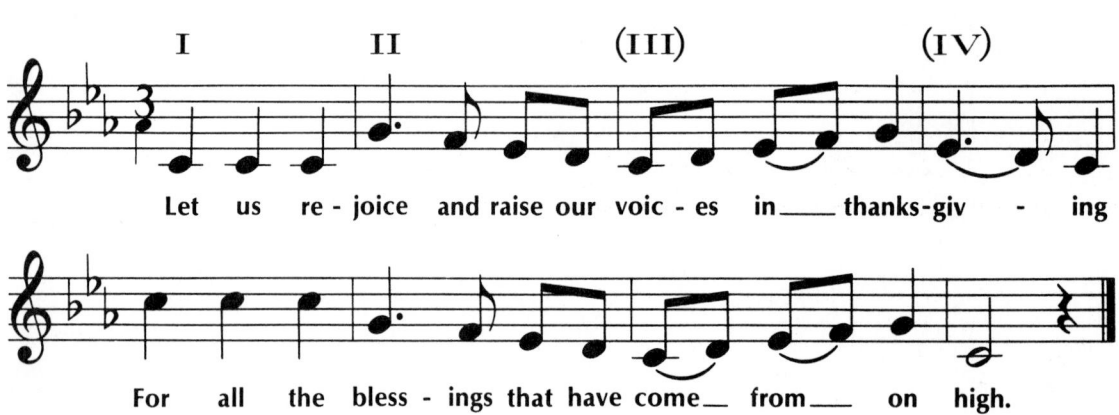

Let us re-joice and raise our voic-es in ___ thanks-giv - ing

For all the bless - ings that have come ___ from ___ on high.

Now trace the melody line of this folk melody from China.

Purple Bamboo   FOLK MELODY FROM CHINA

When one melody line is sung or played all by itself, the musical texture is called *monophonic*. Remember, *mono* means "one." Look on page 98 and find the symbol that shows one melody line.

SEVERAL MELODY LINES TOGETHER

When you are familiar with the tune of "Hallelujah," sing it as a
melody alone.

Hallelujah FOLK ROUND FROM ISRAEL

Hal - le - lu - jah,___ hal - le - lu - jah,___ hal - le - lu - jah, hal -
le - lu - jah. Hal - le - lu - jah, hal - le - lu -
jah.___ Hal - le - lu, hal - le - lu, hal - le - lu - jah.___

When two or more melodies are sung together, the musical
texture is called *polyphonic*. Remember, *poly* means "many."
Find the symbol on page 98 that shows several melodies
together.

You can change the texture of "Hallelujah" from monophonic
(one melody line) to polyphonic by singing it as a two- or
three-part round.

OTHER ROUNDS TO SING TWO WAYS

It's Not That Nina's Naughty, page 21
My Dame Hath a Lame, Tame Crane, page 30
Let Us Rejoice, page 100

ONE MELODY WITH CHORD ACCOMPANIMENT

Sinner Man   BLACK SPIRITUAL

FROM FOLK SONGSTER BY LEON AND LYNN DALLIN   © 1967 WILLIAM C. BROWN CO., PUBLISHERS   USED BY PERMISSION

1. Oh, sin-ner man, where you gon-na run to? Oh, sin-ner man, where you gon-na run to? Oh, sin-ner man, where you gon-na run to, All on that day? / On that day?

2. **Run to the rock, the rock was a-melting,** (*3 times*)
   All on that day.

3. **Run to the trees, trees were a-swaying,** (*3 times*)

4. **Fall to the earth, earth was a-rolling,** (*3 times*)

5. **Run to the sea, the sea was a-raging,** (*3 times*)

6. **Oh, sinner man, you should-a been a-praying,** (*3 times*)

7. **Oh, sinner man, where you gonna run to?** (*3 times*)

102

TWO MELODIES WITH CHORD ACCOMPANIMENT

When Autoharp chords are added to a melody, the musical texture is called *homophonic.* Find the symbol on page 98 that shows a melody with chords (harmony) added.

The Drunken Sailor CAPSTAN SHANTEY

1. What shall we do with a drunk-en sail-or? What shall we do with a
2. Hoist him___ up with a run-ning bow-line, Hoist him___ up with a
3. Put him in the long-boat un-til he's so-ber, Put him in the long-boat un-

drunk-en sail-or? What shall we do with a drunk-en sail-or
run-ning bow-line, Hoist him___ up with a run-ning bow-line,
til he's so-ber, Put him in the long-boat un-til he's so-ber,

Ear-lye in the morn-ing? Way, hey, and up she ris-es, Way, hey, and up she ris-es, Way, hey, and

up she ris-es Ear-lye in the morn - ing.

4. Pull out the plug and wet him all over, . . .   5. Tie him to the mast until he's sober, . . .

6. That's what we do with a drunken sailor, . . .

"Sinner Man" (melody only) and "The Drunken Sailor" can be sung together. When Autoharp chords are added to the performance, the texture is called *mixed texture.* Find the symbol for mixed texture on page 98.

CHECK THE TEXTURE

Before listening to the recording, look at the score of "The Side Show." The music consists of a melody line accompanied by chords written for the piano. Draw a diagram that shows the texture. Then check your diagram with diagram 3 on page 98 in your book.

Notice the meter changes throughout the song. The composer used the meter changes to suggest the stumbling of the old horse as he turns the merry-go-round.

The Side Show
WORDS AND MUSIC BY CHARLES IVES

old horse un - sound,_ turns the mer - ry - go - round, mak - ing poor Mis - ter

Ri - ley look a bit like a Rus - sian dance,_ Some speak of so

high - ly, as _ they do of Ri - ley! _

Sing

MUSIC BY VACLAV NELHYBEL   WORDS BY D. DINAND

I sing when I'm hap-py, I sing when I'm glad.
We sing when we're hap-py, we sing when we're glad.

I sing when I feel like cry-ing, I sing when I am
We sing when we feel like cry-ing, we sing when we are

sad. Glad or sad or mad or snap-py,
sad.

sad or glad or mad or hap-py. My cat
You, too,

meows when hap-py, my dog barks when glad. My dad,
when you're hap-py, you, too, when you're sad, should sing

1.
mad or
moth-er, broth-er, sis-ter sing when they are mad or sad or glad or hap-py.
when you feel like cry-ing

2.
way
and you'll feel right a-way all pep-py glad and hap-py yes, yes.

Hap - py and glad. _____ Sing!

CALL CHART 7: Texture

Bernstein: *Mass,* "Alleluia"

1 Polyphonic (*melody in voices and instruments, percussion accompaniment*)

2 Polyphonic

3 Homophonic (*voices singing in chords*)

4 Polyphonic

CALL CHART 8: Texture

Handel: *Messiah,* "Hallelujah!" Chorus

1 Homophonic (*melody played by strings*)

2 Mixed (*voice melody and orchestra melody with chords*)

3 Monophonic and homophonic alternately

4 Polyphonic (*several melodies in voices and orchestra*)

5 Homophonic (*voices and orchestra have melody together*)

6 Monophonic then polyphonic (*several melody lines in voices*)

7 Polyphonic (*two melodies overlapping*)

8 Polyphonic (*several melodies overlapping*)

9 Polyphonic (*two melodies overlapping*)

10 Mixed (*several melodies plus chords*)

11 Homophonic

FOUR DIFFERENT TEXTURES

You will hear four different performances of the Korean folk song "Ahrirang." The list below will help you name the texture of each performance as you hear it.

1. A melody alone

2. A melody with chords (drone)

3. A melody as a round

4. A melody with countermelody plus chords (drone)

"Ahrirang" is based on a pentatonic (5-tone) scale. To hear its special sound, play the scale on the piano keyboard or on bells.

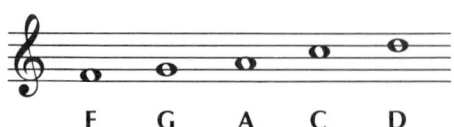

F   G   A   C   D

When you know the song, create different textures by combining the melody with one or more of the instrumental parts on page 110.

Ahrirang

FOLK SONG FROM KOREA   ENGLISH WORDS BY ALICE FIRGAU

1. Ah - ri-rang, Ah - ri-rang, Ah - ra - ri - yo,_____
2. Ah - ri-rang, Ah - ri-rang, Ah - ra - ri - yo,_____

O - ver the___ hills_____ of___ Ah - ri - rang.
O - ver the___ hills_____ of___ Ah - ri - rang.

Voic - es call me from far_____ a - way.___
Years have passed_____ since I went___ a - way._____

I_____ must___ fol - low,___ I___ can - not stay.
Back_____ to___ Ah - ri - rang I'll go_____ some day.

109

ADDED PARTS FOR "AHRIRANG"

Plan your own performance of "Ahrirang," using one or more of the parts below.

Recorder (Play throughout)

Flute

For an Autoharp accompaniment, pluck an F and a C string together. Use one of these rhythm patterns and play it all through the song.

For a bell accompaniment, play the tones F and C, one after the other all through the song. The notation will show you when to play F and when to play C.

For a bell (or other mallet instrument) accompaniment, play this part.

WHAT DO YOU HEAR? 6: Texture

Listen for different textures in music. Use these questions as a guide as you listen to the pieces listed below. You can listen alone or with a group. You may have to listen several times to answer the questions.

Do you hear a melody alone (monophonic)?

Do you hear a melody with harmony (homophonic)?

Do you hear a melody with other melodies (polyphonic)?

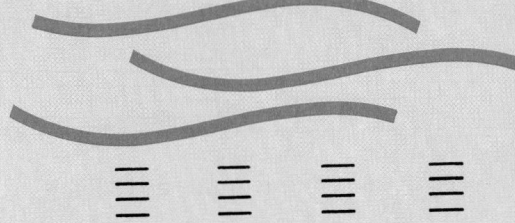

Do you hear several melodies with harmony (mixed)?

1	*Purple Bamboo*	4	Guthrie: *This Land Is Your Land*
2	Bach: *Trio Sonata No. 1*	5	Verdi: *Aida,* "Grand March"
3	Bach: *Chorale*	6	*Gregorian Chant*

Minor   Monophonic   Brass
Percussion   Woodwind
String   Homophonic   Major

Rock of Ages

TRADITIONAL HEBREW MELODY   ENGLISH WORDS BY G. GOTTHEIL

As you listen to the recording of "Rock of Ages," read these
sentences and fill in the blanks.

* The accompaniment uses instruments of the _____ family.
* The melody is based on a _____ scale.
* The voices and instruments create a _____ texture.

Rock of A - ges, let our song   Praise Thy sav - ing pow - er;

Thou, a - midst the rag´-ing foes,   Wast our shel - t'ring tow - er.

Fu - rious they as - sailed   us,   But Thine arm a - vailed _____ us,

Fu - rious they as - sailed   us,   But Thine arm a - vailed _____ us,

And   Thy word   broke their sword When our own strength failed __ us.

And   Thy word   broke their sword When our own strength failed __ us.

Battle Hymn of the Republic

MUSIC BY WILLIAM STEFFE   WORDS BY JULIA WARD HOWE

1. Mine eyes have seen the glory of the coming of the Lord;
   He is trampling out the vintage where the grapes of wrath are stored;
   He hath loosed the fateful lightning of His terrible swift sword;
   His truth is marching on.

2. He has sounded forth the trumpet that shall never call retreat;
   He is sifting out the hearts of men before the judgment seat.
   Oh, be swift, my soul, to answer Him! Be jubilant, my feet!
   Our God is marching on.

For percussion parts, see pp. 230 and 231.

113

TEXTURE: THICK AND THIN

The more parts you add to the texture, the thicker its density.

So My Sheep May Safely Graze

WORDS AND MUSIC BY ROD McKUEN

Ⓐ

1. So   my sheep may safe-ly graze___   I'd climb the high-est hill,___
2. All   good shep-herds watch their flocks___   to the low-est lamb___
3. Last night there were sol-diers on___   the   road___ be-low the town___

___   And keep a watch___ out   for   the hawk___
___   So   that they___ may   safe-ly graze___
___   And crea-tures___ in the   heav-ens with___

and for the howl-ing wolf.___   I   made a friend out
and nev-er come to harm.___   Guard-ed from   the
wings___ of shin-y gold.___   One   of them came

of   the wind___   and got to know   the   snow.   So
hunt-er's horn___   shield-ed from   the   sun.
close   to me___   say-ing,   "Do not be   a - fraid.   A

e - ven   in   the   win-ter-time___   my sheep may safe-ly graze.___
All   my sheep may safe-ly graze___   in   far fields   or at   home.___
child   of God   was born this night;___   Your sheep may safe-ly graze."___

114

[B] REFRAIN

1,2: Call-ing, "Come, sheep, come, I'll count you one by one.

3: Call-ing, "Come, sheep, come, I'll count you one by one.

1,2: One for John and one for Ja - cob, One for Job and one for the

3: Ah _____ And ___ one for the

1,2: child who's born this morn - ing in Beth - le - hem."
(born _____)

3: child who's born in Beth - le - hem."

Alleluia, Amen TRADITIONAL ROUND

I
Al - le - lu - ia, al - le - lu - ia.

II
A - men, a - men.

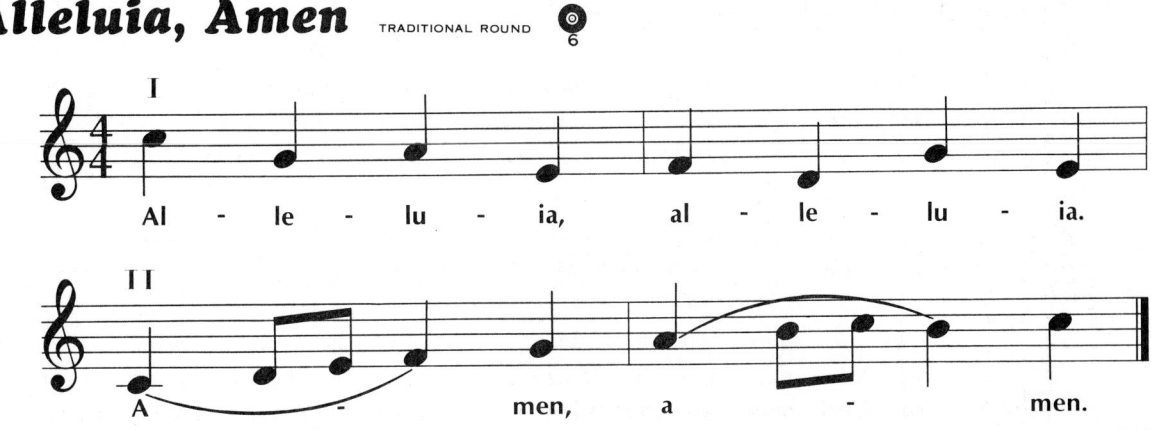

Style: *New Music*

ELECTRONIC SOUNDS

In every period of history some composers have looked for new ways to create music. And as these new ways are created, they are added on to the music that has gone before.

In our times an important thing has happened—the invention of new ways to create sounds by electronic machines. These machines allow composers to do things never before possible with sounds. They can now create extremes of sound that traditional instruments cannot produce.

Here are some of the musical elements that can be extended, or expanded, by using electronic instruments.

steps leaps

thick thin   high low

long short   *loud soft*

In some electronic pieces, the sounds are both produced by the instrument (called a *sound synthesizer*) and changed by the instrument according to the composer's wishes.

In this piece, all the sounds except that of the drum were made by electronic instruments. How would you describe what you hear? Is the piece musically "far-out," or experimental? Or does it sound like music you're used to hearing?

Resnick: *Yummy, Yummy, Yummy*

116

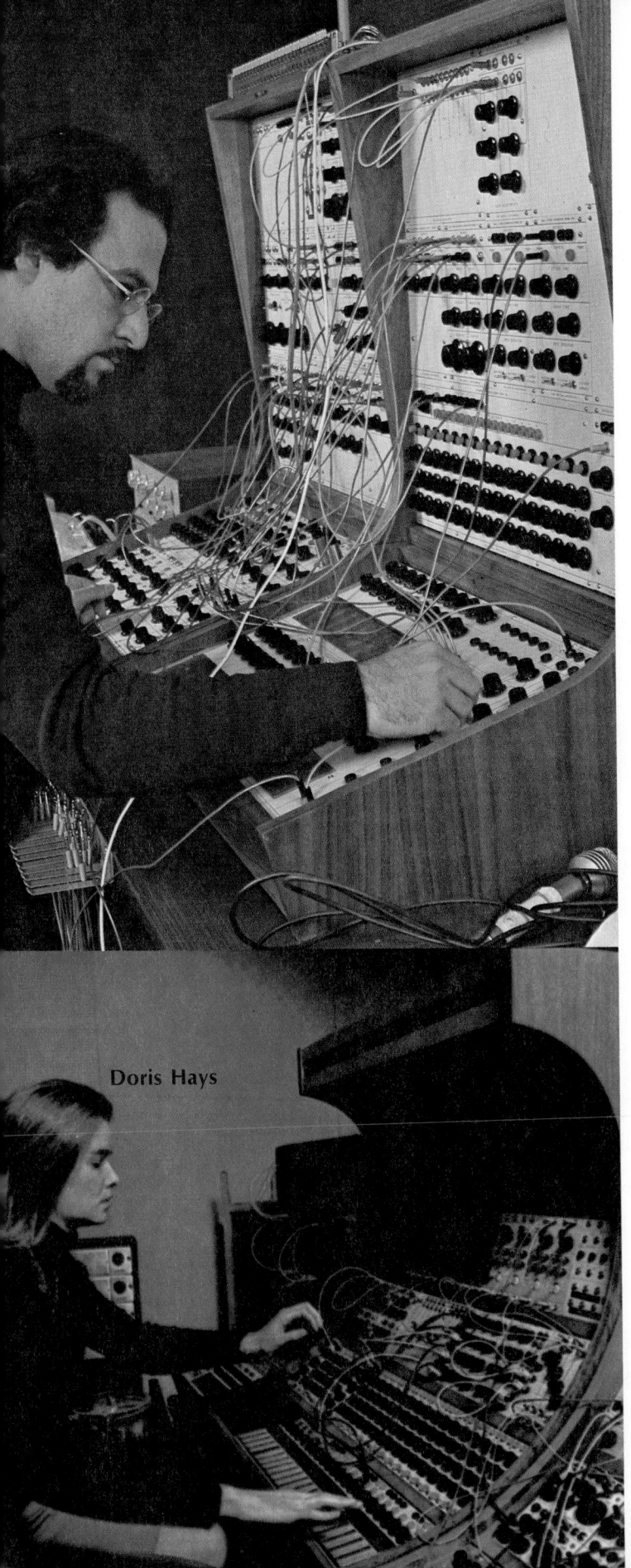

Doris Hays

In this next piece, all the sounds except the voice were made by electronic instruments. Even the voice sounds were changed electronically. Does this piece sound traditional?

⊚ Pousseur: *Trois Visages de Liege,*
6   Movement 1

The next three pieces are different because the original sound for each one was *not* produced by an electronic instrument. In each piece a very common sound was recorded, and then changed by an electronic machine. Can you guess what the original sound was for each piece?

⊚ Le Caine: *Dripsody*
6

⊚ Mimargolu: *Bowery Bum*
6

⊚ Bogusky-Reimer: *Dawn Figures*
6

You can record sounds and then change them in many ways by using a tape recorder. The material on pages 118 and 119 will tell you how to do it.

USING A TAPE RECORDER TO CHANGE SOUNDS   JOYCE BOGUSKY-REIMER

If you have a tape recorder, you can change sounds in several ways.
These sounds can then be used to make a musical composition.

On this recording you will hear how some "everyday" sounds
have been altered using the speed change dial on a tape
recorder. Can you name the original sources? ◎ *Everyday Sound Collage*

SPEED CHANGES

Many tape recorders have two speeds. You can change sounds
by recording at one speed and playing back at the other.

When you record at high speed and play back at low speed,
pitched sounds are one octave lower, the speed is twice as
slow, and the quality of the sound changes.

When you record at low speed and play back at high speed,
pitched sounds are one octave higher, the speed is twice as fast,
and the quality of the sound changes. ◎ *Speed Changes*

SOUND WITH SOUND

If you have a stereo recorder with two *Record* switches, you can
record sound with sound.

Record a sound on *Channel 1.* Rewind the tape and record a
second sound on *Channel 2.* Be sure the Record switch for
Channel 1 is off.

CHANNEL 1	SOUND
CHANNEL 2	SOUND

You can also plan to record on *Channel 2* during silent spaces
you have left on *Channel 1.* Plan the duration of sound on both
channels. Here is an example.

Seconds	0	10"		20"		30"	40"
CHANNEL 1	SOUND				SOUND		
CHANNEL 2			SOUND				SOUND

Follow one of these plans. When you play these back, you hear
separate sounds from each speaker. ◎ *Sound with Sound*

SOUND ON SOUND

When the sounds from two sources are combined on one channel and can no longer be separated, the result is sound on sound. You hear both parts on both speakers.

One way to do this is to play back both channels on which you have recorded sound with sound and record the result on a second tape recorder.

Another way to get sound on sound is to by-pass the erase head (the head closest to the feed reel) when you are recording the second sound.

Either way, record the second sound at a lower volume. ◉ *Sound on Sound*

MAKING A TAPE LOOP

First, record a sound that lasts for 3 or 4 seconds. Make a mark with a white grease pencil or crayon at the beginning and at the end of the sound.

Using a splicing bar, cut out the piece of tape and splice the ends together with splicing tape, forming a loop. Do it carefully so there will be no click or other noise at the point of the splice. Play the loop on a tape recorder and listen to the repeated sound. It can be used as an ostinato in a piece. ◉ *Making a Tape Loop*

Use some of these ideas to create a tape piece of your own. Here is an example. ◉ *Piece for Tape Recorder*

More About Harmony and Texture

LINES OF SOUND

When you can sing the melody of "Hava nashira," the tones of
each phrase create a single horizontal line of sound.

When the tones of all three phrases are sounded together,
vertical lines of sounds (chords) are created.

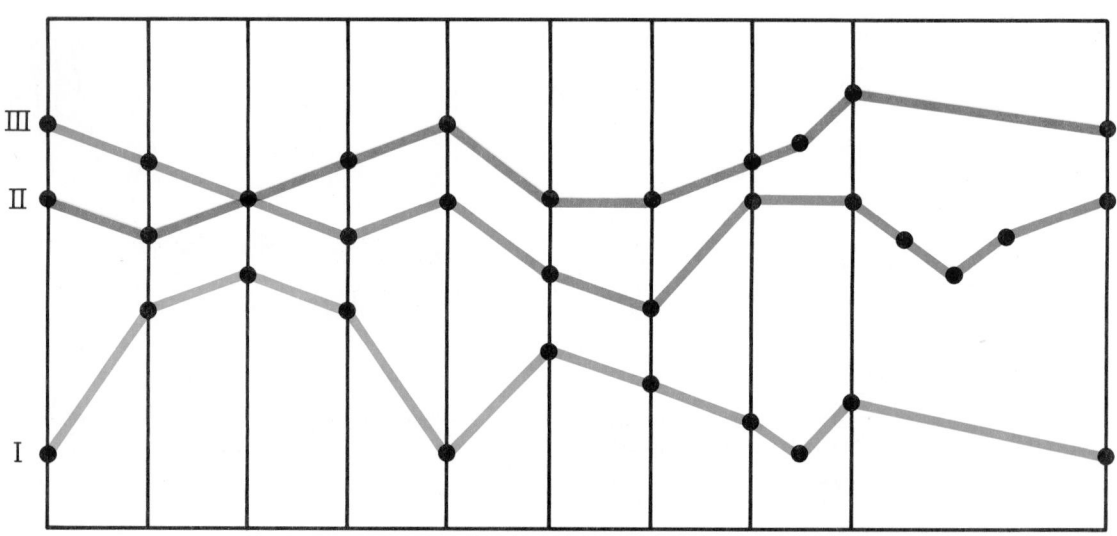

Hava Nashira ROUND FROM ISRAEL

ONE MELODY, DIFFERENT TEXTURES

The color boxes show the first two phrases in this eight-phrase melody. Find other phrases that are like phrase 1 or phrase 2. Recognizing like phrases will help you learn to play the whole melody. Play it on flute, recorder, piano, or bells.

Chorale Melody

MELODY BY JOHANN SCHOP For a recorder ensemble, see p. 213.

When "Chorale Melody" is performed alone, the texture is monophonic. Change this texture to homophonic by playing your part along with this recording.

Chorale Melody, Version 1

Listen to another arrangement of the chorale melody. In this version you will hear a mixed texture. Listen especially for what happens at the end of each phrase.

Chorale Melody, Version 2

AFRICAN RHYTHM COMPLEX

Chant each line of the following set of numbers. Clap on the large-size numbers only as you chant.

1. $\overset{>}{1}$ 2 $\overset{>}{3}$ 4 $\overset{>}{5}$ 6 7 $\overset{>}{8}$ 9 $\overset{>}{10}$ 11 $\overset{>}{12}$

2. $\overset{>}{1}$ 2 3 $\overset{>}{4}$ 5 6 $\overset{>}{7}$ 8 9 $\overset{>}{10}$ 11 12

3. $\overset{>}{1}$ 2 $\overset{>}{3}$ 4 5 6 $\overset{>}{7}$ 8 9 $\overset{>}{10}$ 11 12

4. $\overset{>}{1}$ 2 3 $\overset{>}{4}$ 5 6 $\overset{>}{7}$ 8 9 $\overset{>}{10}$ 11 12

5. 1 2 $\overset{>}{3}$ 4 5 $\overset{>}{6}$ 7 8 $\overset{>}{9}$ 10 11 12

6. $\overset{>}{1}$ 2 $\overset{>}{3}$ 4 $\overset{>}{5}$ 6 7 $\overset{>}{8}$ 9 $\overset{>}{10}$ 11 $\overset{>}{12}$

POLYRHYTHM: COMBINING PATTERNS

Look at the notation for the rhythms you clapped. Choose one of the parts to practice. When the rhythms are added, one at a time, you will hear that each one contributes to the texture of the music.

African Rhythm Complex

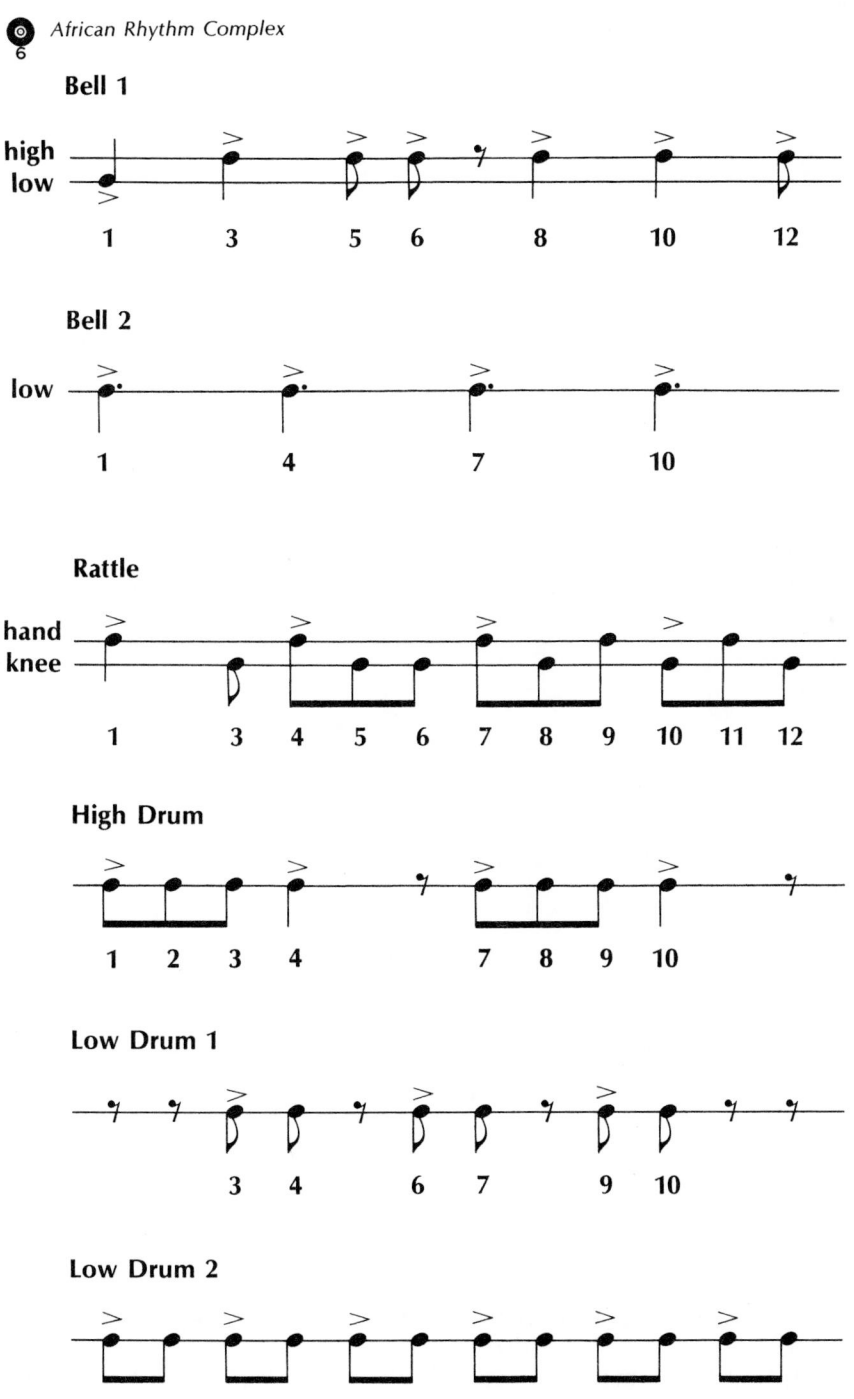

Bell 1

Bell 2

Rattle

High Drum

Low Drum 1

Low Drum 2

CHANT A RESPONSE

Fill in the break after each solo part (response) by chanting and clapping the rhythm pattern made by the words in the title of this song.

Griz - ze - ly Bear___

Grizzely Bear

BLACK WORK SONG   ADAPTED BY ANDREW B. CRANE

6

© COPYRIGHT 1956 BY STORMKING MUSIC, INC. ALL RIGHTS RESERVED. USED BY PERMISSION.

SOLO   *RESPONSE SOLO*

Tell   me who was the griz - ze - ly,   Tell   me

RESPONSE SOLO

who   was the griz - ze - ly,   Jack - o'-Dia-monds was the griz - ze - ly,

RESPONSE SOLO   *RESPONSE SOLO*

Jack - o'-Dia-monds was the griz - ze - ly,   He made a

RESPONSE   *SOLO*

noise   in the bot - tom like a   He made a

RESPONSE SOLO

noise in the bot-tom like a   Well   my ma - ma was scared of that
Well   my pa - pa went a hunt-ing for the

RESPONSE SOLO   *RESPONSE*

Well   my ma - ma was scared of that
Well   my pa - pa went a hunt - ing for the

SING A RESPONSE

Use the rhythm pattern of the title and sing each response part on one of the tones in the D-major chord. Listen as someone strums the chord on the Autoharp and choose the tone that is most comfortable for you to sing.

D   F♯   A   D

You can sing a response that uses more than one tone in the D-major chord. Try one of these.

All the tones of the D-major chord can be sung together. But since one person can sing only one tone at a time, ask three other people to join you and sing the whole chord as a response.

Griz - ze - ly   Bear___

ONE WAY TO MAKE HARMONY

On the recording of the first version of "Banuwa," a guitar plays chords to accompany the melody. As you listen, follow the chord letters in the score to hear which chords the guitarist plays.

Banuwa FOLK SONG FROM LIBERIA

Neh - ni   a - la - no.   Neh - ni   a - la - no.

Neh - ni   a - la - no.   Neh - ni   a - la - no.

Each of the three chords used to accompany "Banuwa" is built
on a tone of the C-major scale.

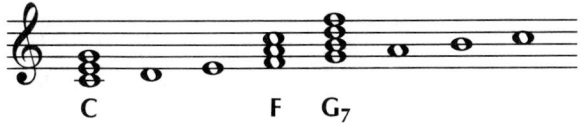

C   F   G₇

ANOTHER WAY TO MAKE HARMONY

Here is another version of "Banuwa." Follow the score below as
you listen to the recording. What makes the harmony in this
version?

Ba - nu - wa,   ba - nu - wa,   ba - nu - wa   yo._____

Ba - nu - wa,   ba - nu - wa,   ba - nu - wa   yo._____   A -

la - no, neh - ni a - la - no,   A - la - no, neh - ni a - la - no.

Neh - ni   a - la - no.   Neh - ni   a - la - no.

Neh - ni   a - la - no.   Neh - ni   a - la   no.

THREE CHORDS—THREE ROOTS

This song uses three chords—D min., G min., and A_7. The tone on which each chord is built is called the *root.*

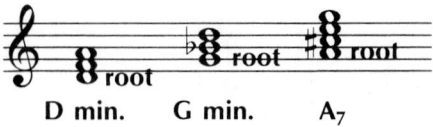

root
root
root
D min.
G min.
A7

To accompany the song, play the root of each chord by plucking the open string D, A, or G on the guitar. The diagram on page 32 will show you which strings to pluck. Follow the chord letters in the score.

Wade in the Water

BLACK SPIRITUAL 6

REFRAIN
D MIN.
A7
D MIN.
Wade in the water, wade in the water, chil - dren,
Fine
D MIN.
G MIN.
D MIN.
A7
D MIN.
Wade in the wa - ter, God's a - gon - na trou - ble the wa - ter.
VERSE
SOLO
D MIN.
CHORUS
G MIN.
1. If Jor - dan's wa - ter is chil - ly and cold,
2. If you get there be - fore I do,
God's a-gon-na trou-ble the
A7
D MIN.
SOLO
wa - ter.
It chills the bod - y but not the soul,
Tell all my friends I'm com - in', too,
CHORUS
G MIN.
D.C. al Fine
A7
D MIN.
God's a - gon - na trou - ble the wa - ter.

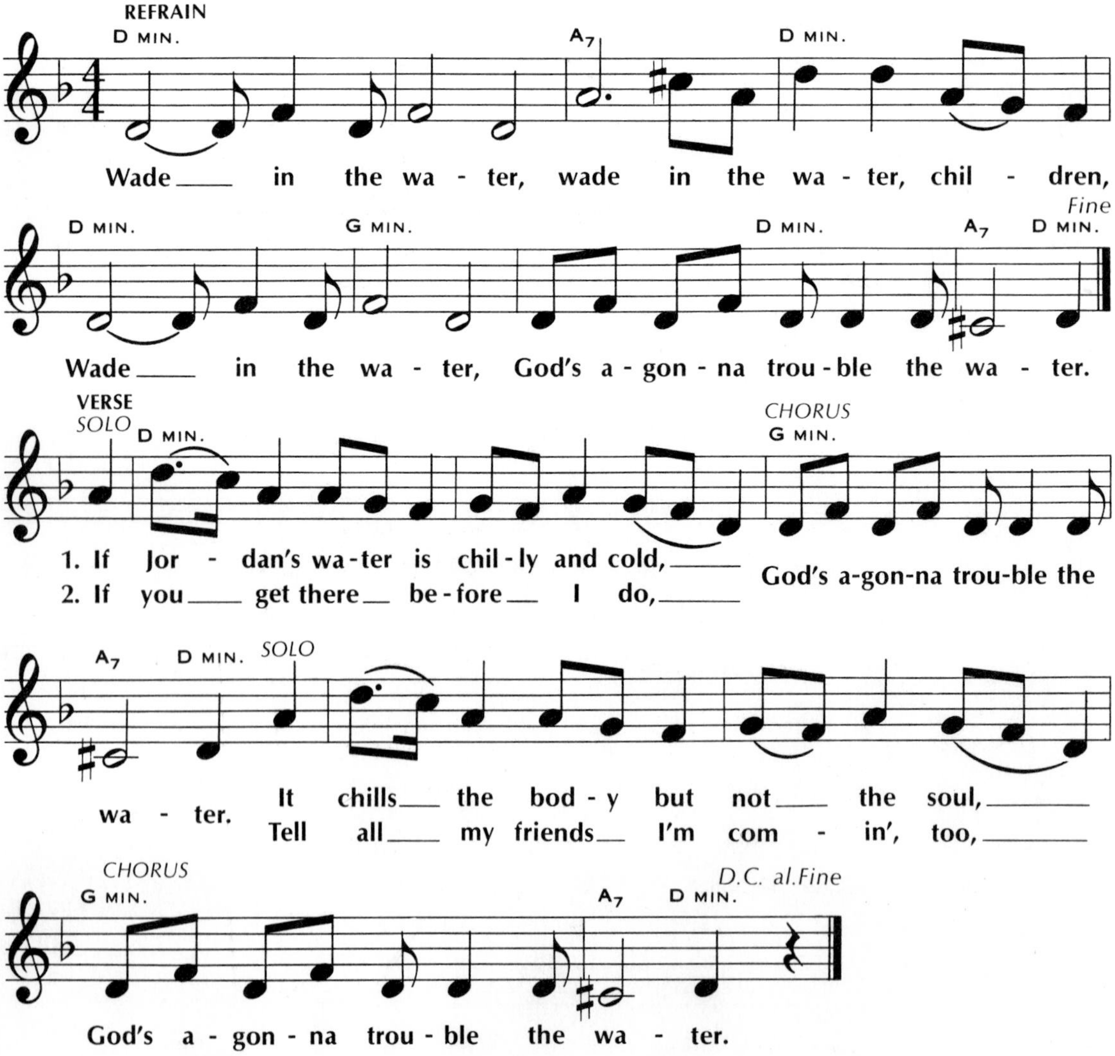

CHORDS: BOOGIE-WOOGIE STYLE

Choose one of the parts described below to play on the keyboard. Each part uses the black keys only, and each part is played in a different register of the keyboard.

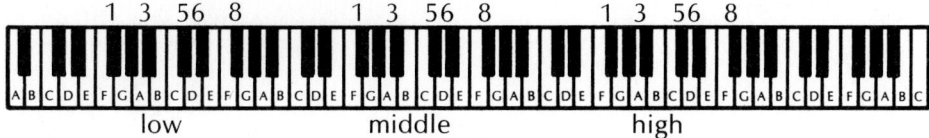

1. Low register

Play the black keys indicated in the low register of the diagram upward, then downward. Don't repeat 8 as you change direction. This is called a *walking bass.* Play a walking bass using one of these rhythm patterns.

2. Middle register

Play the black keys indicated in the middle register as a chord. You can play the chord with one hand or both hands. Use one of these rhythm patterns.

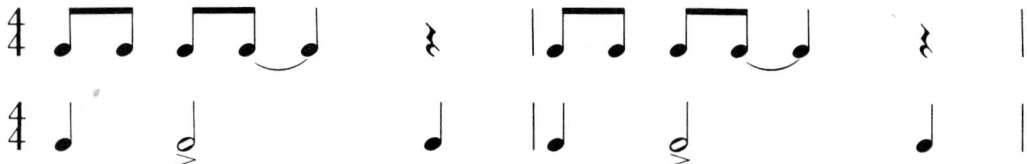

3. High register

Play any of the keys indicated in the high register of the diagram, and improvise a melody using the rhythm.

Now listen to a piano piece played in the boogie-woogie style.

 *Boogie-Woogie Piano*

129

Boogie-Woogie

WORDS AND MUSIC BY CARMINO RAVOSA

Here is a song in boogie-woogie style that was written
especially for you. Listen for the "breaks" in the melody. The
color boxes show you where they are.

(BASS 1)

Boo - gie - woo - gie,   Boo - gie - woo - gie,

(BASS 2)   (BASS 1)

Boo - gie - woo - gie,   Boo - gie - woo - gie,

(BASS 3)   (BASS 1)

Boo - gie - woo - gie,   Boo - gie - woo - gie.

1. There's a kid that plays pi - an - o on the cor - ner of the street,___ He's
2. Now, this kid that plays pi - an - o on the cor - ner of the street, If you
3. Well, this kid that plays pi - an - o on the cor - ner of the street,___ He's

nev - er had a les - son, but he's got the boo - gie beat.   When the
ev - er hear him play___ then you're gon - na have a treat.   Now, you
got a wick - ed left___ hand that no - bod - y can beat.   He can

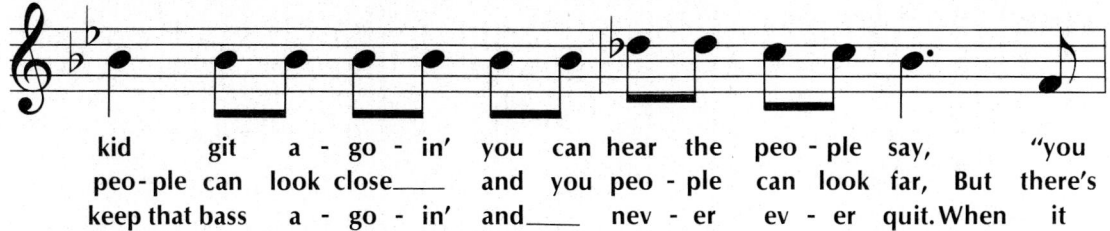

kid git a - go - in' you can hear the peo - ple say, "you
peo - ple can look close___ and you peo - ple can look far, But there's
keep that bass a - go - in' and___ nev - er ev - er quit. When it

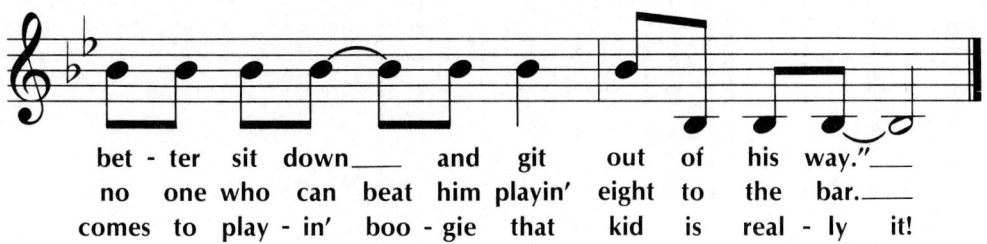

bet - ter sit down___ and git out of his way."___
no one who can beat him playin' eight to the bar.___
comes to play - in' boo - gie that kid is real - ly it!

THINGS TO DO WITH "BOOGIE-WOOGIE"

Fill in the "breaks" in the melody by playing a rhythm pattern
on a percussion instrument. You can play a steady-beat pattern,
or a dotted rhythm pattern.

Here are three walking bass parts you can play on the piano to
accompany section A of the song. The directions in the music
will tell you when to play each one.

Walking bass 1

Walking bass 2

Walking bass 3

Listen to the recording. Each time a number is called, choose
the word that describes the texture.

Calliet: *Variations on the Theme "Pop! Goes the Weasel"*

1	HOMOPHONIC POLYPHONIC	**9**	MONOPHONIC MIXED
2	MONOPHONIC POLYPHONIC	**10**	MONOPHONIC HOMOPHONIC
3	MONOPHONIC POLYPHONIC	**11**	HOMOPHONIC POLYPHONIC
4	HOMOPHONIC POLYPHONIC	**12**	HOMOPHONIC POLYPHONIC
5	MONOPHONIC HOMOPHONIC	**13**	MONOPHONIC HOMOPHONIC
6	MONOPHONIC MIXED	**14**	MONOPHONIC MIXED
7	MONOPHONIC HOMOPHONIC	**15**	MONOPHONIC HOMOPHONIC
8	HOMOPHONIC POLYPHONIC	**16**	HOMOPHONIC POLYPHONIC

Listen to the recording. Each time a number is called, choose
the word that describes the texture. Also, decide whether the
music is major or minor.

Bizet: *L'Arlesienne Suite No. 2,* **"Farandole"**

1	MONOPHONIC	HOMOPHONIC	POLYPHONIC	MIXED
	MAJOR MINOR			

2	MONOPHONIC	HOMOPHONIC	POLYPHONIC	MIXED
	MAJOR MINOR			

3	MONOPHONIC	HOMOPHONIC	POLYPHONIC	MIXED
	MAJOR MINOR			

4	MONOPHONIC	HOMOPHONIC	POLYPHONIC	MIXED
	MAJOR MINOR			

5	HOMOPHONIC
	MINOR

6	MONOPHONIC
	MINOR

7	MONOPHONIC	HOMOPHONIC	POLYPHONIC	MIXED
	MAJOR MINOR			

8	MONOPHONIC	HOMOPHONIC	POLYPHONIC	MIXED
	MAJOR MINOR			

9	MONOPHONIC	HOMOPHONIC	POLYPHONIC	MIXED
	MAJOR MINOR			

Experiencing the Arts:
Representational, Nonrepresentational

When we can easily recognize something in a work of art that represents the world we live in—a person, a house, a flower, an idea—it is said to be *representational*.

What do you think *nonrepresentational* means?

Look at two paintings—the one below, and the one at the top of page 135. Which do you think is representational? Nonrepresentational?

Each kind of art does the same thing—it presents an experience
for us to see and feel.

There is representation or nonrepresentation in other arts.

Find an example of each in sculpture and dance on the
following two pages.

THE PHILLIPS COLLECTION, WASHINGTON

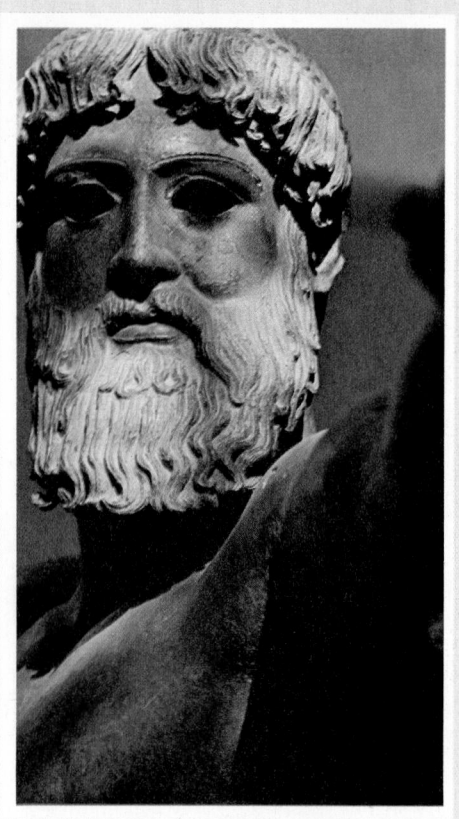

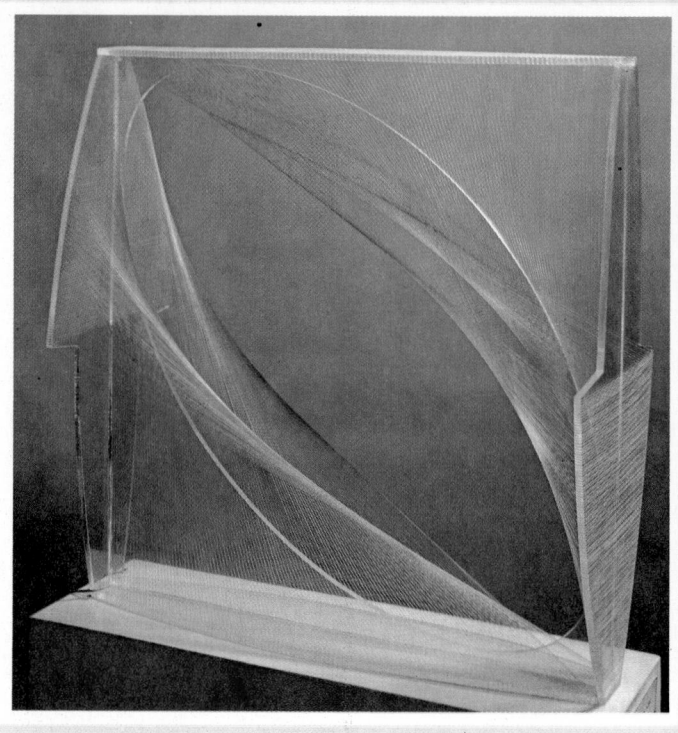

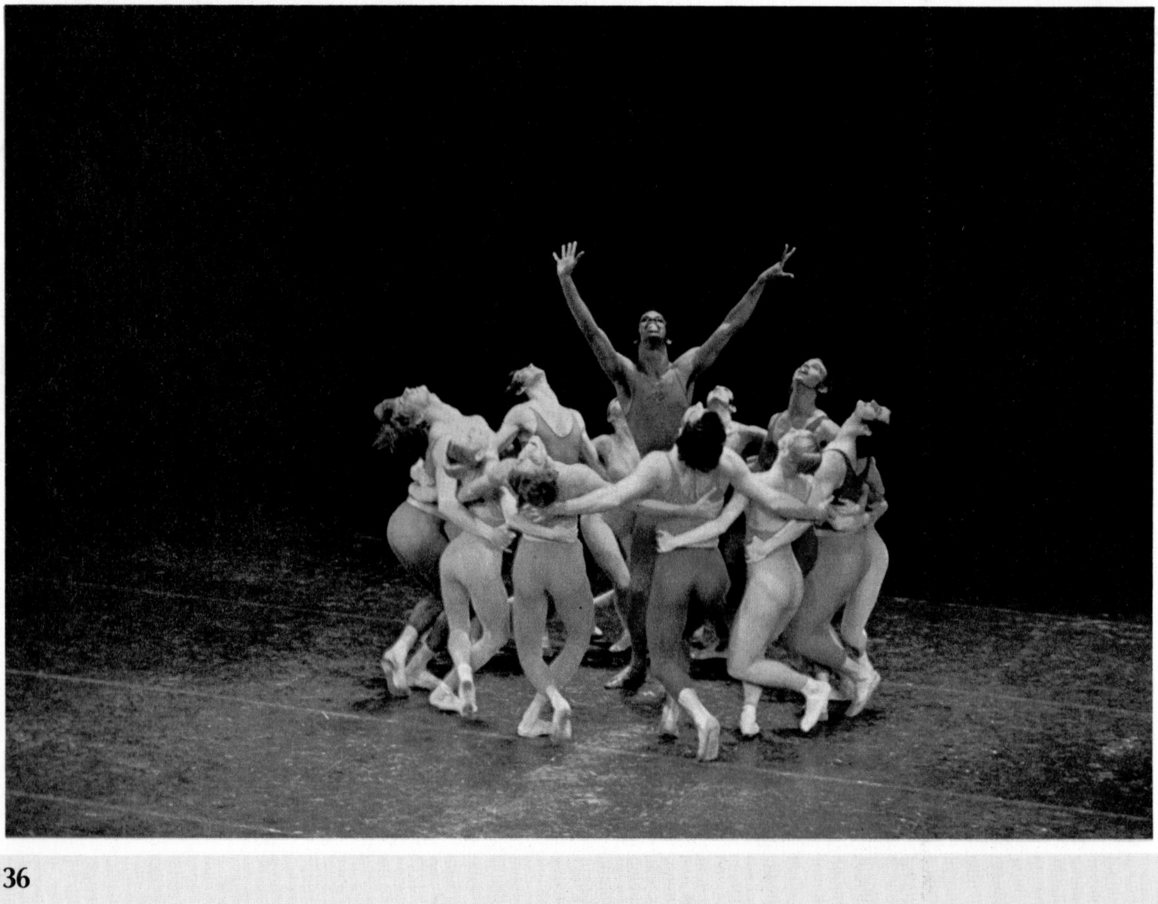

Music can sometimes suggest a thing or a story. Such music is called *program music*. Much music suggests nothing at all except the sounds themselves. Such music is called *absolute music*.

Listen to these three pieces of music. Two are program music. One is absolute music. Can you tell which is which?

Copland: *The Red Pony*, "Circus Music"

Brahms: *Clarinet Sonata*, No. 2

Mussorgsky: *Pictures at an Exhibition*, "Ballet of Unhatched Chicks"

Each work of art is an opportunity for a new experience, whether it represents something we can recognize or is nonrepresentational.

In all works of art, whether we recognize things or not, we *still* perceive and feel.

Using What You Know About Form

INTRODUCTION TO FORM

In this section you will explore several important forms. You will learn how parts of music are put together in ways that repeat and contrast. When you hear musical parts adding up to whole pieces, you become involved in the experience of musical forming.

The way a building is formed, or organized, is a large part of our enjoyment in seeing it.

The famous Taj Mahal in India uses the form ABA over and over. How many ABA arrangements can you find in the building and the grounds?

Can you find repetition and contrast in the painting at the bottom of pages 138 and 139?

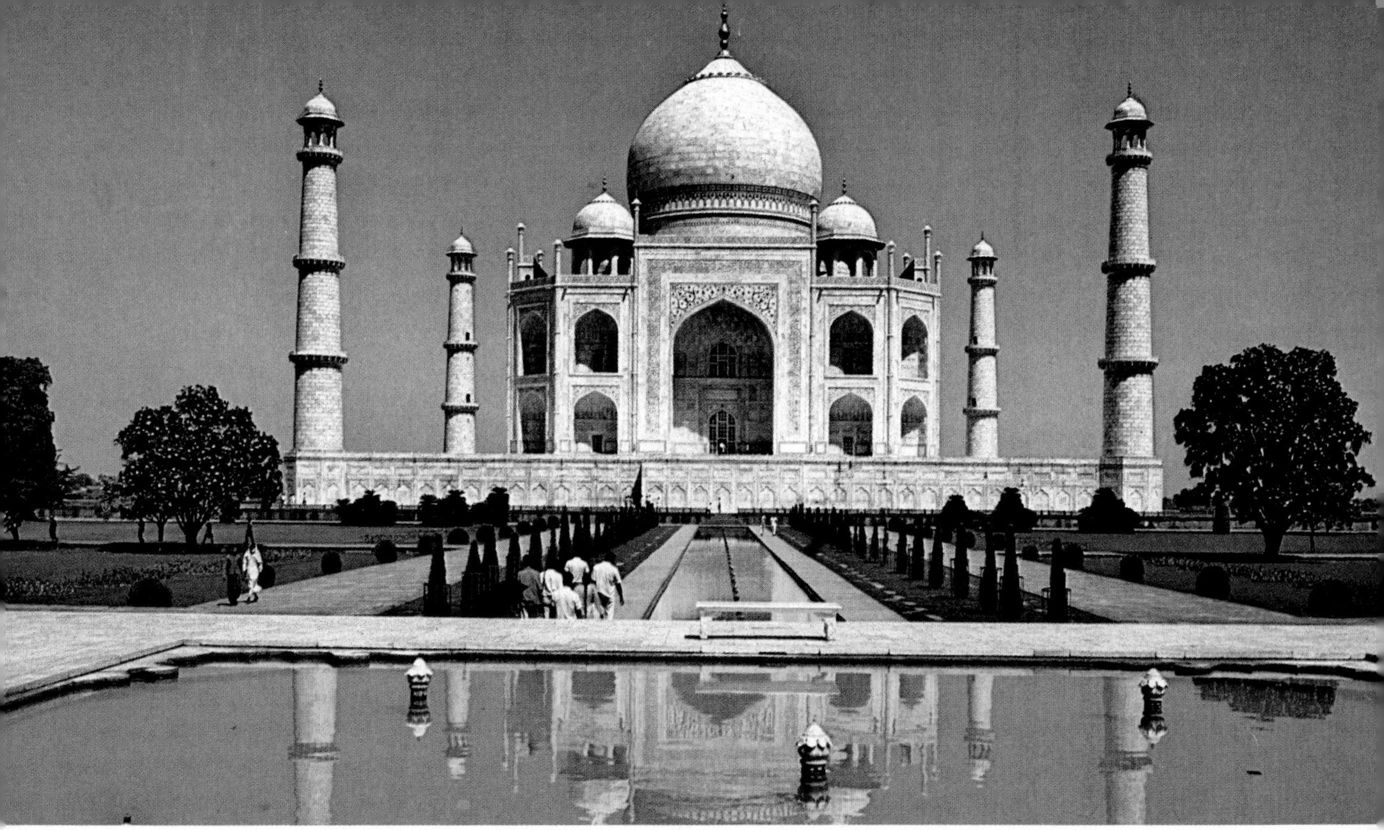

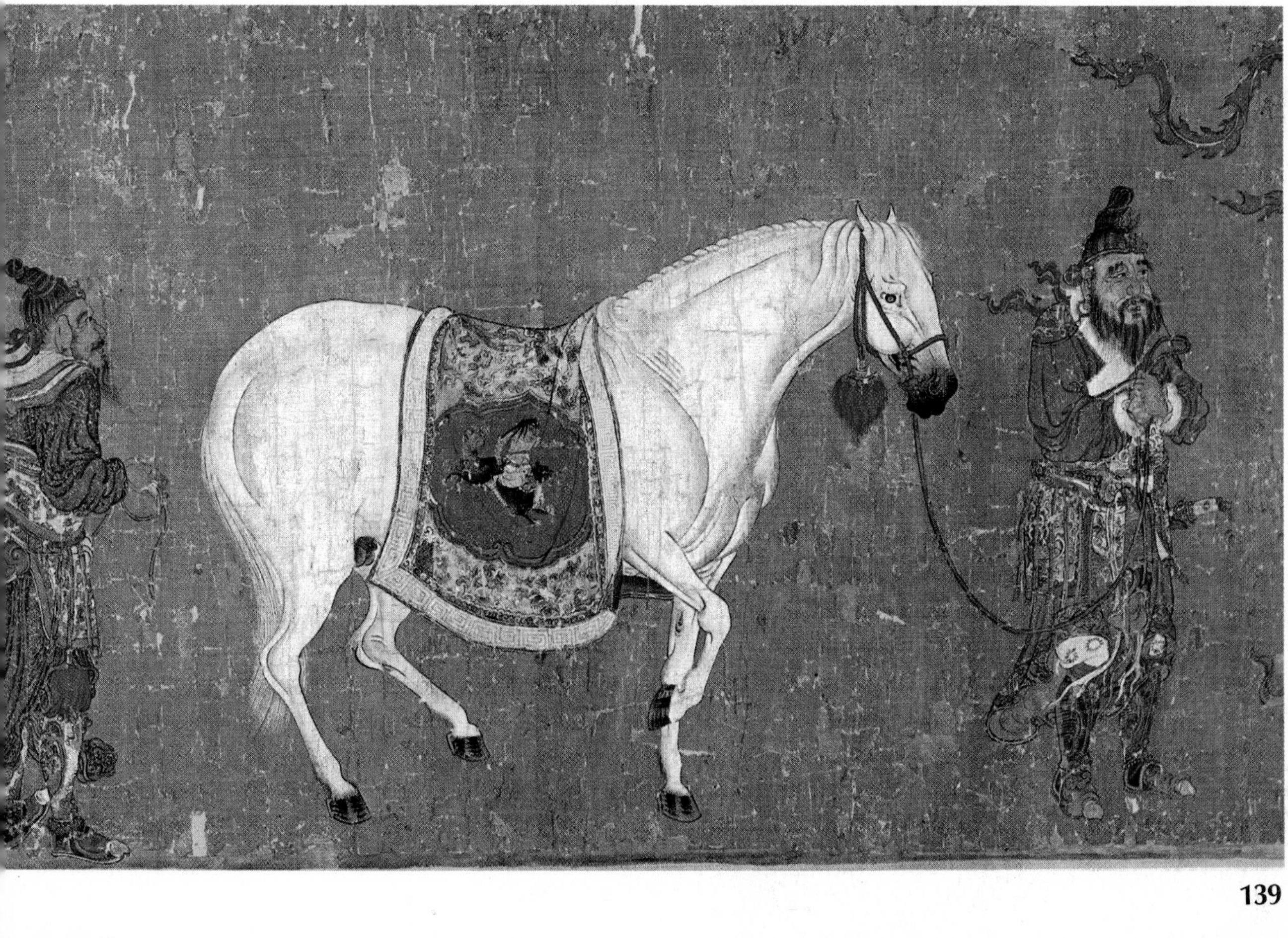

A HIT SONG FROM BROADWAY

This song is from the Broadway musical *Shenandoah*. You can read about it on the next page.

TWO SECTIONS, A AND B

As you listen to the recording, notice that the song has two sections—A and B. Join in on section B when you can.

Freedom (from "Shenandoah")

MUSIC BY GARY GELD   WORDS BY PETER UDELL

© 1974, 1975 GARY GELD & PETER UDELL. ALL RIGHTS CONTROLLED BY EDWIN H. MORRIS & CO., A DIVISION OF MPL COMMUNICATIONS, INC. INTERNATIONAL COPYRIGHT SECURED.

1. Free-dom ain't a state like Maine or Vir-gin-ia,
2. Free-dom ain't a boat that's leav-in' with-out ya,
3. Free-dom is a no-tion sweep-in' the na-tion,

Free-dom ain't a-cross some coun-ty line.
Free-dom ain't a place ya float to find.
Free-dom is the right of all man-kind.

Free-dom is a flame that burns with-in ya,
Free-dom is the how ya think a-bout ya,
Free-dom is a bod-y's 'mag-i-na-tion,

Free-dom's in the state of mind. Free-dom,

free-dom, Free-dom, free-dom.

Free-dom is a flame that
Free-dom is the how ya

burns with-in ya
think a-bout ya, Free-dom's in the state___ of mind.

3.
Free-dom is a no - tion sweep-in' the na - tion, Free-dom is a bod - y's

'mag - i - na - tion, Free-dom is a full time oc - cu - pa - tion,

Free-dom's in the state___ of mind!

A BROADWAY MUSICAL

The Broadway musical is an exciting form of entertainment for people all over the world. Each fall, in New York City, people look forward to the openings of the new shows. If the new musicals are successful, they travel from Broadway to the Main Streets of the United States, then on to the theater districts all over the world.

"Freedom" is one of the songs from the musical *Shenandoah,* which opened on Broadway during the 1975 season. The story is about the Anderson family and how they try to avoid the pain and suffering of the Civil War. The themes of peace and freedom are very important to the plot. "Freedom" is sung by a young slave boy after he has been set free.

CONTRASTING SECTIONS

Listen for the two sections in this song. *Clap* the beat during section A. *Snap* the beat during section B.

The first phrase of each section is shown in a color box. Look at the rhythm patterns made by the words in each color box. Find other phrases that have the same rhythm pattern.

I'm Gonna Sing Out

WORDS AND MUSIC BY DAVID EDDLEMAN

For a percussion ensemble, see p. 235.

PLAN A PERFORMANCE

Plan a performance of "I'm Gonna Sing." Decide how you will use *rhythm, dynamics,* and *texture* to show a contrast between sections. Here are some suggestions:

* contrast of tempo between sections; contrast of rhythm patterns (played on a percussion instrument to accompany the song)
* contrast of melody with harmony to melody alone
* contrast of loud and soft; getting louder, getting softer

Like Phrases · *Rhythm Patterns* · *Melody* · *Harmony* · *Two Sections* · *A B Form*

Baby Day
WORDS AND MUSIC BY MELANIE SAFKA

© 1971 BY APRIL MUSIC INC. AND NEIGHBORHOOD MUSIC PUB. CORP. RIGHTS IN THE U.S.A. AND CANADA ADMINISTERED BY APRIL MUSIC INC. USED BY PERMISSION. ALL RIGHTS RESERVED.

Follow the score as you listen to the recording of "Baby Day."

What can you discover about the music on your own?

1. Why sleep when the day has been called out by the sun? From the
2. "Quite, quite," said___ I, "that's all ver - y well to say, But I
3. And I sing it like I heard it; why I heard it, who knows why? Why___

night, 'Cause the light's gon - na shine on ev - 'ry - one. Why
rose be - fore the dawn to your sing - ing yes - ter - day. I
sleep, when___ you can___ watch the sun a - rise? We were

sleep when the sleep on - ly clos - es up our eyes? Why
could - n't see the rising 'cause the dark was in the sky; I
meant to___ see the be - gin - ning of the day. I be -

sleep when we can watch the sun a - rise?
could - n't see the sun 'cause the sun was in my eye."
lieve___ it was planned to lift us this___ way.

144

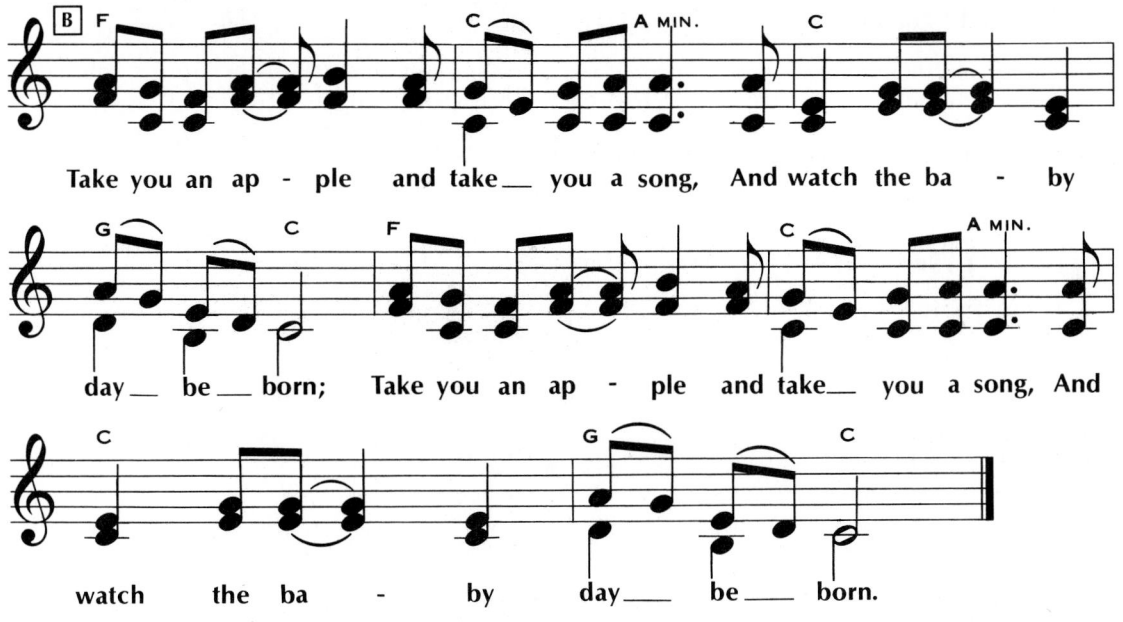

Take you an ap - ple and take__ you a song, And watch the ba - by

day__ be __ born; Take you an ap - ple and take__ you a song, And

watch the ba - by day__ be __ born.

CALL CHART 9: Form

Can you hear sections that repeat and sections that contrast in this piece? Follow the chart to discover the form.

Mexican Cactus

1	INTRODUCTION
2	A
3	REPETITION OF A
4	CONTRAST B
5	REPETITION OF A
6	INTERLUDE
7	REPETITION OF A
8	REPETITION OF A
9	CONTRAST B
10	REPETITION OF A
11	CODA

ABA FORM

Listen to the recording of "Open the Window, Noah" to discover the form. Sing along when you can.

Open the Window, Noah   BLACK SPIRITUAL

FROM AMERICAN NEGRO SONGS AND SPIRITUALS BY JOHN W. WORK. © 1940, 1968 BY CROWN PUBLISHERS, INC. USED BY PERMISSION OF CROWN PUBLISHERS, INC.

O - pen the win - dow, No - ah, O - pen the win - dow, No - ah,

O - pen the win - dow, No - ah, O - pen the win - dow, Let the

dove come in. dove come in.

1. The lit - tle dove flew in the
2. The lit - tle dove brought back the

CHORUS

win - dow and mourned,___ O - pen the win - dow, Let the
ol - ive___ leaf,___

dove come in. The lit - tle dove flew in the win - dow and mourned,___
The lit - tle dove brought back the ol - ive___ leaf,___

CHORUS

O - pen the win - dow, Let the dove come in.

ABC FORM

This song has three sections—A, B, and C. Listen to the recording
to discover how one section is different from the others.

Hahvah Nahgeelah
JEWISH FOLK SONG

Hah - vah   nah-gee-lah, hah - vah   nah-gee-lah, hah - vah   nah-gee-lah,

vuh - nis-muh'kh-hah.   vuh - nis-muh'kh-hah.   Hah-vah nah-rrah-nuh-nah,

hah-vah nah-rrah-nuh-nah, hah - vah nah-rrah-nuh-nah, vuh - nis-muh'kh-hah.

vuh - nis - muh'kh - hah.   Oo - roo,   oo - roo ah'kh - heem,

oo-roo ah'kh-heem buh-lev sah-meh-ah'kh, oo-roo ah'kh-heem buh-lev sah meh-ah'kh

oo-roo ah'kh-heem buh-lev sah-meh-ah'kh, oo-roo ah'kh-heem buh-lev sah-meh-ah'kh,

oo-roo ah'kh-heem, oo-roo ah'kh-heem b'lev sah-meh - ah'kh.

147

Experiencing the Arts: *Creating Tension*

Our lives are full of tension. We often wish there was less of it. But tension, or stress, adds excitement to our lives.

Artists use tension in their works to excite us, to challenge us, to involve our feelings in a new experience.

CREATING TENSION IN THE VISUAL ARTS

In the visual arts (painting, sculpture, architecture, crafts), tension can be caused by these and other qualities.

1. clashes of color
2. irregular lines
3. many different directions
4. things jumbled together
5. contrasting textures
6. distorted shapes
7. off-balance shapes
8. unexpected use of materials

What causes tension in the visual art examples on pages 148–150?

LYONEL FEININGER. VILLAGE STREET. COLLECTION OF THE ART INSTITUTE OF CHICAGO.

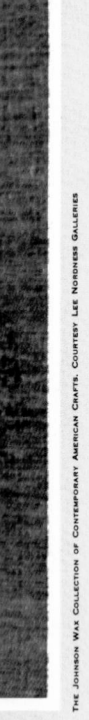

CREATING TENSION IN POETRY

Choose words to finish this familiar little poem. First use words that are very predictable—what everyone would expect. Then choose words that are unexpected, different, thoughtful, challenging.

Roses are _____   Violets are _____

Flowers are _____   And so are _____

What qualities seem to cause tension in this poem?

AFRICAN DANCE

The low beating of the tom-toms,
  The slow beating of the tom-toms,
  Low . . . slow
  Slow . . . low—
Stirs in your blood.

            Dance!

A night-veiled girl
  Whirls softly into a
  Circle of light.
Whirls softly . . . slowly,
Like a whisp of smoke around the fire—
  And the tom-toms beat,
  And the tom-toms beat,
And the low beating of the tom-toms
  Stirs your blood.

Langston Hughes

CREATING TENSION IN MUSIC

In music, tension and release of tension are created by

1. dynamics
2. tempo
3. density
4. accents

5. tone color
6. rhythm patterns
7. register
8. direction

CALL CHART 10: Creating Tension

Beethoven: *Symphony No. 3*, Movement 3

1 *First theme; fast; thin to thick density;
short, even pattern pushes on and on;* < *and* >

2 *Suddenly loud; strong, irregular accents; syncopation;
sudden louds and softs; fast* ♫♫ *pattern drives on;*
< *builds up; contrasting tone colors*

3 *First contrasting theme; change of tone color (French horns);*
♫♫ *pattern still heard;* < *and* >

4 *Second contrasting theme; smooth lines going upward
and downward*

5 *First contrasting theme again; movement slows, then goes on*

6 *First theme again; steady* ♫♫ *pattern, driving on and on;
contrasting registers; contrasting tone colors;* < *builds up*

7 *Loud first theme; strong, irregular accents; syncopation;
loud and soft;* ♫♫ *pattern continues;* < *builds up*

8 *Coda (ending section); soft, then driving to a loud,
strong final cadence*

152

Style: **Improvisation**

If you were to make a tent out of two poles and a blanket, you would be *improvising* a shelter. If you made up two measures of music on the black keys of the piano or on the upper row of the bells, you would be *improvising* a melody.

IMPROVISATION IN JAZZ

In the jazz world, musicians often improvise, or create, music "on the spot." In this recording, a trumpet improvises a melody over an accompaniment played by string bass, piano, and a second trumpet.

12-Bar Blues Improvisation

In the next recording you will hear how Ella Fitzgerald, a famous jazz singer, uses her voice to improvise. First you will hear the melody of *Some of These Days* as it was written. Then you will hear two different improvisations on the melody.

Brooks: *Some of These Days*

In the recording of *When the Saints Go Marching In,* two different brass instruments improvise on the melody. Can you hear which instruments they are?

When the Saints Go Marching In

IMPROVISATION THEN AND NOW

Here is some music for violin and harpsichord that was composed a long time ago. First you will hear the melody as it was written. Then you will hear the performer's improvisation on the melody.

Corelli: *Sonata for Violin and Harpsichord,* No. 3, "Adagio"

In this music from the twentieth century, two performers are heard improvising at the same time. (Two taped performances were combined to make the recording.) One performer improvises on the keyboard of an organ; the other improvises sound from inside the organ.

Wolff: *For 1, 2, or 3 People*

Careers in Music: Conduct

Some music is performed by one person (solo), by two (duet), by three (trio), by four (quartet), by five (quintet). When a piece calls for a larger group of performers, such as a chorus, a band or an orchestra, a leader is needed—a person who keeps everyone together and who makes the musical decisions. This musical leader is called a *conductor*.

A conductor has many special skills and many responsibilities. Listen to Lena McLin, a famous choral conductor, discuss her work.

🔘 *Interview with Lena McLin*
8

🔘 *The Rehearsal*
8

🔘 *The Performance*
8

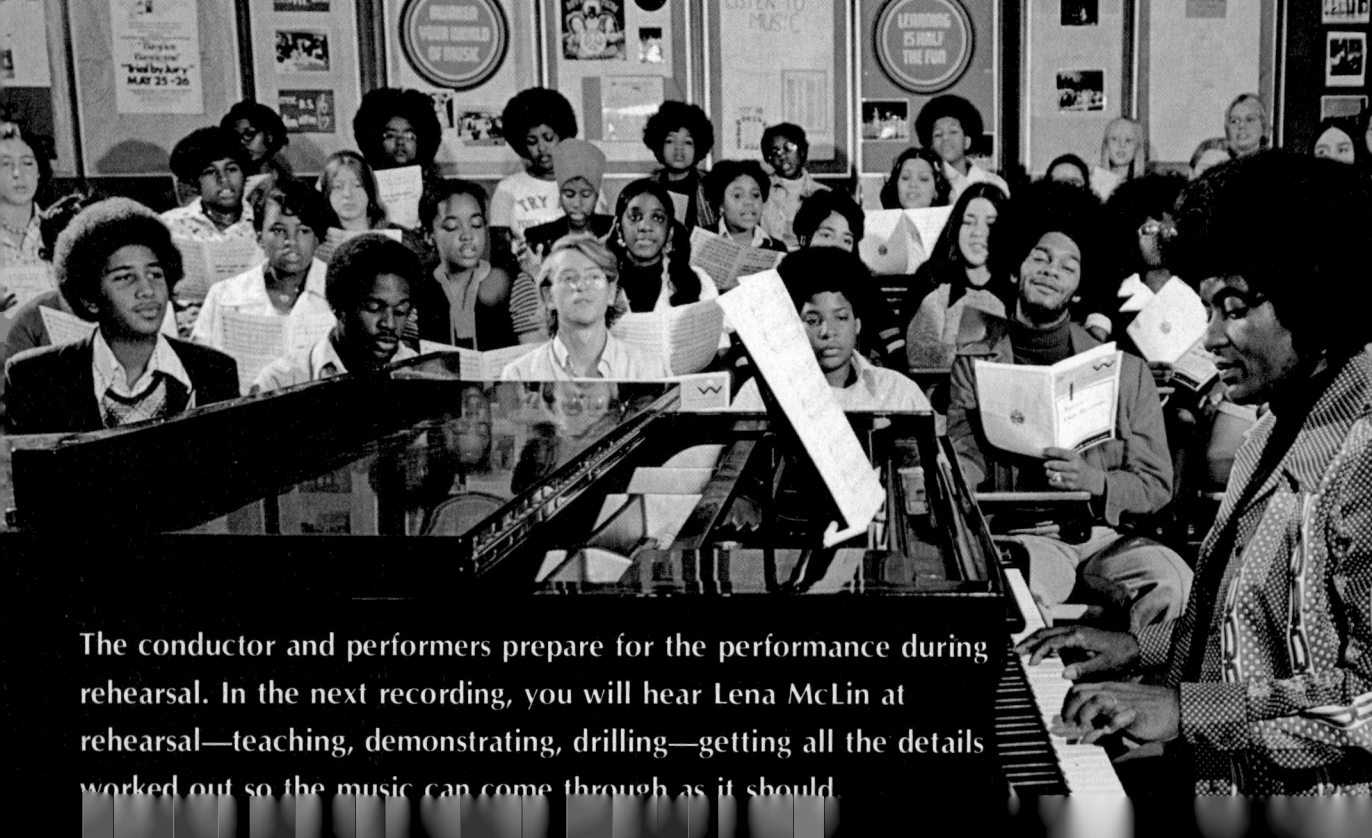

The conductor and performers prepare for the performance during rehearsal. In the next recording, you will hear Lena McLin at rehearsal—teaching, demonstrating, drilling—getting all the details worked out so the music can come through as it should.

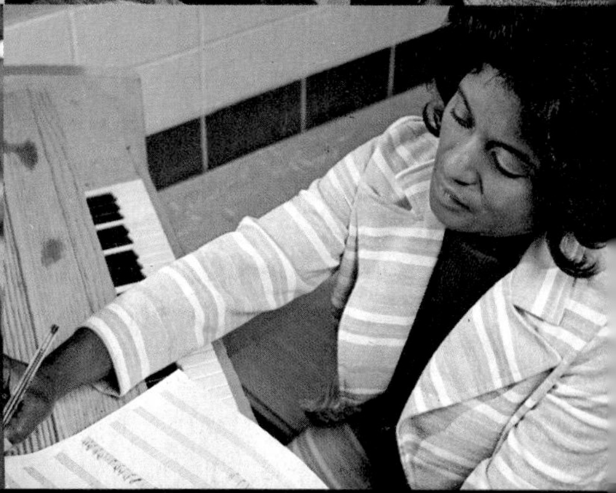

And now the performance. The preparation is over and the final result is shared with the audience.

More About Form

CALL AND RESPONSE

In the piece *Dueling Banjos,* a guitar and a banjo have a
musical duel. Do the phrases use mostly repetition, or contrast?

Listen for some other qualities that are used throughout the piece.

1. low and high registers

2. tempo changes

3. tones that move mostly by step

4. upward and downward direction

Scruggs: *Dueling Banjos*

In conversation, it is natural to *respond* to a question. Some
music uses the question-and-answer, or call-and-response, idea.
In songs, the call is often sung by a solo voice and the response
by a group—the chorus.

Tongo FOLK SONG FROM POLYNESIA SET DOWN BY GLADYS RUSTAY. OBERLIN

FROM TAYOYUMAWIT. COURTESY OF WORLD AROUND SONGS. BURNSVILLE. N.C.

SOLO (Call) *CHORUS (Response)* *SOLO*

Ton - go,___ Ton - go,___ Jim nee bye,___ bye,___ oh,

CHORUS *SOLO* *CHORUS*

Jim nee bye,___ bye,___ oh, Ton - go,___ Ton - go,___

SOLO *CHORUS* *SOLO*

Oom ba de kim bye oh, Oom ba de kim bye oh, Ooh - a - lay,

CHORUS *SOLO* *CHORUS*

Ooh - a - lay, Mah - le - ka - ah lo way. Mah - le - ka - ah lo way.

156

Woke Up This Morning

FREEDOM SONG   ADAPTED WITH NEW LYRICS BY ROBERT ZELLNER

1. I woke up this morn - ing with my mind_____ stayed_____ on
2. Walk-in' and talk - in' with my mind_____ stayed_____ on

free - dom,__ I woke up this morn - ing with my mind_____
free - dom,__ Walk-in' and talk - in' with my mind_____

stayed _____ on free - dom,__ I woke up this morn - ing with my
stayed _____ on free - dom,__ Walk-in' and talk - in' with my

mind _____ stayed_____ on free - dom,__ Hal - le - lu,_____
mind _____ stayed_____ on free - dom,__

_____ hal - le - lu,__ hal - le - lu - - jah!__
Hal - le - lu,   hal - le - lu,

3. **Singin' and prayin' with my mind stayed on freedom, (*3 times*)**
   Hallelu, hallelu, hallelujah!

4. **Body in prison but my mind stayed on freedom, (*3 times*)**
   Hallelu, hallelu, hallelujah!

Listen for the call and response parts in four pieces. For each, decide whether the response is a *repetition* of the call or a *contrast* of the call.

 *Call and Response Collage*

THE 12-BAR BLUES

"Till That Day Blues" is an example of the 12-bar blues form.
Can you guess why the form is called a *12-bar* blues?

Look at the score to discover some things about this form.

How many phrases are there?
Which phrases have the same words?
Do any of the phrases have the same melody contour?

Play the recording of "Till That Day Blues" and notice that the
piano fills in the breaks in the melody at the end of each
phrase. The phrase endings are shown in color boxes.

For a percussion ensemble, see p. 233.

Till That Day Blues

WORDS AND MUSIC BY SOL BERKOWITZ

© 1973 SOL BERKOWITZ

1. I got a big bass fid-dle and a pair of sport-in' ___ shoes._____
2. I got a shiny brass trum-pet ___ that I am gon-na ___ play._____

I got a big bass fid-dle and a pair of sport-in' ___ shoes._____
I got a shiny brass trum-pet ___ that I am gon-na ___ play._____

𝄽 I can tap out a rhy-thm to the beat___ of the blues.
I'm gon-na play that___ trum - pet___ till the Judg-ment Day.

Now, make up your own response and fill in the break in the
melody at the end of each phrase. You can improvise a voice
part to sing on the syllable "doo," or you can make up a
rhythm pattern to play on a percussion instrument.

CHORD PATTERN FOR THE BLUES

Practice the Autoharp chords for "Till That Day Blues." They follow the 12-bar blues form—a form that was developed from black work songs and spirituals early in this century.

Each of the three phrases in the blues form has a special pattern of chords. This diagram shows how the three phrases, with their chords, are used to form a 12-bar blues song. The dotted lines show where the breaks occur in the melody.

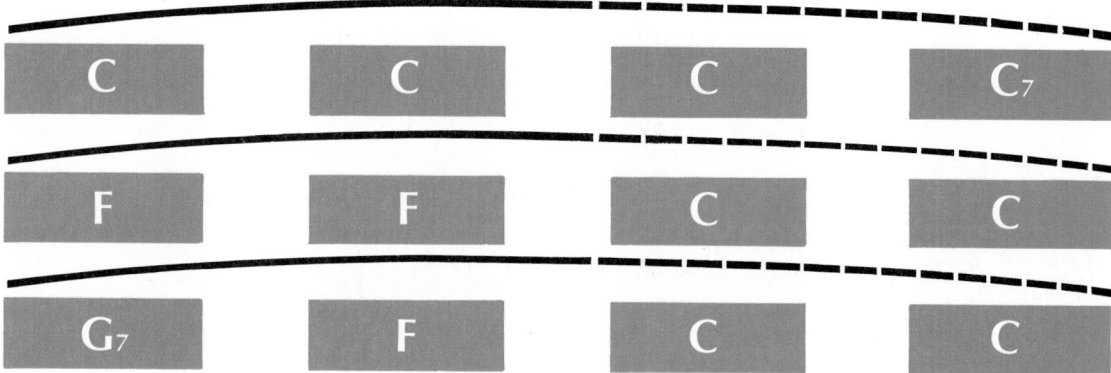

If a stereo record player is available, accompany the melody track of "Till That Day Blues" by playing the chords on the Autoharp. Try strumming this pattern all through the song. Notice the accents.

T means thumb; F means finger.

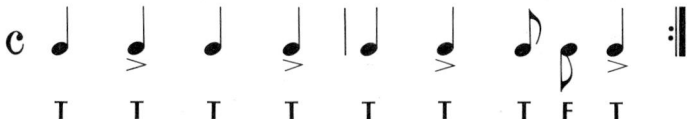

Now listen to two pieces that are based on the 12-bar blues form. The first one is a classical blues piece; the other is a "rock" blues piece that is played on an electronic sound instrument.

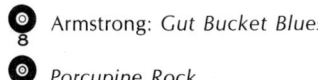 Armstrong: *Gut Bucket Blues*

Porcupine Rock

CALL CHART 11: Rondo Form 🔊

You have heard and performed music with one contrasting section. Now listen for two contrasting sections in this piece.

The chart will help you discover how the sections are put together to create a rondo form.

Rameau: *Gigue en rondeau*

1 *FIRST SECTION A*
Melody in high register; repeated tones in low register; meter

2 *CONTRASTING SECTION B*
Two melodies together; moves mostly by step; polyphonic texture

3 *REPEAT OF A*

4 *ANOTHER CONTRASTING SECTION C*
Starts as a canon (like a round); polyphonic texture

5 *REPEAT OF A*

Letters and shapes can show the form of a rondo.

THE KING OF RAGTIME

In addition to the "blues," ragtime was another style of music developed early in this century. Scott Joplin became known as the "King of Ragtime." His pieces are still popular today.

The chart will help you hear the repeated sections as well as several contrasting sections. Each section is the same length and uses many syncopated rhythms.

CALL CHART 12: Ragtime

Joplin: *Fig Leaf Rag*

1 *INTRODUCTION*

2 *SECTION A: Repeated rhythm pattern; steady beat in lower register; melody mostly outlines chords*

3 *SECTION B: Different rhythm pattern; steady beat continues melody moves mostly by step; harmony in thirds*

4 *SECTION A: Repetition of number 2*

5 *SECTION C: Another rhythm pattern; thicker density; steady beat continues; melody in upward and downward direction*

6 *SECTION D: Melody has many repeated tones; still another syncopated rhythm pattern; melody is ornamented; steady beat continues in lower register; thicker density continues to syncopated ending*

CANON: A FOLLOW-THE-LEADER FORM

In a canon, each voice or instrument performs the same melody, but each starts at a different time. This process is called *imitation*.

When "Alas, Alack" is performed as a canon, the texture is polyphonic.

What is the texture when "Alas, Alack" is performed as a melody alone?

Alas, Alack

MUSIC BY TERENCE GREAVES   WORDS BY WALTER DE LA MARE

Ann, Ann, come quick as you can! There's a fish that talks in the fry - ing pan. Out of the fat, as clear as glass, He put up his mouth__ and moaned, "A - las," Oh, most mourn-ful "A - las, a - lack!" Then turned to his siz-zling and sank him back.

Now listen to a canon played on two recorders.

Telemann: *Six Canonic Sonatas*, No. 1, Movement 3

As you listen again, try to hear other things in the music—wide leaps, trills that decorate the melody, long and short sounds, syncopation, notes that are played staccato (separated, detached).

162

THEME AND VARIATIONS

When one musical idea is repeated in a different version in each section of a piece, the form is theme and variations. The chart will help you hear how a composer uses musical qualities to vary a theme.

CALL CHART 13: Theme and Variations 🎧
9

Handel: *The Harmonious Blacksmith*

	THEME:	*Slow; major; many strong cadences; melodies move by steps and leaps*
1	*VARIATION 1:*	*Many short sounds in higher register, faster tempo; major*
2	*VARIATION 2:*	*Same tempo as variation 1; short sounds in lower register; use of ornamentation*
3	*VARIATION 3:*	*Short sounds in higher register; long sounds in lower register; faster tempo*
4	*VARIATION 4:*	*Short sounds in lower register; long sounds in higher register; same tempo as variation 3*
5	*VARIATION 5:*	*Fastest tempo; many short sounds moving stepwise; downward and upward direction; strong cadence at the end*

Each time a number is called you will hear two musical examples. Decide whether the second example is a repetition of the first, or whether it is a contrast or a variation.

---

1 *REPETITION* *CONTRAST* *VARIATION*

---

2 *REPETITION* *CONTRAST* *VARIATION*

---

3 *REPETITION* *CONTRAST* *VARIATION*

---

4 *REPETITION* *CONTRAST* *VARIATION*

---

5 *REPETITION* *CONTRAST* *VARIATION*

---

6 *REPETITION* *CONTRAST* *VARIATION*

---

7 *REPETITION* *CONTRAST* *VARIATION*

---

8 *REPETITION* *CONTRAST* *VARIATION*

La Sinda
Roll an' Rock
Brahms: *Waltz, Op. 39, No. 2*
Mozart: *Symphony No. 36*, Movement 3

Beethoven: *Variations on "God Save the King"*
Sakura
Chopin: *Waltz in E Flat*, Op. 18
El Capotin

Live! Live!

WORDS AND MUSIC BY MARIA JORDAN

La la la la la la la la, la la la la la la la la, La la la la la la la la,

la la la la.   Run, run, there's worlds to dis-cov - er! Fly, fly wher-
    Do, do, so much is worth do - ing; Try, try what-
    See, see what's hap-pen-ing 'round you; Feel, feel the

ev - er your heart would go! Dance, dance, the mu - sic is call - ing,
ev - er you want to try! Dream, dream, and keep on pur-su - ing,
shake of a friend - ly hand. Taste, taste the sweet and the so - ur,

Sing, sing a song that you know.
Reach, reach for stars in the sky! Look at the world a-round you and you'll see that
March, march, and play in a band!

life's an ad-ven-ture in a way. So get up and go and grab a-hold of it! There's

D.S. (last time al ⊕ *)*

liv-ing to do each day,_____ and no rea-son for de - lay. Come on, let's go and

liv - ing, so much liv-ing to do each day!_____ There's

liv-ing to do!

165

PLAN A PERFORMANCE

Combine the melody of "Turn, Turn, Turn" with the added parts
on the next page to show the two contrasting sections (A and
B) of this song. Think how you will use different tone colors,
different textures, different tempos and dynamics.

Turn, Turn, Turn *(To Everything There Is a Season)*

WORDS FROM THE BOOK OF ECCLESIASTES   ADAPTATION AND MUSIC BY PETE SEEGER   TRO—© COPYRIGHT 1962 MELODY TRAILS, INC., NEW YORK, N.Y. USED BY PERMISSION.

To ev-'ry-thing, (Turn, turn, turn) There is a sea-son (Turn, turn,
turn) And a time for ev-'ry pur-pose un-der heav-en.

1. A time to be born, a time to die; A time to
2. A time to build up, a time to break down; A time to
3. A time of love, a time of hate; A time of
4. A time to gain, a time to lose; A time to

plant, a time to reap; A time to kill, a time to
dance, a time to mourn; A time to cast a-way
war, a time of peace; A time you may em -
rend, a time to sew; A time to love, a time to

heal; A time to laugh, a time to weep.
stones, A time to gath - er stones to - geth - er.
brace, A time to re - frain from em - brac - ing.
hate; A time for

To ev - 'ry peace, I swear it's not too

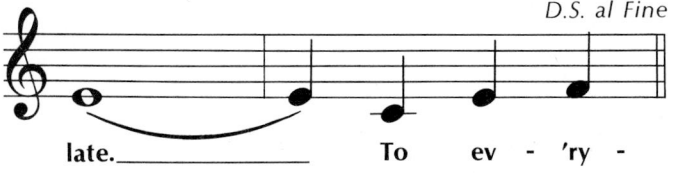

D.S. al Fine

late. _____ To ev - 'ry -

ADD A PART

Section B can be sung as a canon with a countermelody. The countermelody can be sung, or it can be played on recorder and bells.

Recorder or Bells (Section B)

(I)   II

A time to be born, a time to die; A time to plant, a time to

Countermelody

Turn, Turn, Turn, Turn, Turn,

reap; A time to kill, a time to heal; A time to laugh, a time to weep.

Turn, Turn, Turn, Turn, Turn, Turn Turn.

167

Experiencing the Arts: Multimedia

The words in the spinner below describe several qualities of sound. Experiment with different ways to create these sound qualities. Use voices or instruments.

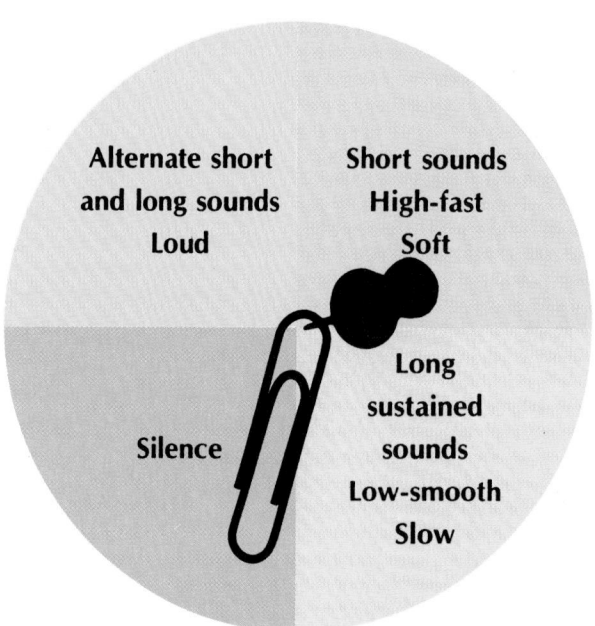

These same words can be used to describe qualities of body movement. They can also be used to describe things you can do with a flashlight—shining it against the ceiling, the walls, or the floor. Experiment with different ways to create movements and light effects, using what the words in the spinner suggest.

Now create a multimedia presentation that combines sounds, movements, and light effects.

1. Make two spinners (like those at the top of page 169) out of heavy cardboard. Use a pushpin to fasten a paper clip in the center of each circle. To spin the paper clip, flick the end with your finger.

I MEDIA EVENTS

Movement and music

Light

Movement

All

Music

Light and movement

II MUSICAL QUALITIES

Alternate short and long sounds
Loud

Short sounds
High-fast
Soft

Silence

Long sustained sounds
Low-smooth
Slow

2. Divide the performers into four groups.

Group 1: voices

Group 2: instruments

Group 3: dancers

Group 4: flashlights

3. Make a plan for your presentation.

• Spin each wheel and write down what it shows. For example, spinner I—Movement and music; spinner II—Long-sustained

• Decide how many such events you will use.

• Decide how long each event will last.

• Decide and practice what will happen for each event.

Here is an example of a plan.

	0″	30″	40″	50″	60″
I	movement and music	light	light and movement	all	
II	long sustained-smooth-low-slow	silence	alternate short and long sounds-loud	short sounds high-fast-soft	

4. Present your multimedia performance.

Afterward, take time to judge the results. Did all parts go well together? Did any part call too much attention to itself?

Experiencing the Arts

What happens when we experience art?

JULES BRETON, THE SONG OF THE LARK, COLLECTION OF THE ART INSTITUTE OF CHICAGO.

OUR SENSES receive the sound of music, the colors in a painting, the movement of dancers, the word-images in a poem. Most experiences of art require seeing or hearing or both.

OUR MINDS AND FEELINGS GET INVOLVED with all the things happening in the music or painting or sculpture or dance. We notice what is there and respond to the qualities as if they were inside our feelings.

WE CREATE ART by singing, playing, composing, painting, dancing, acting. This gives us another way to experience art. We become creators and experiencers at the same time, and produce something others can experience.

WE ANALYZE AND JUDGE ART when we study how a work of art is made and whether we think it is made well—with skill, with sensitivity, with imagination. We analyze and judge our own creations as well as the work of others.

WE VALUE ART if we find excitement in experiencing and creating music, poems, crafts, dances, plays. The arts become part of our lives to enjoy and experience. Just think of how much would be missing from our lives if we didn't have the arts!

171

Gee, It's Nice to be Alone

WORDS AND MUSIC BY ROD McKUEN

Relaxed

Gee, it's nice to be a-lone, To wake up by your-self; To
Gee, it's nice to be a-lone, To get to know your-self; To

own the day a-while, And not have to talk to an-y-bod-y.
waste a-way the time, And

not have to smile for an-y-bod-y. What a deal to stay in your pa-

ja-mas, With noth-in' ver-y much to do, But watch the shad-ows

chang-ing pan-o-ra-mas, When e-ven the shad-ows don't look

back at you. Well, gee, it's nice to be a-lone, To find out for your-

self, What sol-i-tude's a-bout; And not have a need

for an-y-bod-y. Gee, it's nice to be a-lone...some-times.

On My Journey

BLACK-AMERICAN TRADITIONAL SONG   ARRANGED BY LAWRENCE EISMAN

NEW VERSES BY FRED HELLERMAN, LEE HAYS, RONNIE GILBERT, AND ERIK DARLING

© COPYRIGHT 1960, 1968 BY SANGA MUSIC INC. USED BY PERMISSION. ALL RIGHTS RESERVED.

1. When I'm on my jour-ney, oh, don't you weep,_
2. Ev-'ry riv-er must go home to the sea,_
3. On the moun-tain leave my sor-rows be-low,_

1. When I'm on my jour-ney,_ don't you weep af-ter me,_
2. Ev-'ry lone-ly riv-er_ must go home to the sea,_
3. High up on the moun-tain_ leave my sorrows down be-low,_

When I'm on my jour-ney, oh, don't you weep,_
Ev-'ry riv-er must go home to the sea,_
On the moun-tain leave my sor-rows be-low,_

When I'm on my jour-ney,_ don't you weep af-ter me,_
Ev-'ry lone-ly riv-er_ must go home to the sea,_
High up on the moun-tain_ leave my sorrows down be-low,_

When I'm on my jour-ney, oh, don't you weep,_   I don't
Ev-'ry riv-er must go home to the sea,_
On the moun-tain leave my sor-rows be-low,_

When I'm on my jour-ney,_ don't you weep af-ter me,_   I don't
Ev-'ry lone-ly riv-er_ must go home to the sea,_
High up on the moun-tain_ leave my sorrows down be-low,_

want you to weep af-ter me._____

want you to weep af-ter me._____

Waters Ripple and Flow

FOLK SONG FROM CZECHOSLOVAKIA   ENGLISH WORDS BY MARGARET FISHBACK

Smoothly

1. Wa - ters rip - ple and flow,___ Swift - ly flow___ to the sea,
2. Riv - er Tu - ra flow - ing, Hear my yearn - ing___ song.

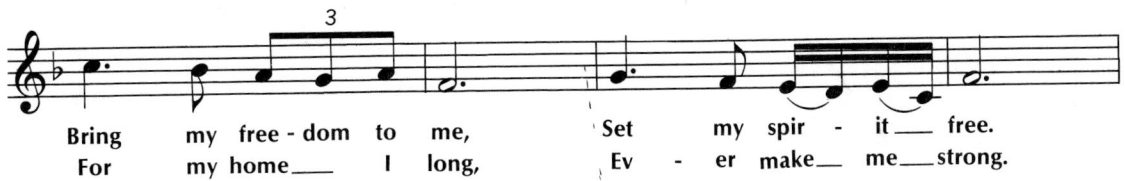

Bring my free - dom to me, Set my spir - it___ free.
For my home___ I long, Ev - er make___ me___ strong.

Riv - er flow - ing by On your way___ to the sky.
Tu - ra flow - ing deep, Let me cour - age___ keep.

3. Sound the cry___ of free - dom, Riv - er, as___ you___ flow,

Then my heart___ might know Vic - t'ry o - ver___ woe.

Tu - ra, flow - ing past, Give me lib - er - ty at last.

Three White Gulls

FOLK SONG FROM ITALY   ARRANGED BY DAVID S. WALKER

ENGLISH WORDS BY MARGUERITE WILKINSON

Original title "The Three Doves" by Marguerite Wilkinson from Botsford collection of Folk Songs—Volume 3. Copyright © 1921, 1922 G. Schirmer, Inc. Used by Permission.

1. There are three____ white gulls____ a - fly - ing;____ There are
2. In the waves____ they dip____ their soft wings;____ In the

three____ white gulls____ a - fly - ing;____ There are three___ white gulls a-
waves____ they dip____ their soft____ wings;____ In the waves____ they dip their

fly - ing;____ By the sea they cry, By the sea they cry, By the sea they
soft wings;____ Then__ soar to the sky, Then__ soar to the sky, Then__ soar to the

cry.
sky.

Ti-ra - li - ra - lu, Ti-ra-li - ra - lu, Ti-ra - li - ra - lu.____

Green, Green

WORDS AND MUSIC BY BARRY McGUIRE AND RANDY SPARKS   ARRANGED BY MILTON FRIEDMAN

With a Steady Beat
INTRODUCTION*

REFRAIN

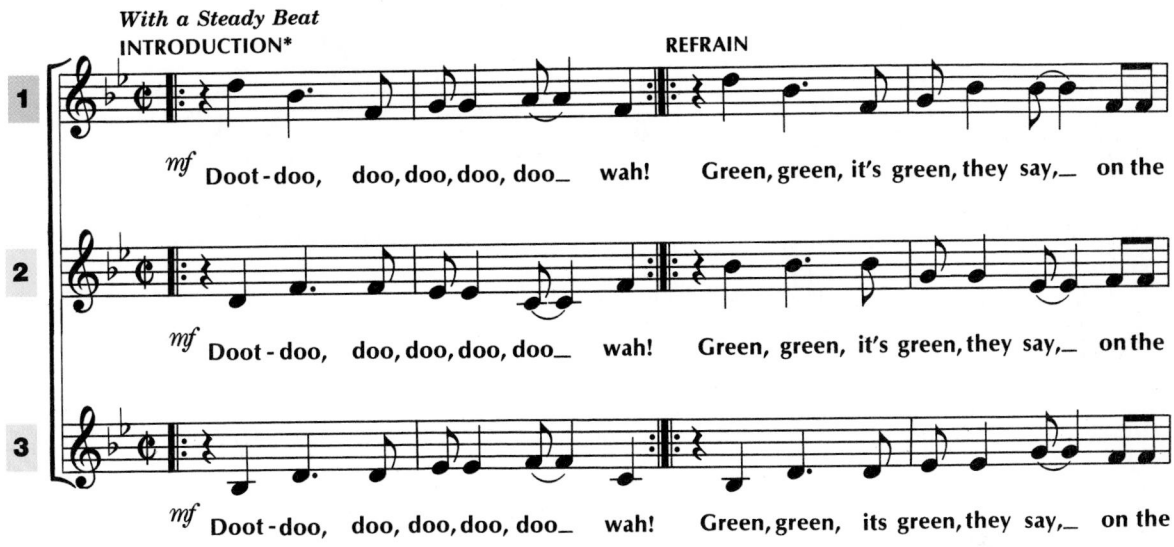

1. *mf* Doot-doo, doo, doo, doo, doo__ wah! Green, green, it's green, they say,__ on the

2. *mf* Doot-doo, doo, doo, doo, doo__ wah! Green, green, it's green, they say,__ on the

3. *mf* Doot-doo, doo, doo, doo, doo__ wah! Green, green, its green, they say,__ on the

1. far side of the hill;__ oo__ Green, green, I'm go-in' a-way__ to where the

2. far side of the hill;__ oo__ Green, green, I'm go-in' a-way__ to where the

3. far side of the hill;__ oo Green, green, I'm go-in' a-way__ to where the

*Voice 3 enters first; add voice 2; add voice 3.

1. Well I told my ma-ma on the day I was born,_ "Don-cha

grass is green-er still._2. No there ain't no-bod-y in this whole_ wide world_ gon-na

3. I don't care_ when the sun_ goes down,_Where I

1. cry when you see I'm gone._

2. tell me how to spend my time._ Ah

3. lay my_ wear-y head._

1. cry when you see I'm gone._

2. tell me how to spend my time._ Ah

3. lay my_ wear-y head._

cry when you see I'm gone._ You know there ain't no - bo - dy gon-na

tell me how to spend my time._ I'm_ just a good _ hap-py

lay my_ wear-y head._ Green, green val-ley or a

got - ta be a - trav - el - in' on.__

bud - dy could you spare me a dime?__   A - sing - in'

there I'm gon - na make_ my bed.__   *(Repeat to Fine.)*

got - ta be a - trav - el - in' on.__

bud - dy could you spare me a dime?__   A - sing - in'

there I'm gon - na make_ my bed.__   *(Repeat to Fine.)*

set - tle me down,_ I just   got - ta be a - trav - el - in' on."__

ram - bl - in' man,____ say   bud - dy could you spare me a dime?__   A - sing - in'

rock - y road,____ It's   there I'm gon - na make_ my bed.__   *(Repeat to Fine.)*

Thou, O Lord, Art My Shepherd

MUSIC BY BENEDETTO MARCELLO   WORDS BY R. J. S. STEVENS

Thou,   O   Lord,_____   art _____ my Shep - herd,

Thou,   O   Lord,_____   art _____ my Shep - herd,

There - fore shall _____   I ____ want noth - ing, There - fore shall

There - fore shall_____   I ___ want noth - ing, There - fore shall

Singing in Chorus   **179**

Bidin' My Time

MUSIC BY GEORGE GERSHWIN   ARRANGED BY SOL BERKOWITZ   WORDS BY IRA GERSHWIN

Slowly

I'm bid - in' my time;_____ 'cause that's the kind - a guy I'm._____ While oth - er folks grow diz - zy I keep bus - y Bid - in' my time. Next year,___ next year,___ some - thin's bound to hap - pen;___ This year,___ this year,___ I'll just keep on nap - pin',___ And bid - in'____ my time _____ 'cause that's the kind-a guy I'm. _____ There's

no re-gret-tin' When I'm set-tin' bid-in' my

1.,2.

time. There's bid-in' my time. _____

pp

3.

pp

Sing a Rainbow

WORDS AND MUSIC BY ARTHUR HAMILTON   ARRANGED BY MARILYN COPELAND DAVIDSON

Moderately Ⓐ
mp

Red and yel-low and pink and green,   pur-ple and or-ange and

mp

Red and yel-low and_ pur-ple, or-ange,

mp

Red and yel-low, pink, green,   pur-ple, or-ange,

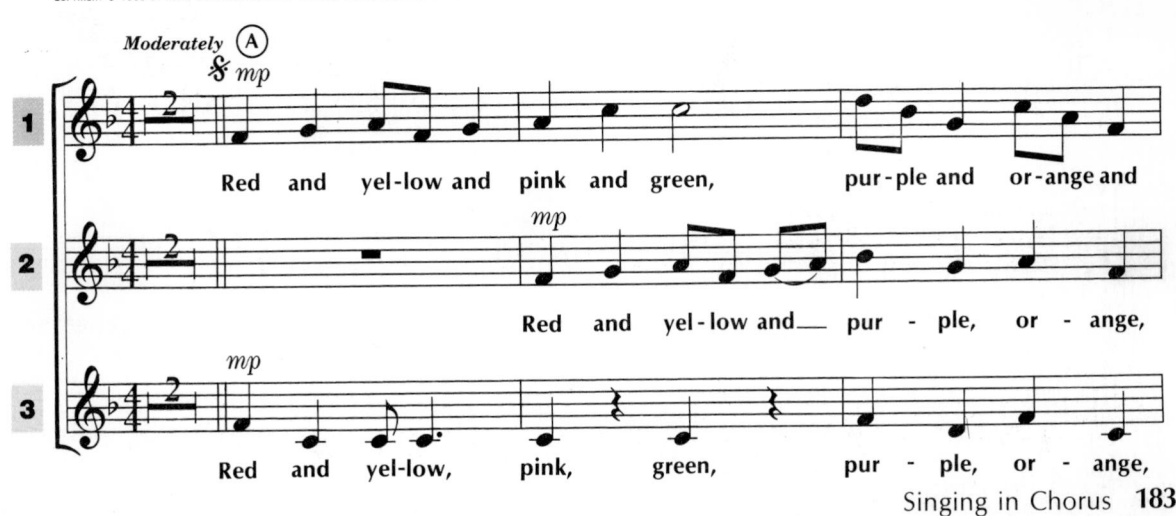

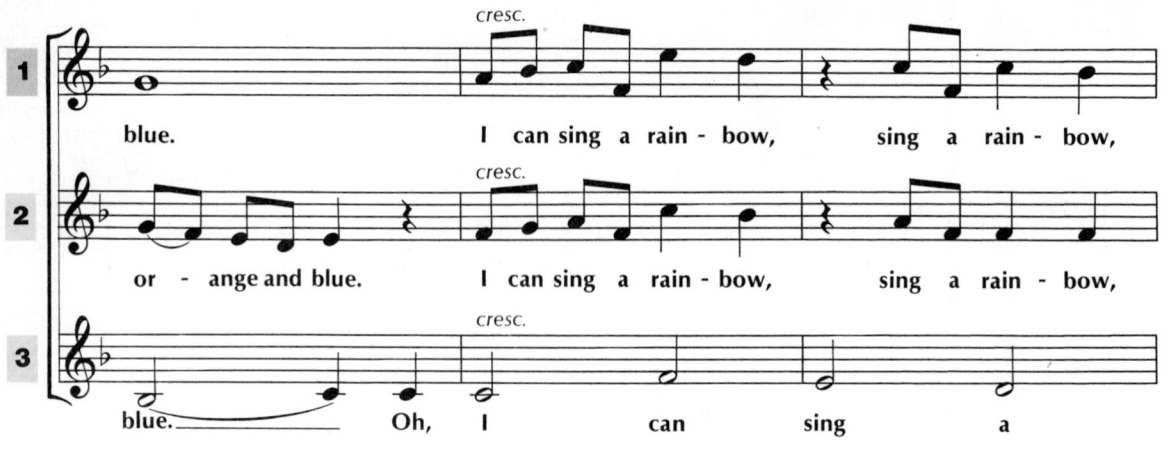

Voice 1: blue. I can sing a rain - bow, sing a rain - bow,

Voice 2: or - ange and blue. I can sing a rain - bow, sing a rain - bow,

Voice 3: blue. Oh, I can sing a

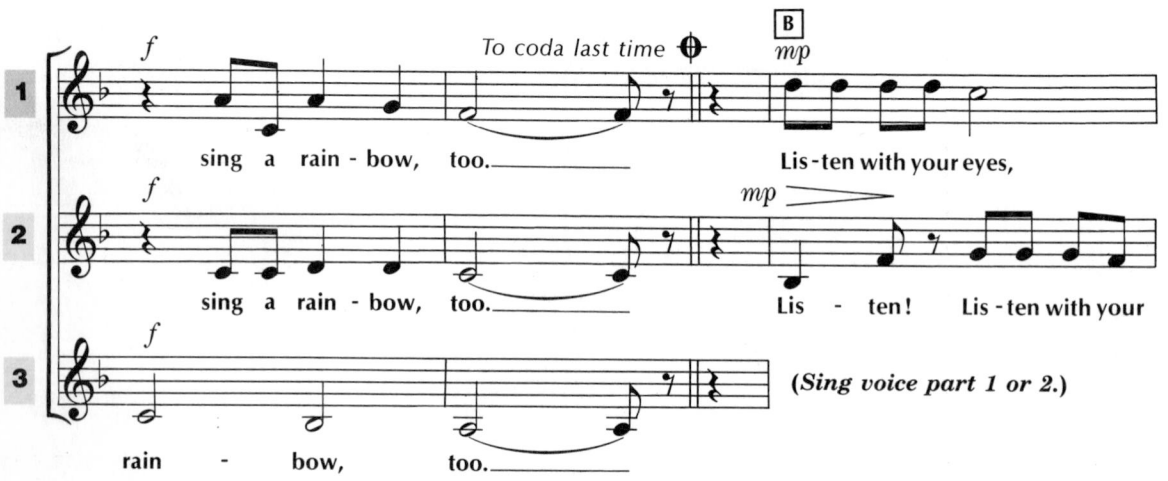

To coda last time

B mp

Voice 1: sing a rain - bow, too. Lis - ten with your eyes,

Voice 2: sing a rain - bow, too. Lis - ten! Lis - ten with your

Voice 3: rain - bow, too. *(Sing voice part 1 or 2.)*

Voice 1: Lis - ten with your eyes and sing ev - 'ry-thing you see.

Voice 2: eyes. Lis - ten with your eyes and sing ev - 'ry-thing you see.

Voice 1: You can sing a rain - bow, sing a rain - bow, Sing a-long with

Voice 2: You, you can sing a rain - bow, You can sing a-long, a-long with

CODA

rit. D.S. al ⊕ f   rit.

1 me. Sing a rain-bow, Sing a rain-bow, too._____

rit. f   rit.

2
3 me. (with me.___) Sing a rain-bow, Sing a rain-bow, too._____

I Don't Mind   WORDS AND MUSIC BY DAVID EDDLEMAN

With a good swing (♪♪ = ⌐³♪)

Ⓐ F   B♭   F   C₇

I don't mind___   if you sing;___   I don't mind___   if you dance;___
La la la___   la la la,   La la la   la la la,

F   B♭

I don't mind___   as long as   you don't mind___   if
La la la___   la la la   la la la___   la

1.,2. *No repeat first time* 3.

F   C₇   C₇   F

I should sing,-   too, just   by chance. *(Section B)*   la la la.___
La la la___   la la la la.   la la la.___

B F   B♭   F   C₇

f You'll nev-er go wrong keep-ing a song sing-ing a-long. You'll
la la la la la la la la la la la la la, La

F   B♭   F

see you've got to be hap-py and free sing-ing a
la la la la la la la la la la la la

1.,2.   3.

C₇   C₇   F

mel-o-dy. La
la la la. La la la la.___

Singing in Chorus **185**

Life Has Loveliness

MUSIC BY ROBERT J. POWELL   WORDS BY SARA TEASDALE

Tranquil

1. Life has love-li-ness to sell, All beau-ti-ful and splen-did things,

Blue waves whit-ened on a cliff, Soar-ing fire that sways and sings,

And chil-dren's fac-es look-ing up, Hold-ing won-der like a cup.

2. Life has love-li-

1 hour of peace Count man - y a year of strife well lost,_____ And for a

2 hour of peace Count man - y a year of strife well lost,_____ And for a

1 breath of ec - sta - sy Give all you have been or could_____ be._____

2 breath of ec - sta - sy Give all you have been or could_____ be._____

Glory to God   MUSIC BY LUDWIG GEBHARDI   WORDS TRADITIONAL

I Glo - ry to God in the high - est!

II Peace on the earth, on the earth_____ peace And good-

III will to men, to_____ all_____ men. A -

IV - - - men, A - men.

Playing the Guitar

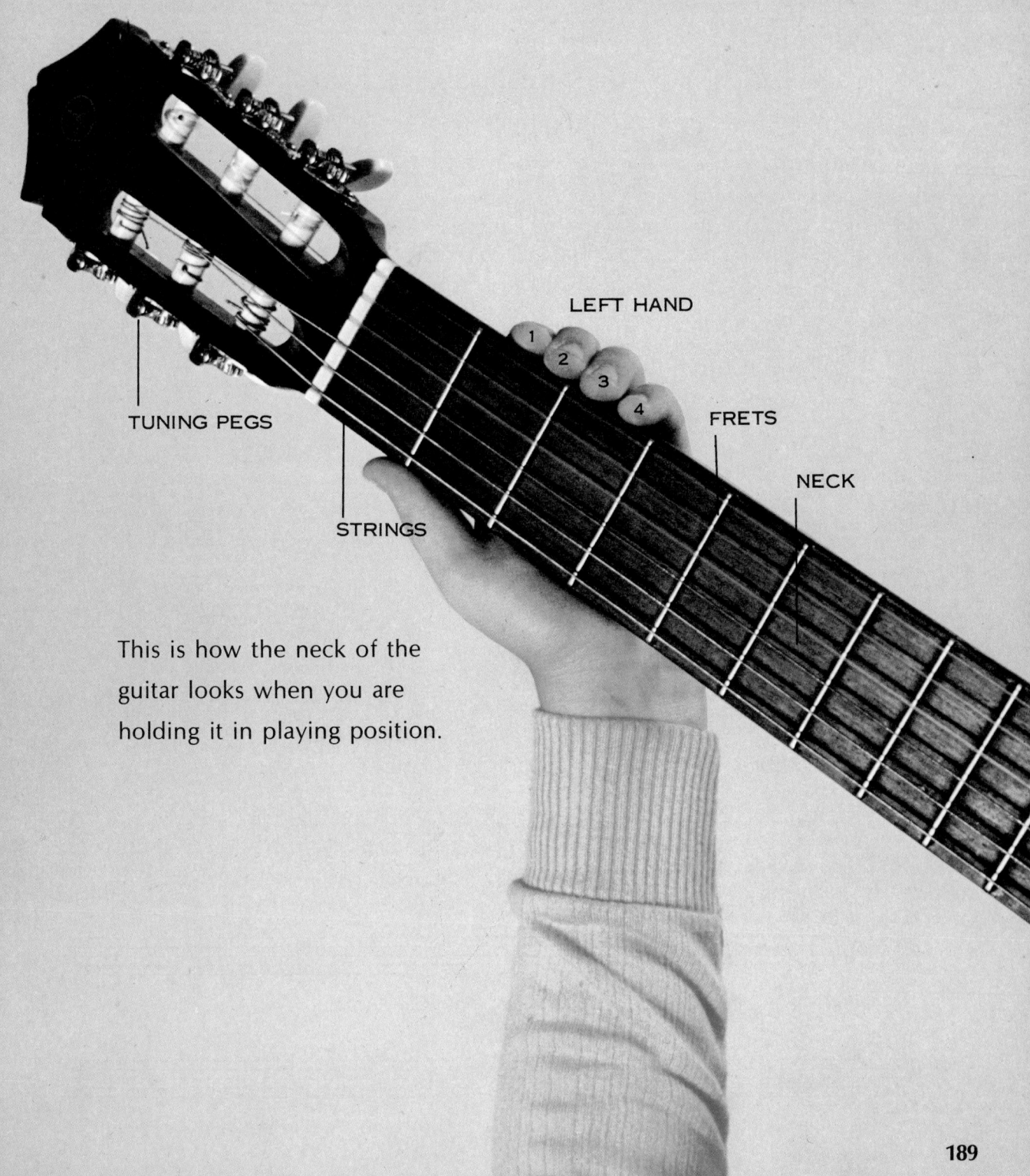

TUNING PEGS

STRINGS

LEFT HAND

1
2
3
4

FRETS

NECK

This is how the neck of the guitar looks when you are holding it in playing position.

THE C AND G₇ CHORDS

These diagrams will show you a simplified way to play the
C and G₇ chords on the guitar.

To play the C chord, put finger 1 (your index
finger) on the B string. Strum the strings
shown in red.

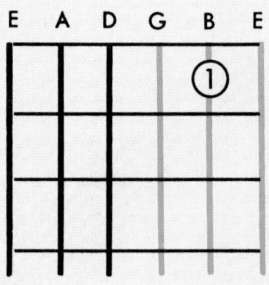

To play the G₇ chord, move finger 1 to the
high-E string and strum the strings shown in
red.

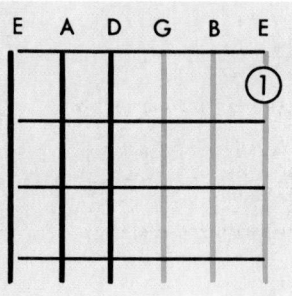

If you have already played the simplified C
and G₇ chords, try the full chords.

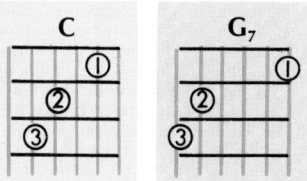

Use the C and G₇ chords to accompany this song.

Goodby, Old Paint   AMERICAN FOLK SONG

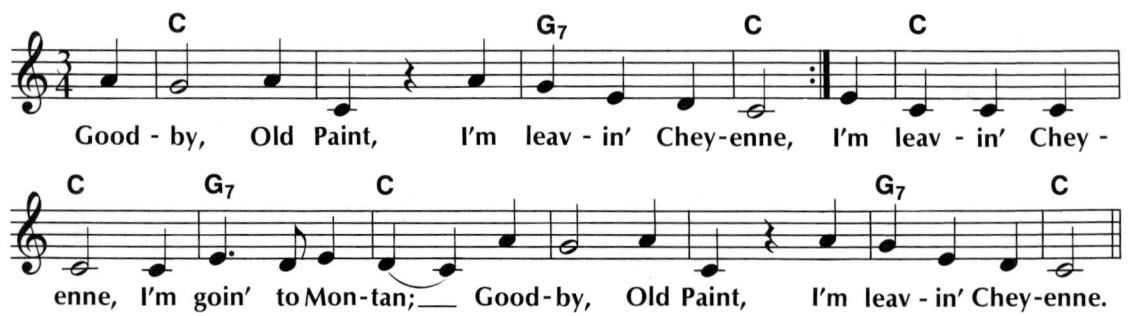

Practice changing back and forth from the C chord to the G_7
chord by accompanying one of the songs you may know.

- "Chumbara," page 33
- "Puttin' On the Style," page 34
- "La Sinda," page 35

If you cannot play the full C and G_7 chords easily, team up with
a friend who will play a bass part while you strum the
simplified chords.

To play a bass part, alternate these two bass
notes when the simplified C chord is played.

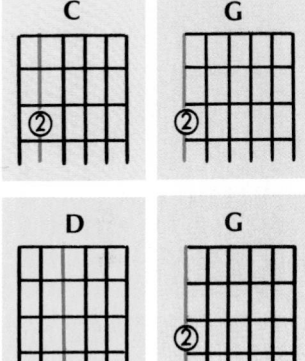

Alternate these two bass notes when the
simplified G_7 chord is played.

Use the C and G_7 chords to accompany "Mary Ann."

Mary Ann   TRADITIONAL CALYPSO

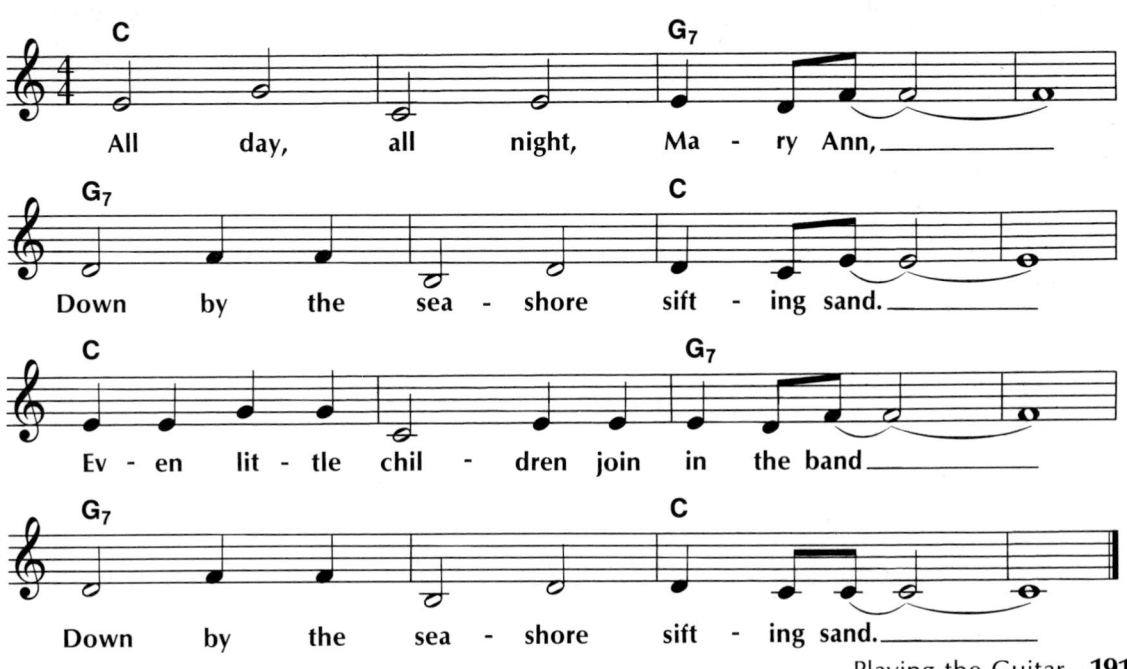

THE A AND E₇ CHORDS

When you can play the A and E_7 chords, you will be able to accompany more songs. The photographs and diagrams will show you where to place your fingers.

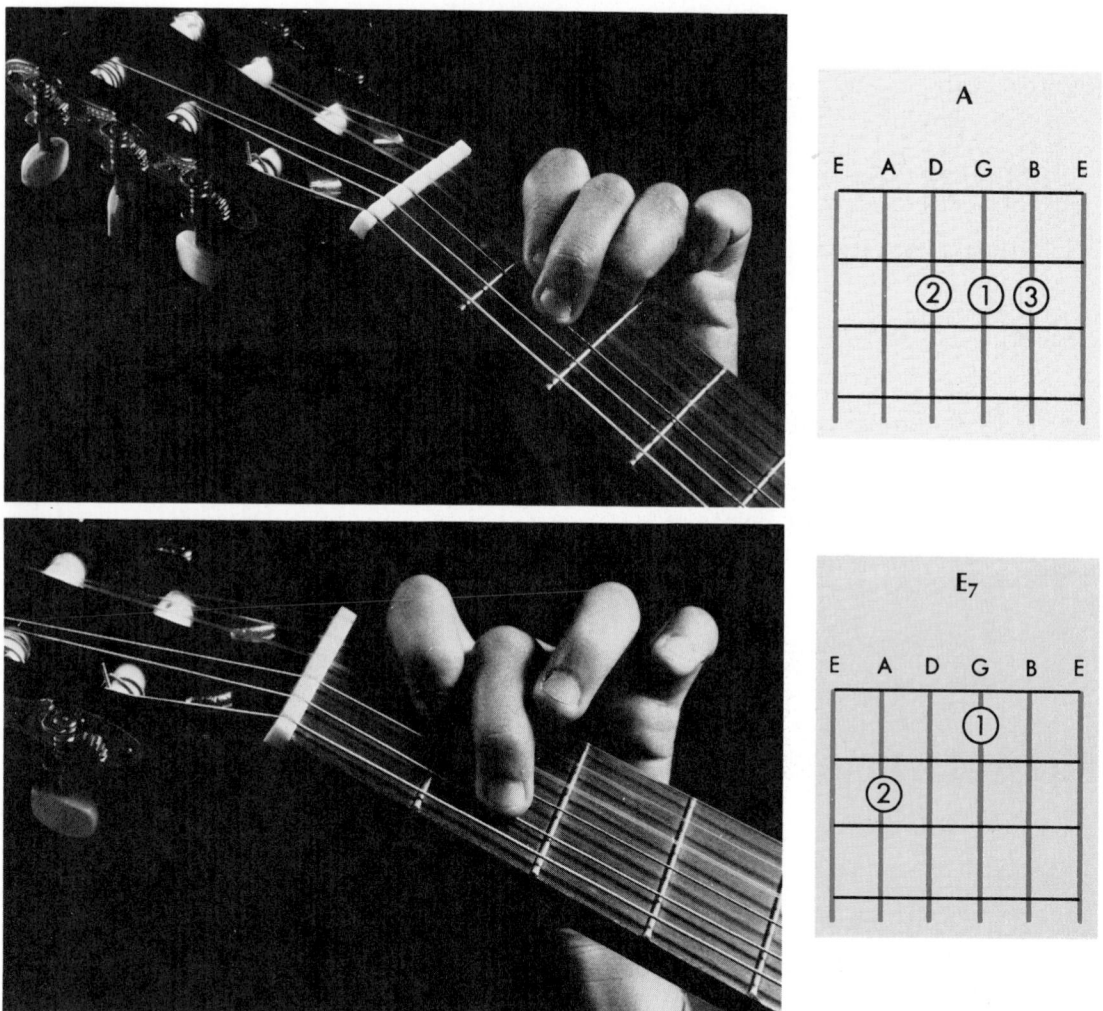

Sing and accompany by ear some two-chord songs you know using the A and E_7 chords.

- "I'se the B'y," page 10
- "La Raspa," page 26
- "There's a Fiesta," page 27
- "Take Time in Life," page 31
- "Gonna Build a Mountain," page 78

The easiest way to strum is to brush your thumb down across the strings in a rhythm that fits the song you are accompanying.

BACK-AND-FORTH STRUM

Brush your thumb across the strings, moving away from your body. This is the *downstroke,* shown by an arrow (↓). Between downstrokes, strum the strings again, moving toward your body. This is the *upstroke,* shown by an arrow (↑).

Begin with a simple pattern of downstrokes and upstrokes in a regular rhythm. Be careful to strum only the strings needed for the chord you are playing.

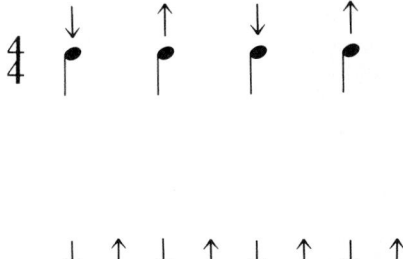

Play the A and E$_7$ chords to accompany "Ain't Gonna Rain." Follow the arrows above the words and use the back-and-forth strum.

Ain't Gonna Rain   AMERICAN FOLK SONG

THE D-MINOR AND A₇ CHORDS

Practice playing two more chords. The photographs and the diagrams will show you where to place your fingers.

THE D-MINOR CHORD

Here is the fingering for the D-minor chord.

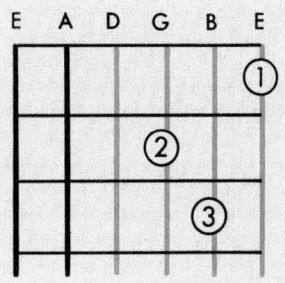

THE A₇ CHORD

When you accompany "Joshua Fit the Battle of Jericho," use this fingering for the A₇ chord.

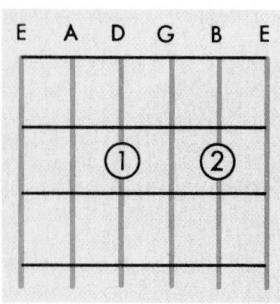

Joshua Fit the Battle of Jericho   BLACK SPIRITUAL

Use the back-and-forth strum to accompany "Joshua Fit the Battle of Jericho." Try one section at a time. Follow the arrows above the words and play the same strumming rhythm throughout.

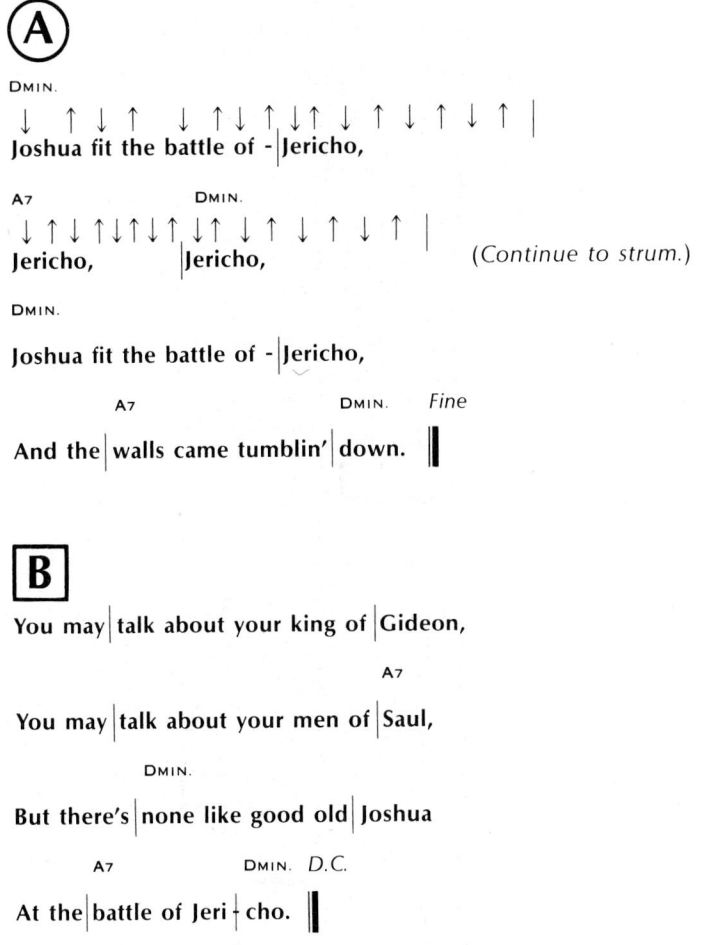

(A)

DMIN.

↓ ↑ ↓ ↑   ↓ ↑ ↓ ↑ ↓ ↑ ↓ ↑ ↓ ↑ ↓ ↑ |
Joshua fit the battle of - |Jericho,

A7   DMIN.

↓ ↑ ↓ ↑ ↓ ↑ ↓ ↑ ↓ ↑ ↓ ↑ ↓ ↑ ↓ ↑ |
Jericho, |Jericho,   (Continue to strum.)

DMIN.

Joshua fit the battle of - |Jericho,

      A7   DMIN.   *Fine*

And the |walls came tumblin' |down.   ‖

B

You may |talk about your king of |Gideon,

                              A7

You may |talk about your men of |Saul,

            DMIN.

But there's |none like good old |Joshua

      A7   DMIN. *D.C.*

At the |battle of Jeri + cho.   ‖

Now, use the D-minor chord with the C chord to accompany these songs.

- "Sinner Man," page 102
- "The Drunken Sailor," page 103

He's Got the Whole World in His Hands

BLACK SPIRITUAL

Notice the fingering for the D chord in the diagram below.
Compare it with the fingering for the D-minor chord on
page 194.

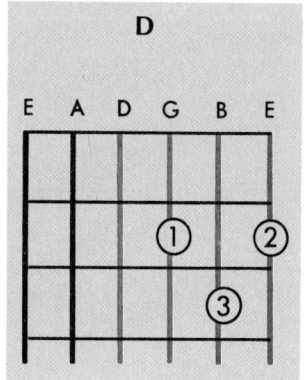

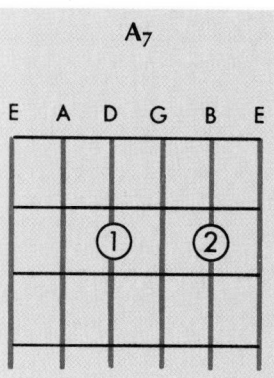

Use the D and A_7 chords to accompany "He's Got the Whole
World in His Hands." Try one of the strums suggested on
page 197.

   (A7)   D

1. He's got the | whole   /   world   / | in His hands, |

            A7   D

He's got the | whole wide world   / | in His hands,

He's got the | whole   /   world   / | in His hands,

            A7   D

He's got the | whole world in His | hands. / /

2. He's got the wind and the rain . . .

3. He's got the little bitty baby . . .

4. He's got you and me brother . . .

5. He's got the whole world . . .

MORE ABOUT STRUMS

Here are some rhythm patterns to use when playing the back-and-forth strum.

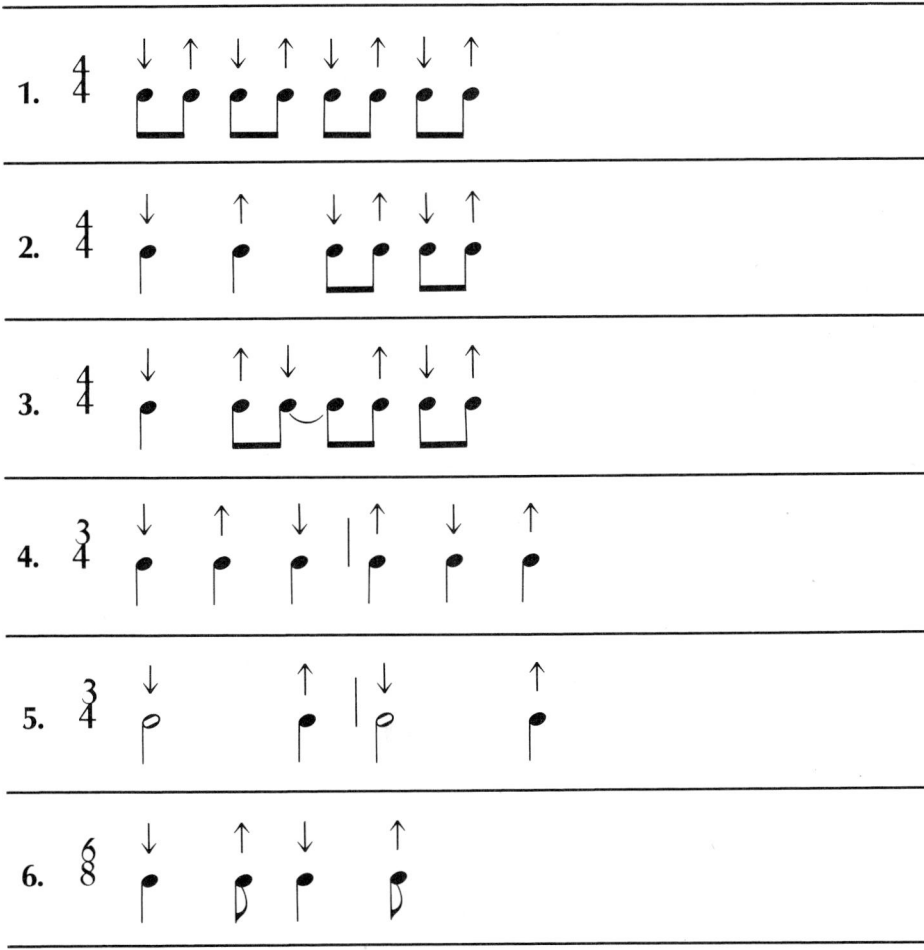

You can create your own rhythm pattern to match the style of the song you are accompanying. Experiment! You might invent a strumming rhythm nobody has ever used before.

To vary the sound of the back-and-forth strum, use the tips of your fingers rather than your thumb. As you strum on the downstroke with your fingers, you will hit the strings with your fingernails, making a sharp sound.

Remember to hold your fingers loosely so they will brush the strings easily. Experiment to find the sound you like.

Old Blue

SOUTHERN MOUNTAIN SONG

Practice the D and A$_7$ chords by accompanying this song. Make up a strum of your own.

1. I had an old dog,_____ And his name was Blue,_____

_____ And I bet-cha five dol-lars he's a good dog, too. Come on

Blue,___ you good dog,_ you;___ Come on Blue,___ you good dog,_ you.___

2. I grabbed my axe and I tooted my horn,
   Gonna git me a 'possum in the new-ground corn. *Refrain*

3. Chased that ol' 'possum up a 'simmon tree,
   Blue looked at the 'possum, 'possum looked at me. *Refrain*

4. Blue grinned at me, I grinned at him,
   I shook out the 'possum, Blue took him in. *Refrain*

5. Baked that 'possum all good and brown,
   And I laid them sweet potatoes 'round and 'round. *Refrain*

6. Well, old Blue died, and he died so hard,
   That he shook the ground in my back yard. *Refrain*

7. I dug his grave with a silver spade,
   I let him down with a golden chain. *Refrain*

8. When I get to heaven, first thing I'll do,
   Grab me a horn and blow for old Blue. *Refrain*

CHORD FAMILY, KEY OF A (A E$_7$ D)

Practice these fingerings, then accompany the songs below.

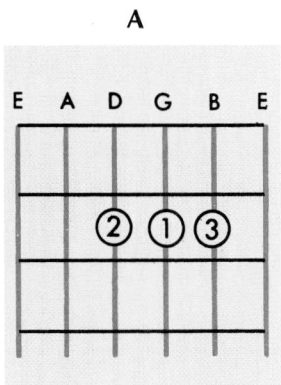
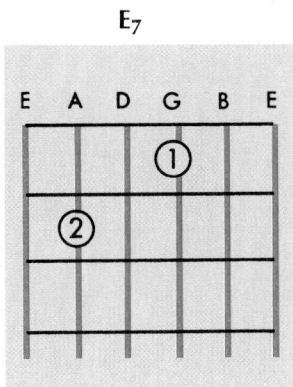
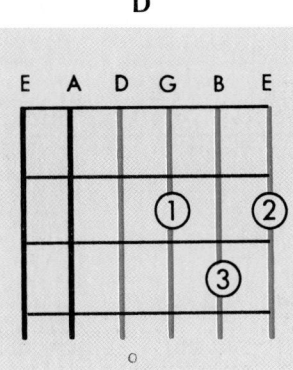

On Top of Old Smoky   FOLK SONG FROM KENTUCKY

On top of old Smok - y,_____   All cov-ered with snow,_____

I lost my true lov - er,_____   A - court-in' too slow._____

Silent Night   FRANZ GRUBER

A   E$_7$ A
Silent night, holy night, All is calm, All is bright

D   A
Round yon Virgin, Mother and Child.

D   A
Holy Infant so tender and mild,

E$_7$ A   E$_7$ A
Sleep in heavenly peace, Sleep in heavenly peace.

CHORD FAMILY, KEY OF D (D A₇ G)

Practice these fingerings, then accompany "Tzena, tzena" and the songs on page 201.

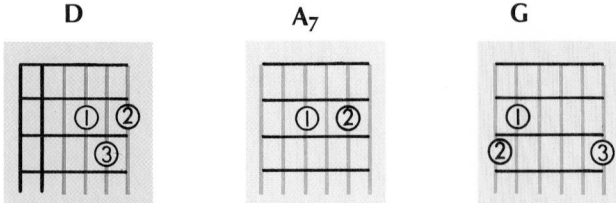

Tzena, Tzena

FOLK SONG FROM ISRAEL   ENGLISH WORDS BY PHYLLIS RESNICK

Tze - na, tze - na, tze - na, tze - na, come in - to the fields and we'll be -
Hoe - ing, sow - ing, new things grow - ing, pi - o - neer - ing all to - geth - er,

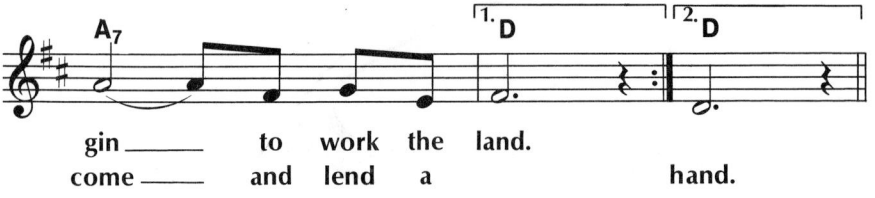

gin _____ to work the land.
come _____ and lend a hand.

Tze - na, tze - na, build - ing a new na - tion, toil - ing bus - i - ly all

day. _____ Soon we'll dance and have a cel - e - bra - tion, But

first we'll work and then we'll play.

New River Train

AMERICAN FOLK SONG

REFRAIN D

1. I'm rid - in' on that new ri - ver train. I'm rid - in' on that new ri - ver

A₇   D   G   A₇

train. The same old train that brought me here, gon - na car - ry me back a -

D   VERSE D   A₇

gain. Oh, dar - lin' you can't love_ one, Oh, dar - lin' you can't love_ one, You

D   G   A₇   D

can't love one and have a - ny fun, Oh, dar - lin' you can't love one.

John Jacob Jingleheimer Schmidt

NONSENSE SONG

D   A₇   D

John   Ja - cob Jing - le - heim - er Schmidt, That's   my name too.   When -

D   G

ev - er I go out,   The peo - ple al - ways shout, "There goes

A₇   D   A₇   D

John   Ja - cob Jing - le - heim - er Schmidt," Da Da   Da   Da   Da   Da   Da   Da.

Playing the Guitar   **201**

CHORD FAMILY, KEY OF G (G D₇ C)

G	D₇	C
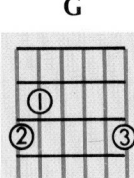	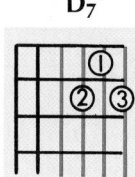	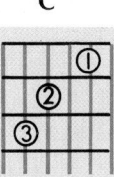

Practice using the G, D₇, and C chords by accompanying songs you know. Some of these songs use two chords (G, D₇), others use three chords (G, D₇, C).

- "I'se the B'y," page 10
- "The *John B.* Sails," page 14
- "La Raspa," page 26
- "There's a Fiesta," page 27
- "Take Me Home, Country Roads," page 28
- "Take Time in Life," page 31
- "Gonna Build a Mountain," page 78
- "Amazing Grace," page 96

You can accompany "Viva l'Amour" with the G, D₇, and C chords.

Viva l'Amour   COLLEGE SONG

Let ev-'ry good fel-low now join in a song, *Vi-va la com-pa-gnie!* Suc-

cess to each oth-er and pass it a-long, *Vi-va la com-pa-gnie!*

Vi-va la, vi-va la, vi-va l'a-mour, vi-va la, vi-va la, vi-va l'a-mour,

*Vi-va l'a-mour, vi-va l'a-mour, Vi-va la com-pa-gnie!*____

Rock Island Line   RAILROAD SONG

Make up your own strumming pattern to accompany the singing
of "Rock Island Line." For suggestions, see page 197.

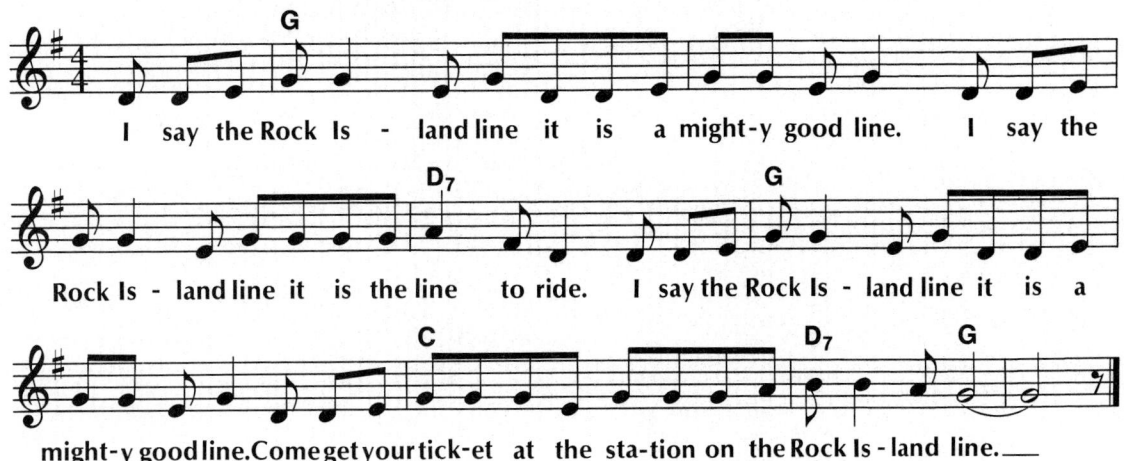

I say the Rock Is - land line it is a might-y good line.   I say the
Rock Is - land line it is the line   to ride.   I say the Rock Is - land line it is a
might-y good line. Come get your tick-et at the sta-tion on the Rock Is - land line. __

HAVE A SING-A-LONG

With the chords that you now know, you will be able to
accompany two- or three-chord songs in the following keys.

Key of C	C		G_7
Key of D MIN.	D MIN.		A_7
Key of D	D	G	A_7
Key of G	G	C	D_7
Key of A	A	D	E_7

A WORD ABOUT TUNING

Tune the low-E string to a piano or to a pitch pipe. Place your finger just behind the fifth fret as shown in the diagram. You will be fingering the correct pitch for the next string, the A string. As you pluck the fingered string, tune the A string until the pitches match.

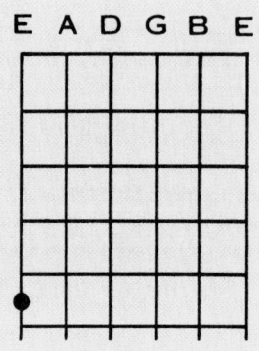

These pairs of strings should sound the same pitch when one of them is fingered as shown.

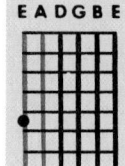 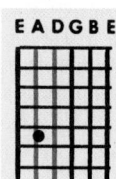 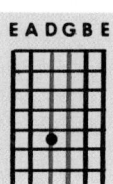 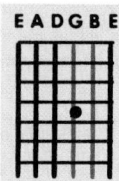 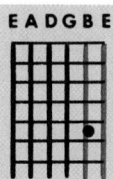

When you first start, it will be easier to have someone tune the guitar for you. Watch carefully and listen to learn how it is done. Then try tuning it by yourself.

Remember, a good guitar player always plays on a well-tuned instrument.

This section will help you learn to play
the soprano and alto recorders. If you
need help with the fingerings for the first
few pages, study the fingering chart on
page 220.

PRIVATE PRACTICE

Review these notes: B A G on the soprano recorder;

E D C on the alto recorder.

Suo Gan WELSH FOLK MELODY

Dance Tune

ENSEMBLE

Add these parts while others sing "La Raspa." Ask someone to play an Autoharp or guitar accompaniment.

La Raspa (SONG ON PAGE 26.)

PRIVATE PRACTICE

Review these notes: high C and D on the soprano recorder;

high F and G on the alto recorder.

Winter, Ade! (Winter, Goodby!) FOLK SONG FROM GERMANY

SOPRANO

Win - ter, a - de! Win - ter, a - de! It may be sad to ___ part

But laugh - ter fills my ___ heart, Win - ter, a - de! Win - ter, a - de!

ALTO

ENSEMBLE

The soprano and alto parts for *Winter, Ade!* can be played
together. Ask someone to play an Autoharp accompaniment.

PRIVATE PRACTICE

Review these notes: low E D C on the soprano recorder;

low A G F on the alto recorder.

Tideo

SOPRANO

ALTO

PRIVATE PRACTICE

Review F♯ on the soprano recorder and B on the alto recorder by practicing the refrain of "Open the Window, Noah." Then practice the other parts on pages 208 and 209.

Open the Window, Noah (SONG ON PAGE 146)

The Streets of Laredo AMERICAN COWBOY SONG

As I_____ walked out in the streets of La - re - do, As

I_____ walked out in La - re - do one day, I spied a young cow-boy wrapped

up in white li - nen, wrapped up in white li - nen as cold as the clay.

Michael Finnegan

ENSEMBLE

Organize an ensemble by "mixing and matching" the melodies
and countermelodies on pages 208 and 209.

Open the Window, Noah (SONG ON PAGE 146)

Scarborough Fair FOLK SONG FROM ENGLAND

Are you go-ing to Scar-bor-ough fair, Pars-ley,

sage,___ rose-ma-ry, and thyme; Re-mem-ber me___ to

one who lives there, For once she was___ a true love of mine.

This Old Man

This piece uses notes you know. Choose a part to practice.

Then team up with other recorder players to make an ensemble.

Bransle de Champaigne BY CLAUDE GERVAISE

"BRANSLE DE CHAMPAIGNE" FROM RENAISSANCE DEBUT ARRANGED BY MAURICE C. WHITNEY. REPRINTED BY PERMISSION OF CONSORT MUSIC., A DIVISION OF MAGNAMUSIC.

A NEW NOTE

SOPRANO
high E

ALTO
high A

PRIVATE PRACTICE

The soprano recorder can practice the melody of "Lonesome Valley" on page 59.

Lonesome Valley

ALTO

A

ENSEMBLE

When the soprano recorder plays the melody of "Lonesome Valley," the alto recorder can add this countermelody.

ALTO

PRIVATE PRACTICE

The soprano recorder can practice the melody of "Purple Bamboo" on page 100.

Purple Bamboo

ENSEMBLE

After you can play these melodies, team up with other recorder players. Then play each melody through at least two times. Parts II, III, and IV follow in turn, two measures apart.

Canon in C BY DAVID EDDLEMAN

Canon in F BY DAVID EDDLEMAN

ENSEMBLE

Choose a part to practice. Then team up with another recorder player to make an ensemble.

Chorale Melody

ANOTHER NEW NOTE

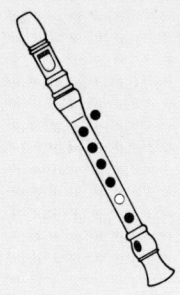

PRIVATE PRACTICE

I'll Begin Ahead of You FOLK TUNE FROM HUNGARY

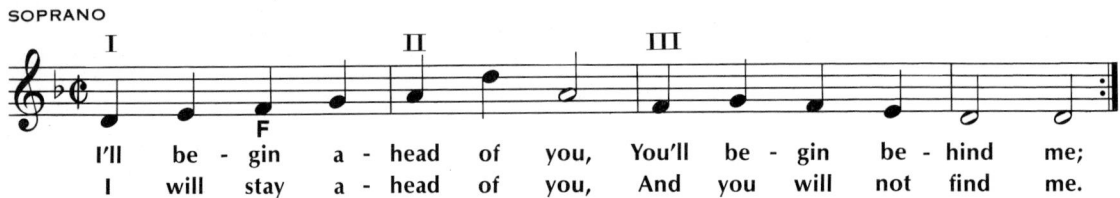

I'll be - gin a - head of you, You'll be - gin be - hind me;
I will stay a - head of you, And you will not find me.

ENSEMBLE

Team up with other recorder players and play "I'll Begin Ahead of You" as a two- or three-part round. Add these parts to the ensemble.

ALTO (PLAY WITH SOPRANO ABOVE.)

SOPRANO (PLAY WITH ALTO ABOVE.)

TWO NEW NOTES

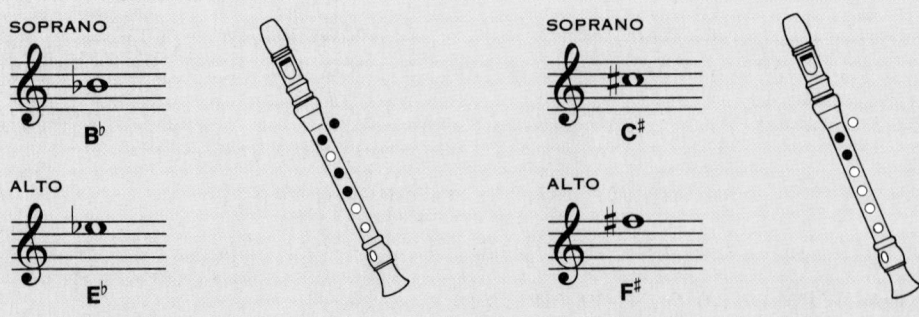

PRIVATE PRACTICE FOR SOPRANO RECORDER

Now that you know the fingerings for B♭ and C♯, you can play
the following melodies on the soprano recorder.

The *John B.* Sails, page 14   Carol from an Irish Cabin, page 49

The Baby Boy, page 50   Everybody's Got a Song, page 58

PRIVATE PRACTICE FOR ALTO RECORDER

Now that you know the fingerings for E♭ and F♯, you can play
the following melodies on the alto recorder.

My Dame Hath a Lame, Tame Crane (countermelodies), page 30

Take Time in Life (countermelody), page 31

Anthony Mayberry (verse), page 56

Amazing Grace (countermelody 2), page 97

Read about the 12-bar blues on pages 158 and 159 in your book.

Then practice this blues song on the soprano or the alto recorder.

Cornbread, Peas, and Black Molasses   BLUES SONG

SOPRANO AND ALTO

1. I don't want no,_____ corn - bread, peas, and black mo - las - ses._____
2. I ain't got no,_____ got no read - y made_____ mon - ey.

I don't want no,_____ corn-bread, peas, and black mo - las - ses._____
I ain't got no,_____ got no read - y made_____ mon - ey.

At sup - per time, Lord, at sup - per_____ time._____
To call my own, Lord, to call my_____ own._____

ENSEMBLE

Ask someone to play the Autoharp chords when you play
"Cornbread, Peas, and Black Molasses" on the recorder. Have
others sing the song to fill out the ensemble.

Double Round

ALTO
SOP
I
II
III
IV

Add these ostinatos to the ensemble.

SOPRANO RECORDER
ALTO RECORDER
DRUM

Add this part for bells or mallet instruments to the ensemble.

1.
2.

FINAL ENSEMBLES

Play the ensembles on pages 217–219 with friends who play the soprano or the alto recorder.

Polka   F. M. HIMMEL

SOP I / SOP II

MELODY
Al-though I do not like to dance, I real-ly must ad-mit when

ALTO

some-one plays a pol-ka tune, I sim-ply can't re-sist. MELODY At

an-y time of day or night, If sud-den-ly by chance,

MELODY
That pol-ka sound should fill the air, my feet be-gin to dance.

Deep Blue Sea

AMERICAN FOLK SONG

Deep   blue   sea,   ba - by,   deep   blue   sea,

*A# FINGERING SAME AS B♭

Deep   blue   sea,   ba - by,   deep   blue   sea,

Deep   blue   sea,   ba - by,   deep   blue   sea,

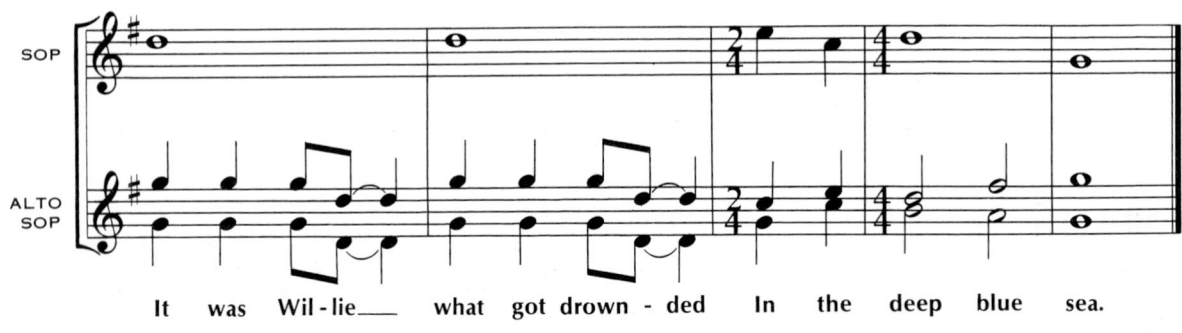

It   was Wil - lie____ what got drown - ded In   the deep blue sea.

Angels We Have Heard on High

TRADITIONAL CAROL FROM FRANCE

An - gels we have heard on high, Sweet - ly sing - ing o'er the plains,
And the moun-tains in re - ply, Ech - o - ing their joy - ous strains.

Glo - - - - - - - - ri - a

in ex - cel - sis De - o, De - o.

FINGERING CHART

Reading Rhythm

You have already played some
percussion parts to accompany songs
you know. Sometimes you play alone
and sometimes in an ensemble. This
section contains arrangements for two
or more percussion instruments that
can be used to accompany songs in
your book. Play any one of the parts
alone with the recording. Or organize
a group of friends to play in an
ensemble.

La Raspa (SONG ON PAGE 26)

To feel the steady beat in "La Raspa," play an Autoharp accompaniment as you sing the song.

This Autoharp part is in $\frac{4}{4}$ meter. The steady beat is shown as a quarter note (♩). The beats are measured in sets of 4—four beats in each measure. Notice that the measures are separated by bar lines.

Press the G or D_7 button as indicated and strum each quarter note.

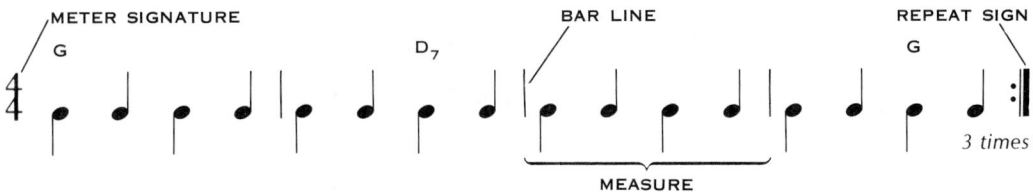

For a special Autoharp strum, play short strokes with your thumb on the lowest strings for the notes with the stems down. For notes with stems up, brush the strings in the opposite direction with your fingers.

Here are two percussion parts to play with "La Raspa." The tambourine part shows the steady beat in quarter notes and quarter rests (𝄽). In the castanets part, some beats are divided into two equal sounds. These sounds are shown as eighth notes (♫).

Remember: In $\frac{4}{4}$ meter
- a quarter note (♩) shows a beat of sound;
- a quarter rest (𝄽) shows a beat of silence;
- 2 eighth notes (♫) show the beat divided into two equal sounds.

Joy to the World (Song on page 4)

Here is an Autoharp part you can play with the refrain of "Joy to the World."

The meter signature ($\frac{4}{4}$) tells you that there are four beats in a measure and that a quarter note gets one beat.

The Autoharp part uses quarter notes (♩) and half notes (♩).

The chord letters will tell you when to play the D, A₇, or G chord.

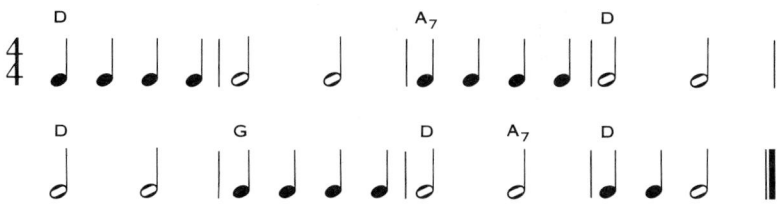

Here are two percussion parts to play with the refrain of "Joy to the World." The tambourine part uses half notes (♩) and half rests (▬). The wood block part uses quarter notes (♩) and quarter rests (𝄽).

TAMBOURINE

WOOD BLOCK

Remember: In $\frac{4}{4}$ meter
• a half note (♩) shows two beats of sound;
• a half rest (▬) shows two beats of silence.

La Sinda (SONG ON PAGE 35)

To feel the steady beat in "La Sinda," play a percussion part as you listen to the song.

This percussion part for wood block is in $\frac{3}{4}$ meter. The steady beat is shown as a quarter note. The beats are measured in sets of 3—three beats in each measure.

Start playing on the first strong beat.

WOOD BLOCK

Play throughout.

In this percussion part for tambourine, you will play only on the first beat of every measure. Start playing on the first strong beat.

TAMBOURINE

Play throughout.

Team up with a friend and play both percussion parts together.

Now try an Autoharp accompaniment for "La Sinda" that uses dotted half notes (𝅗𝅥.). In $\frac{3}{4}$ meter you will hold a dotted half note for three beats.

Start playing the Autoharp on the first strong beat. The chord letters will tell you when to change from one chord to another.

AUTOHARP

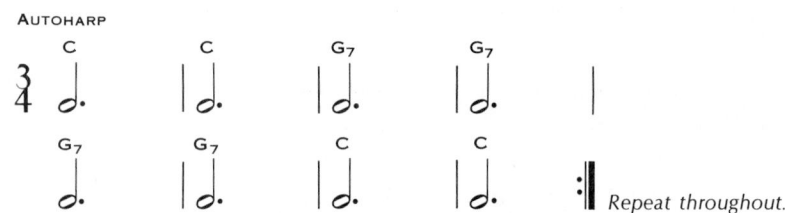

Repeat throughout.

Remember: In $\frac{3}{4}$ meter

• a dotted half note (𝅗𝅥.) is held for three beats.

There's a Fiesta <small>(SONG ON PAGE 27)</small>

To feel the beat moving in sets of 3, play an Autoharp accompaniment as you listen to "There's a Fiesta." Play short strokes with your thumb for notes with stems down. For notes with stems up, brush the strings in the opposite direction with your fingers.

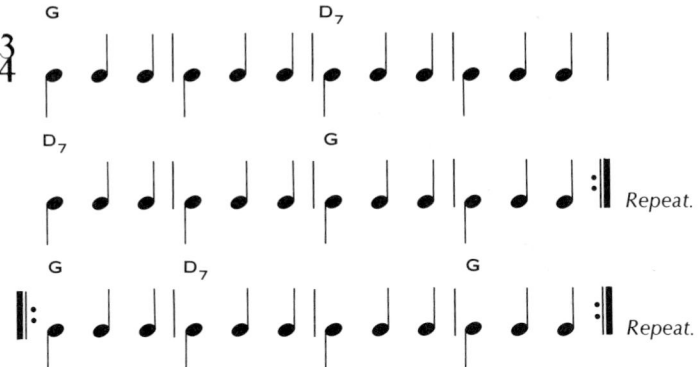

In "La Raspa" (page 222) you played two equal sounds for one beat.

The beat can also be divided into three equal sounds—this is called a *triplet*.

Try one of the parts in this arrangement for tambourine and wood block as you listen to the recording of "There's a Fiesta."

I'se the B'y (SONG ON PAGE 10)

This song is in $\frac{6}{8}$ ($\frac{2}{J.}$) meter. The steady beat is shown as a dotted quarter note (J.).

To feel the steady beat, play this Autoharp accompaniment as you sing "I'se the B'y."

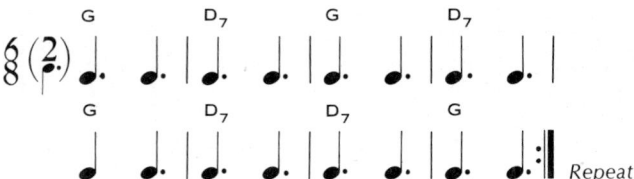

You will find these three different rhythms in the percussion arrangement at the bottom of the page.

Now try playing one of these parts with the recording.

Gonna Build a Mountain <small>(SONG ON PAGE 78)</small>

The meter signature ¢ tells you that there are two beats in a measure and that a half note (𝅗𝅥) gets one beat. Which part shows the steady beat in the percussion arrangement below?

Choose one of the parts to practice.

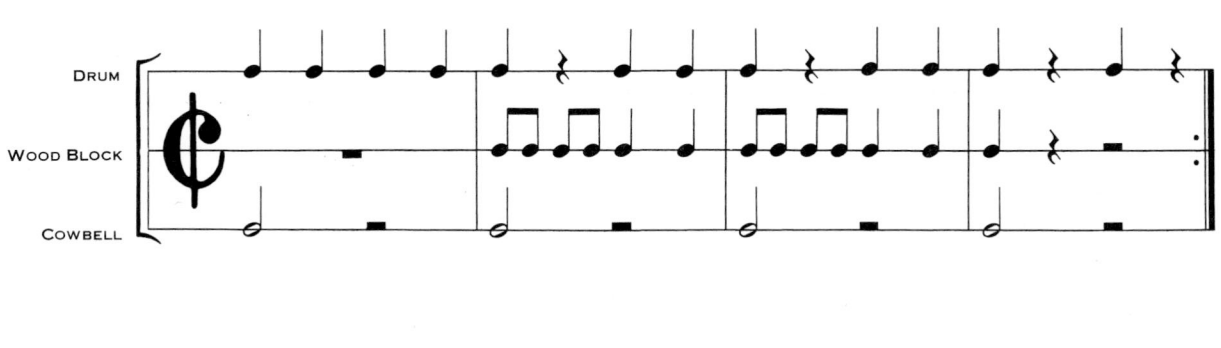

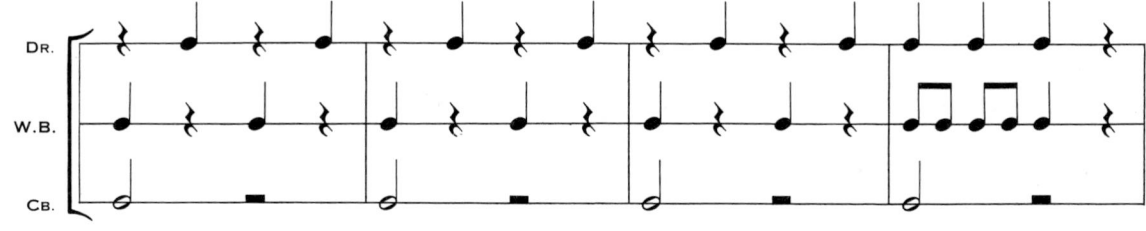

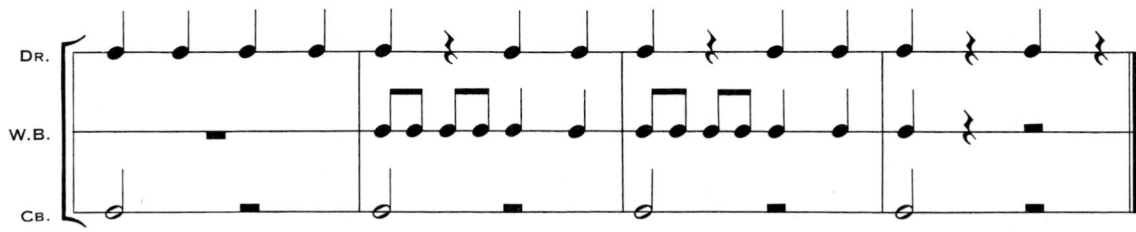

After you have practiced your part, add it to the other two parts and form an ensemble to accompany the singing. Before you play, decide how fast or how slow you will play.

Orion (Song on page 70)

Practice one of the parts to accompany "Orion." Notice that the meter changes from $\frac{4}{4}$ to $\frac{3}{4}$ in the middle of the music. The quarter note will get one beat throughout the piece, but the top number shows a change in the number of beats in a measure.

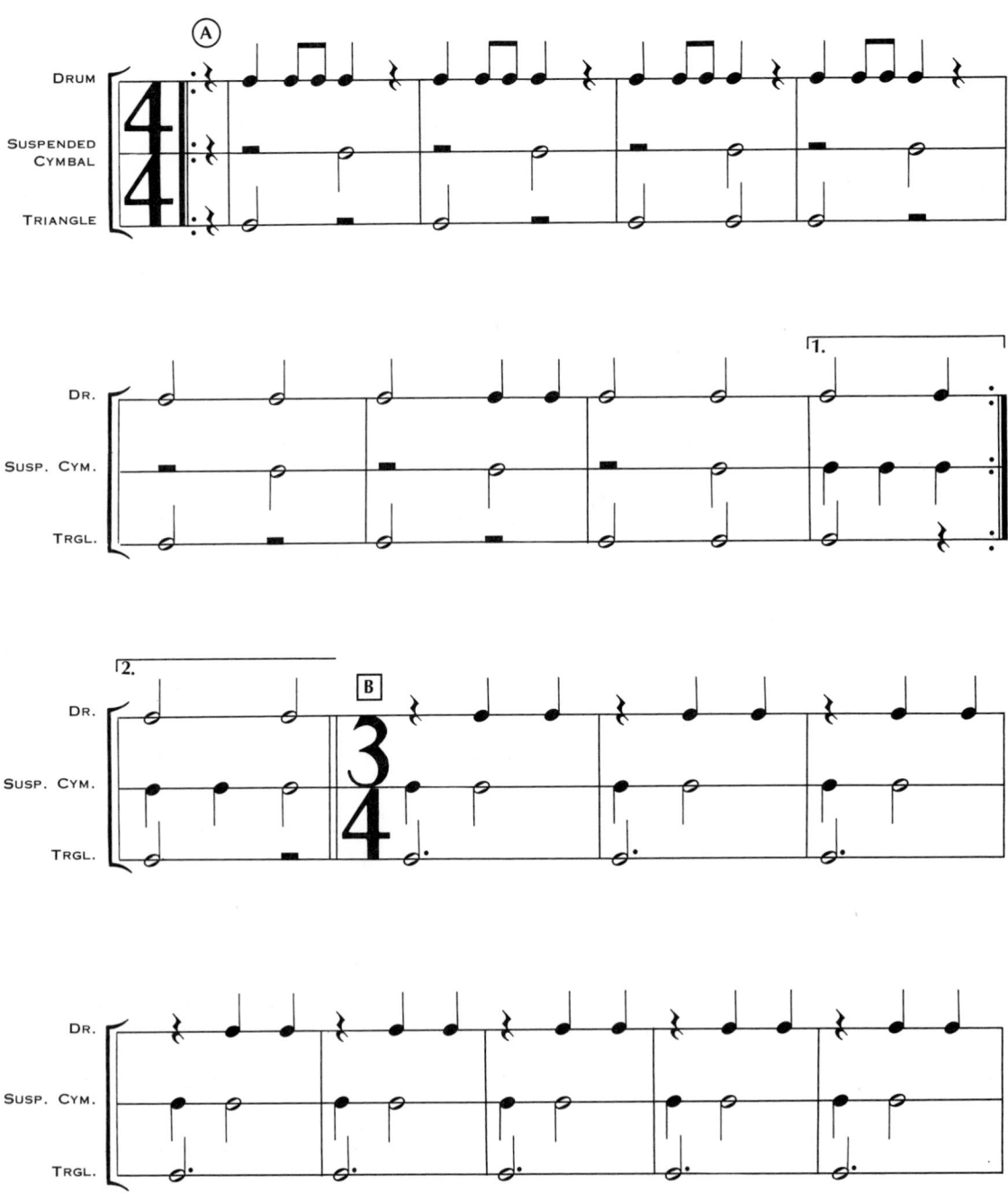

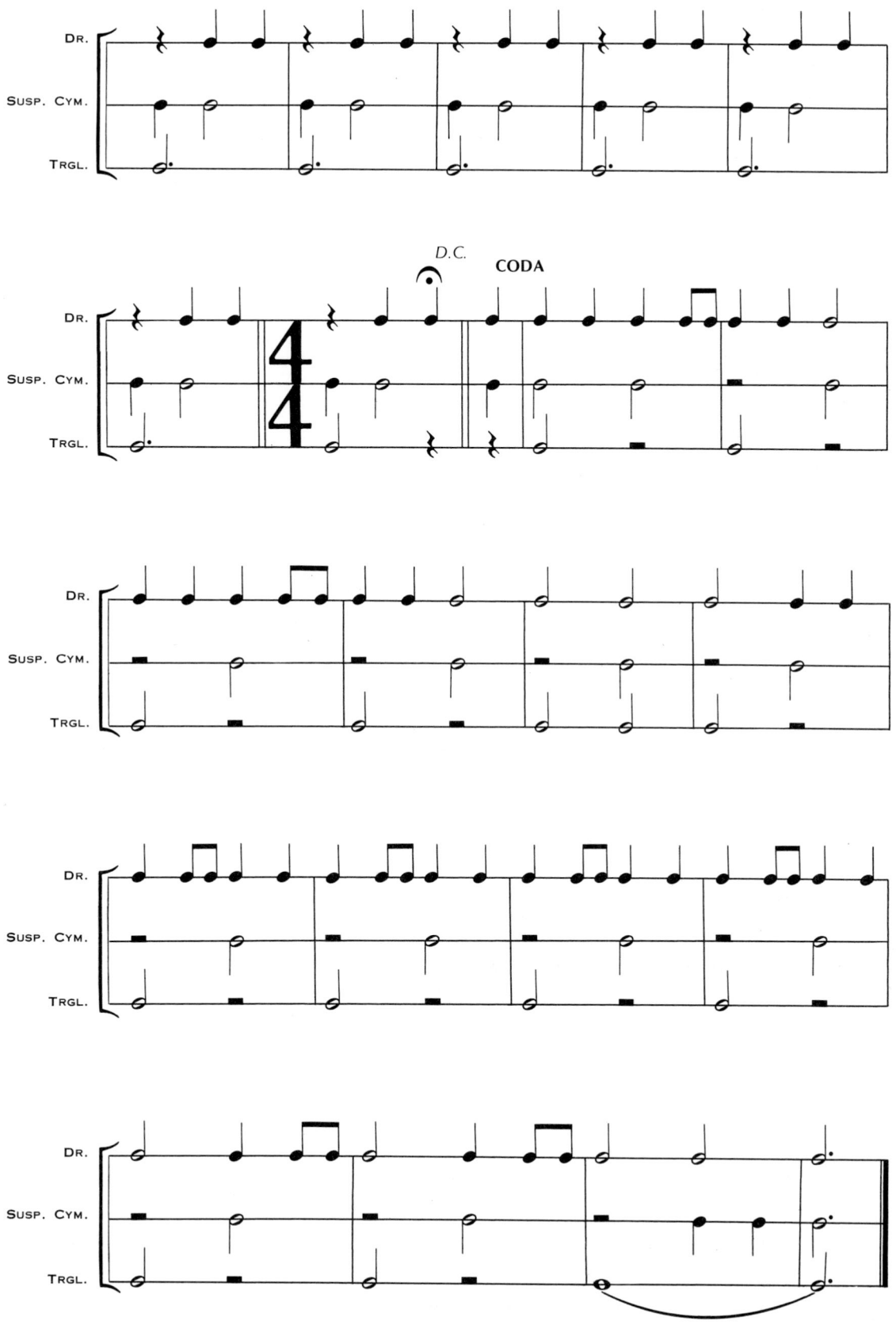

SIXTEENTH NOTES

While one person plays the steady beat on a drum, clap each of the lines below. Notice that the beat can be divided into

- two equal sounds 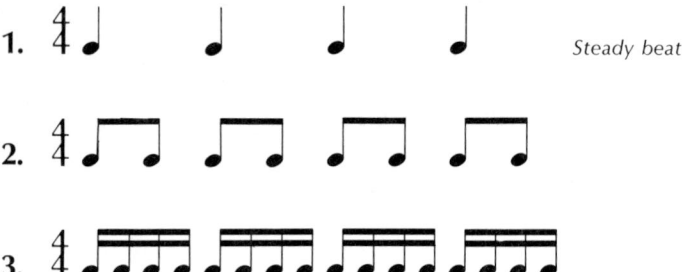 eighth notes
- four equal sounds sixteenth notes

1. Steady beat

2.

3.

Now clap a pattern that uses both eighth notes and sixteenth notes to divide the beat.

4.

Battle Hymn of the Republic I (SONG ON PAGE 113)

Play this snare drum part to accompany the refrain of "Battle Hymn of the Republic."

SNARE DRUM

DOTTED RHYTHMS

A dot after a note makes it longer by half its value. Notice how dotted rhythms are used in songs you may know. Play these rhythms on any percussion instrument.

An - tho - ny May - ber - ry seemed ver - y sad as he turned to look back one last time.

There once was a ship, and a stur - dy craft was she;

Glo - ry, glo - ry, hal - le - lu - jah!

Battle Hymn of the Republic II (Song on page 113)

Here are parts for small drum and cymbals. Add them to the snare drum part on page 230 and, with others, play an accompaniment for the refrain of "Battle Hymn of the Republic."

For the quarter rests (𝄽) in the cymbals part, dampen the sound by holding the cymbals against the body.

The John B. Sails

While listening to the recording of "The *John B.* Sails," play
each line below on a muted cowbell. Notice that in line 4 the
dot takes the place of the tie.

Play one of these parts as others sing "The *John B.* Sails."
Someone can add the steady beat on the Autoharp. The chord
letters in the music on page 14 show when to change from one
chord to another.

Play throughout verse.

Play throughout refrain.

232   Reading Rhythm

Till That Day Blues (SONG ON PAGE 158)

Practice one of these parts and play it with the recording of "Till That Day Blues," or form an ensemble with your friends to accompany the song in class.

SYNCOPATION

Listen to the recording of "Artsa alinu" and play this pattern on a tambourine when it comes in the song.

(Art - sa   a - li - nu,   Art - sa   a - li - nu)

The special feeling of syncopation comes from playing some notes on the weak part of the beat. Clap the following lines to discover how a syncopated pattern develops from the steady beat.

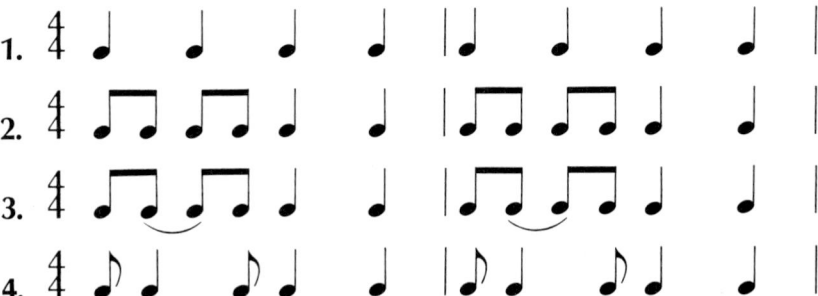

Artsa Alinu (SONG ON PAGE 81)

Practice one of the parts to play with the recording, or form an ensemble with your classmates to accompany the class singing of "Artsa alinu."

I'm Gonna Sing Out (SONG ON PAGE 142)

Look through the claves part and notice that syncopation is created in two ways.

Sound on weak beats in section A

Silence on strong beats in section B

Practice syncopated patterns by playing the claves part. Then choose another part to add to the accompaniment.

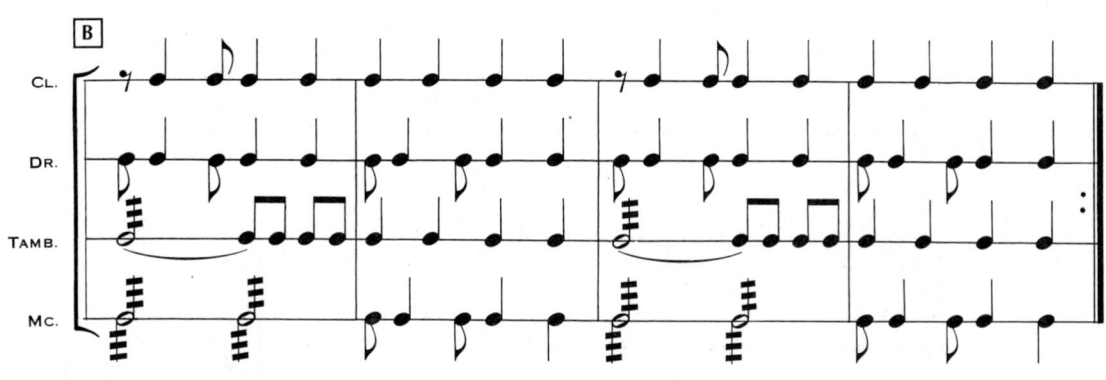

Green, Green (SONG ON PAGE 177)

Here is an arrangement you can use to accompany "Green, Green." Be sure to follow the repeat signs.

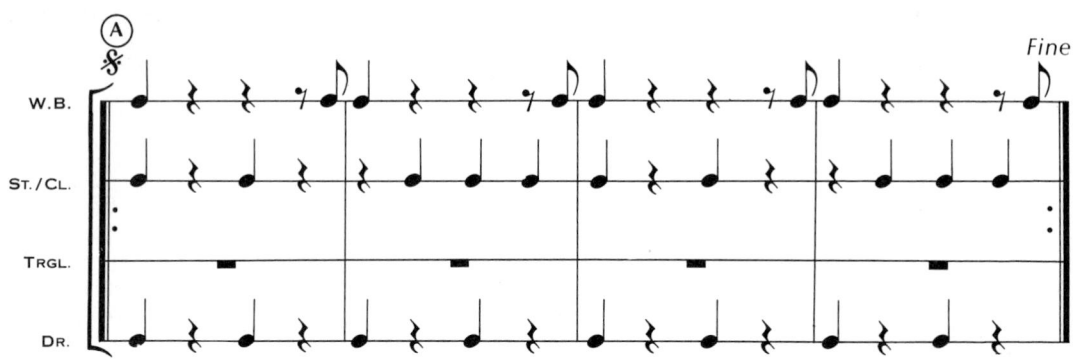

*Wood block enters first with voice 1; add sticks/claves with voice 2; add triangle and drum with voice 3.

Working with Sounds

COMPILED BY DORIS HAYS

The world is full of sounds—sounds that can be organized in an endless variety of ways. Part of the excitement of learning about music is discovering the many ways in which composers use sounds. The following pages suggest ways in which *you* might choose and organize sounds.

ADAPTED FROM

COMING TOGETHER   BY BOB BECKER

© 1973 Bob Becker

Here is a rhythm game for two players. Each player should:

1. Choose a number from 1 to 5. Don't tell the other player what your number is.

2. Clap a rhythm pattern that has as many beats as the number you chose, plus one beat of rest. For example, if your number is 4, your rhythm pattern would be.

Both players together set a tempo and, beginning at the same time, clap their rhythm patterns over and over until they "come together." The patterns will come together when both players have a rest at the same time. If one player chooses number 4 and the other chooses number 3, the patterns would look like this.

Player 1:

Player 2:

As you clap your rhythm pattern, think of a new number between 1 and 5 so that when your rhythms come together you can begin to clap a new pattern without losing a beat.
Here is an example in another kind of notation. Each block stands for one beat. Empty blocks stand for rests.

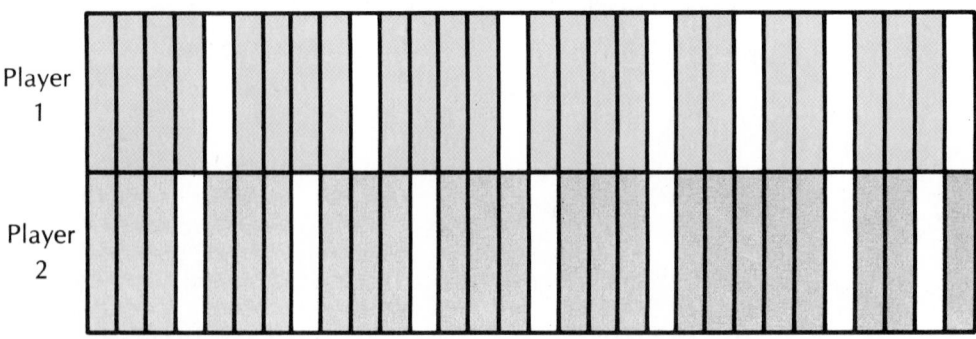

Find the places where the patterns come together.

WAYS TO VARY "COMING TOGETHER"

Continue in this way until both of you choose the same number. When that happens, clap the rhythm pattern three times and stop. The game is over.

1. Make the tempo twice as fast.

2. Accent some of the beats in your rhythm patterns, for example, the first and last beats.

3. Make your rhythm patterns more interesting. If you choose the number 3, clap ♩ ♫♩ ♩ 𝄽 instead of ♩ ♩ ♩ 𝄽

4. Play your rhythm patterns on a percussion instrument.

5. Play your rhythm patterns on a melody instrument; change to a new pitch each time you choose a new number.

6. Play the game with more than two players.

Can you think of other rhythm games to play? Can you think of ways to vary them?

IMPROVISE A RHYTHM ACCOMPANIMENT

Play a recording of your favorite song. As you listen, use a percussion instrument or a sound like clapping or pencil-tapping to discover different rhythm patterns that fit the song.

Try playing two different rhythm patterns one after the other to form a longer pattern. Notate your rhythm patterns so that another player can read and play them from your score. You may use *traditional* notation or *graphic* notation. A rhythm pattern that looks like this in traditional notation

♫♩ 𝄾 ♪ ♫♩ 𝄾 ♪ ♫♩

might look like either of these in graphic notation.

LIGHT-SOUND MOVEMENT

These symbols can be expressed in light, in sound, and in movement. As you move a flashlight beam across a dark surface, use the on-off button to turn the symbols into a "light design." How will you show the lines? the dots? How will you show "no light"? Experiment with moving the flashlight closer to the surface, then farther away.

Another time, turn the symbols into sound by playing an instrument. Which symbol will stand for a long sound? A short sound? Where will the pitch get higher? Where will it get lower? What will be the symbol for the loudest sound?
You can turn the symbols into movement by using a different body movement—bending, sliding, turning, etc.—for each symbol.

Have some friends help you turn the symbols into a light-sound-movement ensemble by doing all three activities at the same time.

Try making up new symbols that can be turned into a light design, into sound, and into movement. Have your friends help you interpret them in a light-sound-movement ensemble.

DANCE ON THE SPIRALS

BY DORIS HAYS   © 1979 TALLAPOOSA MUSIC

Dance on the Spirals combines light, sound, and movement.
The red line stands for the motion of the dancer. The black dots
stand for drum beats or triangle taps. The green dots stand for
short flashes of light from a flashlight. The wash of blue color
stands for the sweep of light from other flashlights around the
dancer.

Do the dance starting from the center of the big spiral. Follow
the lines around and out to the edge and top and over to the
smaller spirals. Then try beginning at the outer edge and circling
inward. Do the dance at different speeds.

Working with Sounds   **241**

ADAPTED FROM

FOLLOW THE LEADER BY DORIS HAYS © 1973 TALLAPOOSA MUSIC

Use these symbols to write a piece for voices.

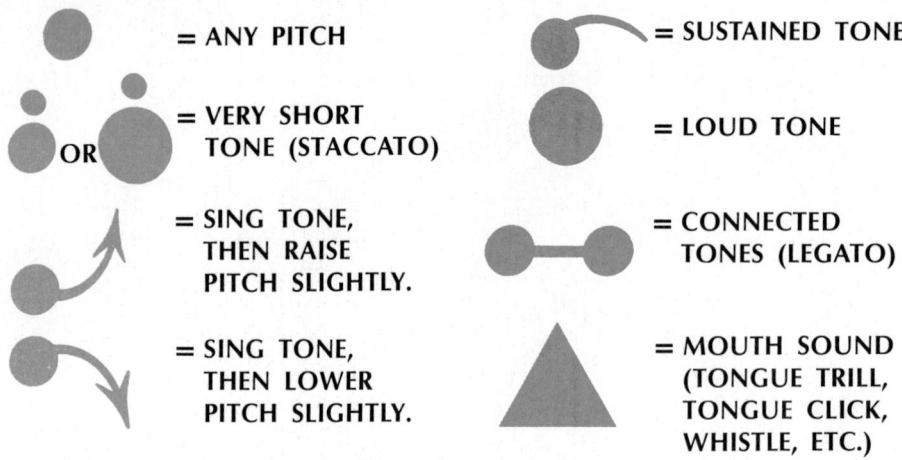

Choose your "lyrics" from the following words and syllables.

SEE! OH? LAH! MMM! UGH!!! NOK! AH. . . MEE!

Your score might look something like this.

MMM!   MEE!   LAH!   MMM!   UGH!!!

When you have written your score, conduct a "follow-the-leader" performance of it. Choose five or more performers to stand in a semicircle, facing you. Since the performers will be imitating your sounds, they will not need copies of your score. Perform the sounds in your score, one at a time. After each sound, signal the performers to imitate the sound you have made. Your signal should tell the performers whether you want them all to imitate your sound at the same time (ensemble) or whether you want each performer to imitate the sound alone, one after the other (in sequence).

MY NAME IS

FOR
1 OR MORE PERFORMERS
3 OR MORE TAPE RECORDERS
AND AUDIENCE

Members of the audience are recorded saying, "My name is —" (first name only).

Three or more identical tape loops are made from each "my name is —". This dubbing and editing process may be performed in view of the audience, and it may be done silently if the performer(s) wear earphones. Thus some other audible performance may happen simultaneously while this process is going on.

Each set of three or more identical loops is then played on three or more tape recorders for about two minutes or more. Because of slight differences in motor speed, tape tension and loop length (even in 'identical' loops) the loops proceed to move slowly in and out of phase with each other.

When changing from one set of loops to the next one should change one loop first, pause, then the second, pause, and then the third (and so on if there are more recorders). Eg., if set 1 has played for two minutes or more then the first loop of set 2 is substituted on the first recorder resulting in one loop of set 2 and two loops of set 1. Then the second recorder is changed resulting in two loops of set 2 and one of set 1. Finally the third recorder is changed resulting in three loops of set 2.

The piece is over when all sets of three or more loops have been played.

Steve Reich 5/67

MY NAME IS BY STEVE REICH

ACTIVITY 1

Here is one way to do *My Name Is.*

1. Make a tape recording of a friend saying his or her name, for instance, "My name is Rosalyn."

2. On separate tapes record two other friends saying their names. One might say, "My name is Fred." The other might say, "My name is Alice."

3. Make two copies of each recording. (When you copy the sounds from one tape onto another tape, you are *dubbing.*) You should have three tapes that say "My name is Rosalyn," three that say "My name is Fred," and three that say "My name is Alice."

4. Make each of the tapes into a tape loop. Directions for making tape loops are on page 119. Be certain that the three tape loops for each name are the same length.

5. Using three tape recorders, take the loops that say "My name is Rosalyn" and put one loop on each tape recorder. Start all three tape recorders at the same time. Let the loops play for two minutes.

Listen to the changes in sound as the loops play. At first, the names will all sound at the same time (*in phase*). As the loops continue to play, the names will not stay together—the loops will get *out of phase.*

This happens because one of the tape recorders may be running a little faster than the others, or because all the tape loops may not be exactly the same size.

6. At the end of two minutes, change to the tape loops that say "My name is Fred." Change the loop on one tape recorder at a time. As you change each loop, let the other two tape recorders keep playing. Let the "My name is Fred" loops play for two minutes.

After two minutes, change to the "My name is Alice" tape loops, one at a time. Let the loops play for two minutes.

To end the piece, turn the tape recorders off.

Listen to *My Name Is*. How is it like your piece? How is it different?

ACTIVITY 2

Here are some other things you can do with tape.

1. Make a version of *My Name Is* that uses more than three tape recorders and more than three tape loops for each name.

2. Join (splice) two or more *My Name Is* loops together to make a longer loop. For example, you might splice a "My name is Rosalyn" loop to a "My name is Fred" loop. Make a different loop for each tape recorder that you use. Plot a duration chart for each loop. If you use three tape recorders (TR's), your chart might look like this:

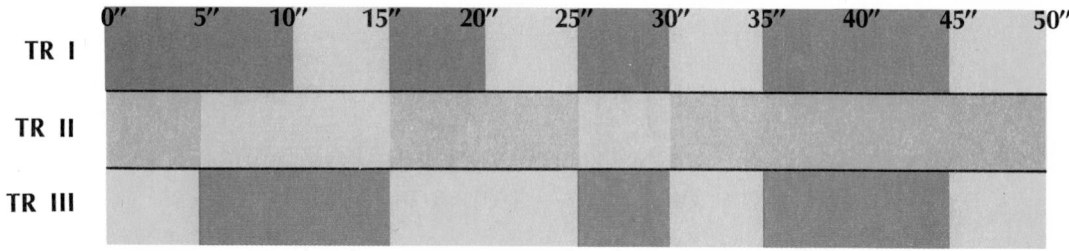

Control the length of sound from each tape recorder by fading the volume in and out.

3. Use tape loops of various lengths to experiment with other sounds besides voice. Some sound sources you might use are water dripping, water running, footsteps, whistling, paper crumpling, paper ripping, horn honking.

Try playing the sounds back at speeds that are faster or slower than the ones at which they were recorded.

ADAPTED FROM

ON THE WAY TO . . . , BY DORIS HAYS © 1973 TALLAPOOSA MUSIC

On the Way to . . . is a piece of music theater. It consists of a story that is "told" by a narrator and a piano. Read the story and then listen to it on the recording.

Every morning my brother and I get up early. We have eggs and cereal with bananas and milk for breakfast. After eating our eggs and our cereal with bananas and milk my brother and I get ready for school. My brother and I ride the bus to school when the weather is nice. On rainy days our father drives us to school so we don't get wet waiting for the bus. One rainy day when we were late for school my brother and I ran out the front door and slipped on a banana peel. Our father came running out the door behind us and he slipped on the banana peel. Our mother had just finished washing the dishes after our breakfast of eggs and cereal with bananas and milk when she noticed that we had forgotten our lunch. Our mother came running out the front door with our lunch and she slipped on the banana peel. I don't think I will ever forget that morning when my brother and I were late for school and we all slipped on a banana peel as we ran out the front door. My friend Marsha still can't understand why I yelled at her later that morning when she tried to share her lunch with me. All she said was, "Would you care for a banana?"

Try performing *On the Way to . . .* with some of your friends. Choose a different percussion instrument for each new underlined word in the story. For example, someone might play finger cymbals on the word "morning" or a wood block on the word "late." Try using hand sounds, too, and sounds that can be made with objects in the room. When you have assigned a sound to each word, choose someone to be narrator. As the narrator reads the story he should leave out the underlined words. An instrument should play whenever a word is left out. Try several different versions of *On the Way to . . .* to find the one you like best.

IMPROVISE ON A KEYBOARD INSTRUMENT

BY DORIS HAYS

© 1973 TALLAPOOSA MUSIC

Experiment with playing single tones and clusters of tones in different places on a keyboard instrument (piano, organ, accordion, electronic keyboard, bells). Make up a sound pattern that uses clusters and single tones.

You may wish to notate your sound pattern so that you can remember it and so that others can play it. One way is to place symbols within a box.

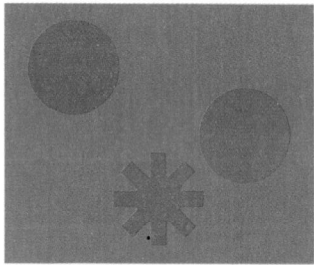

In this example, a dot (•) stands for a single tone, and a star (*) stands for a cluster of tones. The symbol near the top of the box stands for a high tone; the one near the bottom stands for low tones. The symbol halfway between the top and the bottom stands for a tone in the middle of the keyboard.

Follow the score for this sound pattern. Do you see the pattern of two high tones followed by a low cluster and a middle tone?

Now write your own sound pattern. You may use dots and stars, or any symbols that you like. Play your sound pattern on a keyboard instrument. Does it sound as good as it looks?

MAKE A MELODY—MAKE A SONG   BY DORIS HAYS

Make up a melody of your own. If you like, you can choose the tones for your melody by chance. Tear a piece of paper into 14 smaller pieces. Write one tone name from A through G on each piece of paper. You should have two A's, two B's, two C's, and so forth.

Mix the papers and then close your eyes and pick 6 pieces, one at a time. The order in which you pick the tones will determine their order in your melody. If the first paper you pick says "C," C will be the first tone of your melody. If the second paper says "D," D will be the second tone of your melody.

After you've chosen your tones, experiment with different rhythm patterns. You may decide that your melody should have only quarter notes, as in this example.

Or you may want to give it a rhythm pattern that uses long and short sounds

or a pattern that has a dotted rhythm.

Try putting words to your melody. You may have to change the rhythm of your melody a little to make the words fit.

Won-der what   this song   is?

Now try repeating the first two or three notes a few times before going on to the rest of the melody.

Won - der, won - der, won - der

Decorate your melody by adding some notes in between the original ones (ornamentation). Besides decorating the melody, the extra notes can make the words that are sung on them more important.

Won - der, won - der, won - der what _____ this song ____ is?

Play your melody to discover whether it falls into a pattern of strong beats and weak beats. Do the strong beats group the beats into sets of 2, 3, or 4? Write the meter signature next to the treble clef sign. Put a bar line before the note on the first beat in each set of 2, 3, or 4.

In this example, the beats fall into sets of 3. The meter signature is $\frac{3}{4}$.

Won - der, won - der, won - der what _____ this song ____ is?

Now you have a good beginning for a song. Your melody can be the first phrase of the song. Repeat the phrase two or three times. Each time you repeat it, change it in some way. You can make the rhythm a little different or add some notes to the melody or take some notes away.

Make up a new phrase to end the first part of your song. Your ending phrase might be a contrasting phrase. If so, it will not sound like the phrases you've written so far.

One way to make a contrasting phrase is to write the notes of
the original phrase in reverse order (retrograde).

When you have your ending phrase, make up words for it.
You may have to repeat some tones or change the rhythm to
make your words fit.

It's   just   a   lit - tle   bit   of mel - o - dy.

Try adding some notes to "ornament" your closing phrase. You
may want to change the words slightly.

It's ___   just ___   a ___   lit - tle   bit   of mel - o - dy.

Now that you have the first part of your song, you can write the
rest of it by yourself. As you write, try some of the things that
you did in the first part of your song—use different rhythm
patterns; use ornamentation; repeat phrases, changing them in
some way.

Listen to *Wonder What This Song Is?* Is your song in the same
style, or is it in a different style?

Hays: *Wonder What This Song Is?*

Songs from Our Heritage

This Is My Country

MUSIC BY AL JACOBS   WORDS BY DON RAYE

There is a familiar tune in the countermelody of this song. Can you name it?

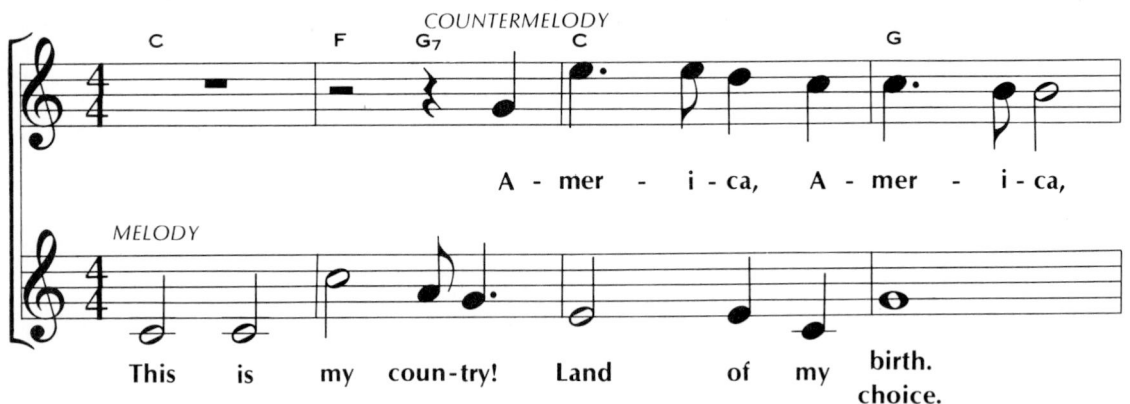

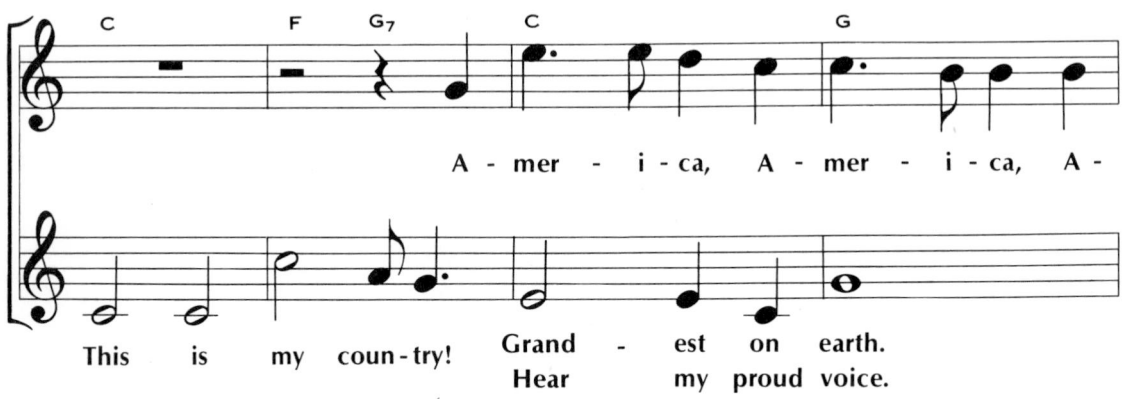

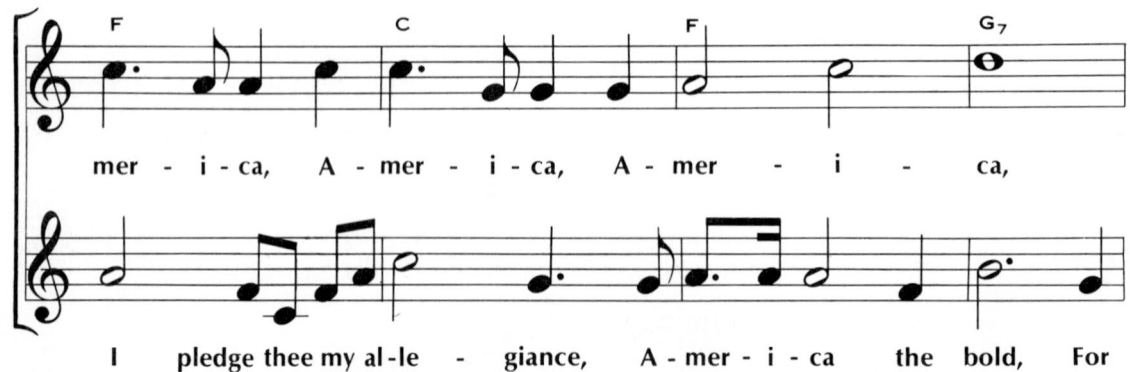

To have ____ and to hold!

this is my coun-try, to have and to hold!

Use this Autoharp part to accompany the singing.

OUR MUSICAL ROOTS

Music has always played an important part in the lives of people all over the world. The thousands upon thousands of people who emigrated to the United States brought their music with them. And all through the years, this music has contributed to America's musical roots.

On the following pages, you will find some of the songs that are part of our musical heritage.

The Glendy Burke

WORDS AND MUSIC BY STEPHEN C. FOSTER

Stephen Foster was a pop-song writer of his day. His songs were influenced by the music he heard on the riverboats that traveled the Ohio and Mississippi rivers in the early steamboating days.

In this song, "The Glendy Burke" refers to the *Glen D. Burk,* an actual riverboat that picked up passengers on its way down the Ohio to Louisiana.

1. The Glen - dy Burke is a might - y fast boat, With a might - y fast cap - tain
2. The Glen - dy Burke has a fun - ny old crew, And they sing___ the boat-man's

too; He sits up there on the hur - ri - cane roof, And he keeps his
song; They burn the pitch and the pine___ knot, too, For to shove the

eye on the crew. I can't stay here, for the work's too
boat a - long. The smoke goes up and the en - gine

hard, I'm___ bound to leave this town; I'll take my duds and
roars, And the wheel goes round and round; So fare ye well, for I'll

tote 'em on my back, When the Glen - dy Burke comes down.
take a lit - tle ride, When the Glen - dy Burke comes down.

B REFRAIN

Ho! for Lou' - si - an - a! I'm bound to leave this town; I'll

take my duds and tote 'em on my back, When the Glen - dy Burke comes down.

Shenandoah   RIVER SHANTEY   13

The "rolling river" mentioned in this shantey is thought to be named after the great Indian chief Shenandoah. As you listen to the recording, join in on the chorus parts.

SOLO

1. Oh, Shen - an - doah, I long to hear you,_____
2. I long to see your smil - ing val - ley,_____

CHORUS

A - way,_____ you roll - ing riv - er._____

SOLO

Oh, Shen - an - doah, I long to hear you,_____
I long to see your smil - ing val - ley,_____

CHORUS

A - way,_____ I'm bound a - way, 'Cross the wide Mis - sou - ri.

3. 'Tis seven long years since last I see thee . . .

255

The Boatmen's Dance

AMERICAN MINSTREL SONG

During the last half of the nineteenth century, the minstrel show was the most popular musical entertainment in our country. The first part of the traditional minstrel show was made up of song-and-dance routines. These were accompanied by tambourines, spoons, and banjos.

Try a tambourine routine as you listen to "The Boatmen's Dance." Sit in a chair and hold the tambourine in your right hand. Raise your left arm and keep the elbow bent. Use the following striking pattern:

R knee L knee L elbow L hand

Hi - ho, the boat-men row, Float-in' down the riv - er, the O - hi - o.____

Hi - ho, the boat-men row, Float-in' down the riv - er, the O - hi - o.____

VERSE

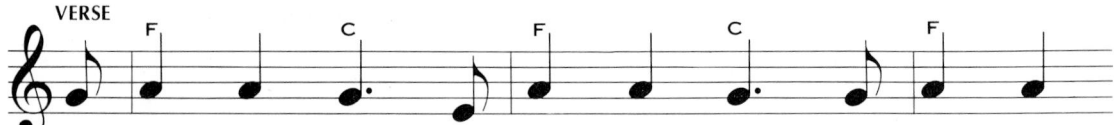

1. The boat - men dance, The boat - men sing, The boat - men
2. The oys - ter boat should keep to the shore, The fish - ing
3. When you go to the boat - men's ball,_____ Dance with your

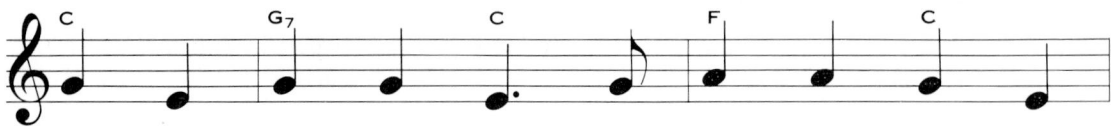

up to ev - 'ry - thing. And when the boat - man
smack should ven - ture more, The schoon - er sails be -
wife or not at all; ‿ Sky - blue jacket and

gets on shore, He spends his cash and works for more.
fore the wind, The steam - boat leaves a streak be - hind.
tarpau - lin hat, Look out, my boys, for the nine - tail cat.

REFRAIN
Then dance, the boat - men, dance! Oh, dance, the boat - men, dance!

Oh, dance all night till the broad day - light, And go

D.C. al Fine

home with your pals in the morn - ing.

A TAMBOURINE SPECIALTY ACT

Formation: Five or six people seated in a row

Phrase 1: Hold the tambourine in the right hand and play the striking pattern on page 256.

Phrase 2: Switch the tambourine to the left hand and repeat the striking pattern.

Phrases 3-4: Continue the striking pattern, switching the tambourine from right hand to left hand in each successive measure.

Phrases 5-6: With right hand held high, walk around the chair, shaking the tambourine as you go.

Every Night When the Sun Goes In

APPALACHIAN FOLK SONG

FROM ENGLISH FOLK SONGS FROM THE SOUTHERN APPALACHIANS BY CECIL SHARP, COPYRIGHT, OXFORD UNIVERSITY PRESS, LONDON.

The country music of today started long ago with people who came from the British Isles and settled in the Appalachian mountains.

The mountains were lonely places and the settlers were cut off from the "outside" world. They had to depend on themselves and their neighbors for entertainment. So they sang the songs they had sung at home. Here is one of the songs they sang.

1. Ev - 'ry night _____ when the sun goes in, _____
Refrain True love, don't weep, _____ true _____ love, don't mourn;

Ev - 'ry night _____ when the sun goes in, _____
True love, don't weep, _____ true _____ love, don't mourn;

Ev - 'ry night _____ when the sun goes in _____
True love, don't weep, _____ true _____ love, don't mourn.

I hang _____ my head _____ and mourn - ful cry. _____
I'm go - ing a - way _____ to Mar - ble - town. _____

2. How I wish that train would come (*3 times*)
   And take me back where I come from.
   Refrain

Good Morning, Blues

WORDS AND MUSIC BY HUDDIE LEDBETTER

New words & new music arrangement by Huddie Ledbetter. Edited with new additional material by Alan Lomax. TRO—© Copyright 1959 Folkways Music Publishers, Inc., New York, New York. Used by permission.

Blues is the name given to a type of song first sung in America and now known throughout the world. The melodies of these songs often include blue notes which give a mournful or melancholy feeling.

Listen for the blue note in this song.

1. Good morn - ing, blues; blues, how do you do?
2. Called yes - ter - day, here you come to - day.

Good morn - ing, blues; blues, how do you do?
Called yes - ter - day, here you come to - day.

I'm do - ing all right,___ good morn - ing, how are you?
Your mouth's ___ wide o - pen but you don't know what to say.

PLAN A PERFORMANCE

• As you sing "Good Morning Blues," clap a rhythm pattern to fill in the break in the melody at the end of each phrase.

• Improvise a rhythm pattern as you strum the Autoharp chords.

• Fill in the break at the end of each phrase by playing a pattern on a percussion instrument of your choice.

Springtime (La Primavera)

SPANISH FOLK SONG FROM CALIFORNIA

ENGLISH WORDS BY MARGARET MARKS

The Spanish-speaking people who settled in California brought their songs with them. They also brought the sounds of soft-strumming guitars and clicking castanets.

Here is a rhythm pattern you might find in many songs of Spanish origin. Try playing it on castanets as an introduction and throughout the song.

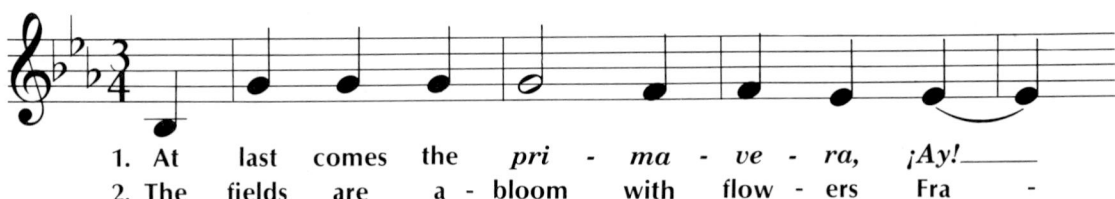

1. At last comes the *pri - ma - ve - ra,* ¡Ay!____
2. The fields are a - bloom with flow - ers Fra -

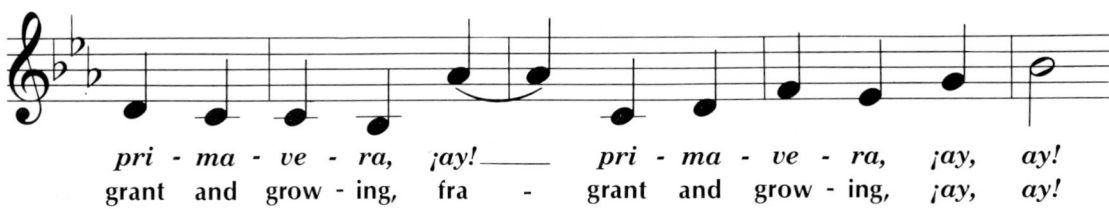

pri - ma - ve - ra, ¡ay!____ *pri - ma - ve - ra,* ¡ay, ay!
grant and grow - ing, fra - grant and grow - ing, ¡ay, ay!

The deep win - ter snows are melt - ing high____
The or - chards are bright with blos - soms ra -

in the sier - ra, high____ in the sier - ra.____
diant and glow - ing, ra - diant and glow - ing.____

MELODY

Soft winds are blow - ing,_____ Blue_____
Birds sing a greet - ing,_____ Birds_____

COUNTERMELODY

Ah_____ Ah_____

sky is show - ing._____ Through the emp - ty a -
sing a greet - ing._____ Neigh - bors walk in the

Ah_____

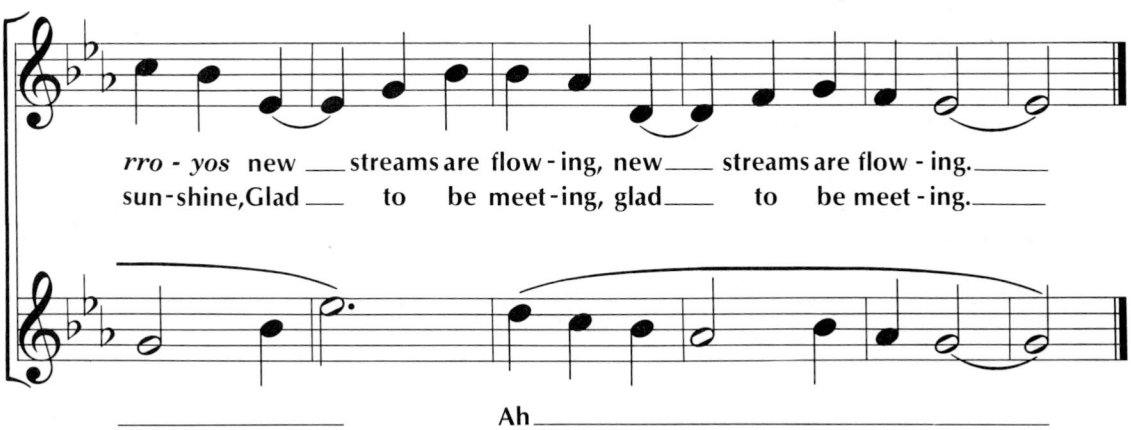

rro - yos new ___ streams are flow - ing, new ___ streams are flow - ing._____
sun - shine, Glad ___ to be meet - ing, glad ___ to be meet - ing._____

Ah_____

3. At evening the sounds of music
   Fill my *hacienda*, fill my *hacienda*, ¡ay, ay!
   A Spanish guitar is throbbing,
   Thrilling and tender, thrilling
      and tender.

   Heels start a-tapping,
   Hands in rhythm clapping.
   Castañetas are clicking,
   Fingers are snapping, fingers
      are snapping.

La Jesusita

FOLK SONG FROM MEXICO   ENGLISH VERSION BY M. BUDLONG AND R. JACQUES

Aaron Copland, a well-known American composer, used the melody of this Mexican folk song in a piece for orchestra called *El Salon Mexico.*

A light gui-tar in the dusk soft-ly strum-ming,_____

From near and far now the danc-ers are com-ing._____

The gold-en lan-terns a-bove them are swing-ing,_____

And on the soft eve-ning air voi-ces ring, tra la la la!

And then there comes Je-su-si-ta, The stars twin-kle far a-bove;___

She danc-es with grace and beau-ty, And ten-der-ly sings of love.

Crescent Moon

CHINESE FOLK SONG   ENGLISH WORDS BY ELAINE NIENOW

13

Many of the folk songs we sing in this country came from faraway places. This one comes from China.

1. Cres - cent moon float-ing on a cloud   O'er the crest of the
2. Night - in - gale sing-ing in the wood,   Ser - e - nad - ing the
3. Lo - tus blooms rise a-bove the streams,   Love - ly wax - en per-

mount - tain.   Sil - ver gem in a sat - in crown,
for - est,   Fills the air with a sad re - frain
fec - tion,   Slow - ly o - pen to view the world,

Rest - ing on the roy - al moun - tain.   Pale moon, new moon,
In the qui - et of the eve - ning.   Sweet song, fair song,
Slow - ly spread their silk - en pet - als.   Wild flow'r, pink flow'r,

cres-cent moon____ Shin - ing bright-ly o - ver K'an - ting.
lone - ly song____ Ech - o ing through all of K'an - ting.
fleet - ing flow'r____ Grow - ing in the streams of   K'an - ting.

Recorder

Recorder   **Last measure**

263

So Long (Dusty Old Dust)

WORDS AND MUSIC BY WOODY GUTHRIE

13

Woody Guthrie composed more than a thousand songs. Most of them are written in the style of folk songs. Like all folk songs, they tell about people and their ways of living. Woody called his songs *singing history.*

Guthrie wrote this song during the 1930s, when most of the Southwest was turned into a "dust bowl." Although dust and gloom hung like a curtain over much of the land, people managed to keep a sense of humor.

When you know the melody of "So Long," you might want to try singing the countermelody in the refrain.

1. I've sung this song but I'll sing it a - gain, Of the place where I
2. A dust storm hit and it hit____ like thunder, It____ dust - ed us

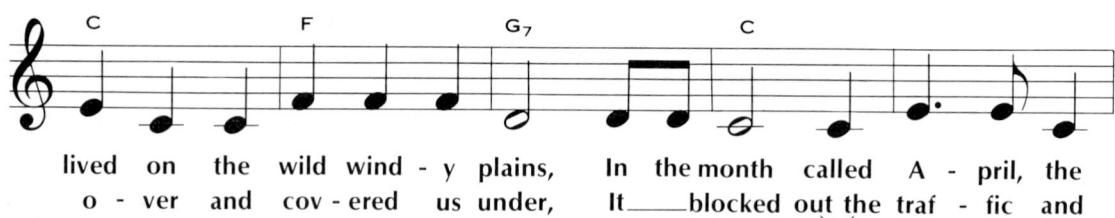

lived on the wild wind - y plains, In the month called A - pril, the
o - ver and cov - ered us under, It____blocked out the traf - fic and

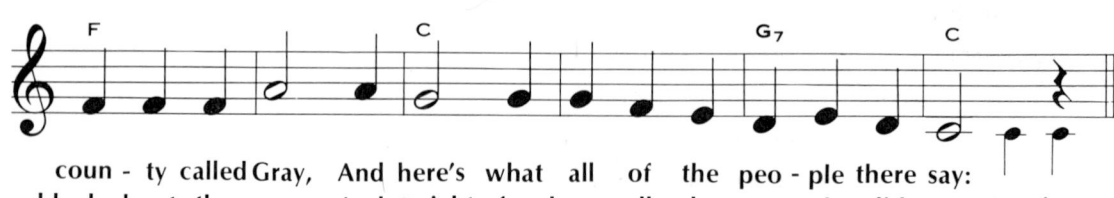

coun - ty called Gray, And here's what all of the peo - ple there say:
blocked out the sun, And straight for home all the peo - ple did run, sing - ing:

264

REFRAIN

COUNTERMELODY

So long! So long!

MELODY

"So long, it's been good to know you, So long, it's

So long!_____ So_____

been good to know you, So long, it's been good to

long! So long! So

know you, This dust-y old dust is a-get-ting my

long! So_____ long!_____

home, I've got to be mov-ing a-long."_____

3. We talked of the end of the world, and then
   We'd sing a song, and then sing it again.
   We'd set for an hour and not say a word,
   And then these words would be heard:
   Refrain

265

The Stars and Stripes Forever

WORDS AND MUSIC BY JOHN PHILIP SOUSA

13

John Philip Sousa was best known as a band conductor and a composer of marches. He was often referred to as "The March King." For many years Sousa was the leader of the Marine Band, the official band of the President of the United States. Many of Sousa's marches are still heard today in parades and at football games.

Hur - rah for the flag of the free,_____ May it

wave as our stand - ard for - ev - er, The gem of the

land and the sea,_____ The ___ ban - ner of the right.__

____ Let des - pots re - mem - ber the day_____

When our fa - thers with might - y en - deav - or

Pro - claimed as they marched to the fray_____

That by their might and by their right it waves for - ev - er!

Glossary

absolute music Music that has no suggestion of any nonmusical thing, idea, story, or event (see program music).

accent A single tone or chord louder than those around it.

accompaniment Music that supports the sound of a solo performer.

atonal Music in which no single tone is a "home base" or "resting place."

ballad In music, a song that tells a story.

beat A repeating pulse that can be felt in some music.

cadence A group of chords or notes at the end of a phrase or piece that gives a feeling of pausing or finishing.

call and response A musical device with a portion of a melody (call) followed by an answering portion (response). The response may imitate the call or it may be a separate melody that repeats each time.

canon A device in which a melody begins in one part, and then is imitated by other parts in an overlapping fashion (see round).

chant To sing in a manner approximating speech.

chord Three or more different tones played or sung together.

chord pattern An arrangement of chords into a small grouping, usually occurring often in a piece.

chorus (See refrain.)

clef A sign that tells where pitches are located on the staff. The sign 𝄞 (G clef, or treble clef) shows that G above middle C is on the second line. This clef is used for music in higher registers. The sign 𝄢 (F clef, or bass clef) shows the tone F below middle C on the fourth line. It is used for music in lower registers.

cluster A group of tones very close together performed at the same time; used mostly in modern music.

composer A person who makes up pieces of music by putting sounds together in his or her own way.

contour The "shape" of a melody, made by the way it moves upward and downward in steps and leaps, and by repeated tones.

contrast Two or more things that are different. In music, slow is a *contrast* to fast; section A is a *contrast* to section B.

countermelody A melody that is played or sung at the same time as the main melody.

density The thickness or thinness of sound.

duration The length of sounds, from very short to very long.

dynamics The loudness and softness of sounds.

elements The parts out of which whole works of art are made: for example, music uses the *elements* melody, rhythm, texture, tone color, form; painting uses line, color, space, shape, etc.

ensemble A group of players or singers.

fermata A sign (⌒) indicating that a note is held longer than its written note value, stopping or "holding" the beat.

frets Strips of metal across the fingerboard of guitars and similar instruments. The player raises the pitch of a string by pressing it into contact with a fret.

form The overall plan of a piece of music.

fugue A musical procedure based on imitation, in which the main melody (subject) and related melodies are repeated in higher and lower registers and in different keys. The texture is polyphonic.

ground A melody pattern repeated over and over in the bass (lowest part) of a piece, while other things happen above it.

harmony Two or more tones sounding at the same time.

improvisation Making up music as it is being performed; often used in jazz.

interval The distance between tones. The smallest interval in traditional Western music is the half-step (f–f♯, f♯–g, etc.), but contemporary music and music of other cultures often use smaller intervals.

jazz A style that grew out of the music of black Americans, then took many different substyles—ragtime, blues, cool jazz, swing, bebop, rock, etc.

key The particular scale on which a piece of music or section is based, named for its tonic, or key-tone, or "home-base" tone. (The key of D major indicates that the major scale starting and ending on the tone D is being used. *See* tonality.)

major scale An arrangement of eight tones in a scale according to the following intervals, or steps: whole, whole, half, whole, whole, whole, half.

267

measure A grouping of beats set off by bar lines.

melody A line of single tones that move upward, downward, or repeat.

melody pattern An arrangement of pitches into a small grouping, usually occurring often in a piece.

meter The way the beats of music are grouped, often in sets of two or in sets of three. The meter signature, or time signature, such as $\frac{3}{4}$ or $\frac{4}{4}$, tells how many beats are in the group, or measure (top number), and the kind of note that gets one beat (bottom number).

minor scale Several arrangements of eight tones in a scale, such as *natural minor* (whole, half, whole, whole, half, whole, whole) and *melodic minor* (upward: whole, half, whole, whole, whole, whole, half; downward: whole, whole, half, whole, whole, half, whole).

notes Symbols for sound in music.

octave The distance of eight steps from one tone to another that has the same letter name. On the staff these steps are shown by the lines and spaces. When notes are an *octave* apart, there are eight lines and spaces from one note to the other.

ornamentation In the arts, the addition of decorations, or embellishments, to the basic structure of the work.

ostinato A rhythmic or melodic phrase that keeps repeating throughout a piece or a section of a piece.

pattern In the arts, an arrangement of an element or elements into a grouping, usually occurring often in the work (*see* elements).

phrase A musical sentence. Each *phrase* expresses one thought. Music is made up of *phrases* that follow one another in a way that sounds right.

pitch The highness or lowness of a tone.

polyrhythm Several different rhythm patterns going on at the same time, often causing conflicts of meter among them.

program music Music that suggests or describes some nonmusical idea, story, or event (*see* absolute music).

range In a melody, the span from the lowest tone to the highest tone.

refrain A part of a song that repeats, with the same music and words. It is often called the "chorus," since it is usually sung by all the singers, while the verses in between are often sung by one voice.

register The pitch location of a group of tones (*see* pitch). If the group of tones are all high sounds, they are in a high *register*. If the group of tones are all low sounds, they are in a low *register*.

repetition Music that is the same, or almost the same, as music that was heard earlier.

rests Symbols for silences in music.

rhythm The way movement is organized in a piece of music, using beat, no beat, long and short sounds, meter, accents, no accents, tempo, syncopation, etc.

rhythm pattern A pattern of long and short sounds.

rondo A musical form in which a section is repeated, with contrasting sections in between (such as A B A C A).

round A kind of canon that leads back to the beginning of the melody and starts all over again (circle canon).

scale An arrangement of pitches from lower to higher according to a specific pattern of intervals. Major, minor, pentatonic, whole-tone, and chromatic are five kinds of scales. Each one has its own arrangement of pitches.

sequence The repetition of a melody pattern at a higher or lower pitch level.

solo Music for a single player or singer, often with an accompaniment.

staff A set of five horizontal lines on which music notes are written.

style The overall effect a work of art makes by the way its elements are used (*see* elements). When works of art use elements similarly, they are said to be "in the same style."

subject *See* fugue.

syncopation An arrangement of rhythm in which prominent or important tones begin on weak beats or weak parts of beats, giving a catchy, off-balance movement to the music.

tempo The speed of the beat in a piece of music (*see* beat).

texture The way melody and harmony go together: a melody alone, two or more melodies together, or a melody with chords.

theme An important melody that occurs several times in a piece of music.

tonal Music that focuses on one tone that is more important than the others—a "home base"—or resting tone.

tonality The kind of scale, major or minor, on which a piece of music or section is based (*see* key).

tone color The special sound that makes one instrument or voice sound different from another.

tone row An arrangement of the twelve tones of the chromatic scale into a series in which there is no focus on any one of them as the home tone. When the series is played backward, it is called the "retrograde."

triplet A rhythm pattern made by dividing a beat into three equal sounds.

variation Music that is repeated but changed in some important way.

Index

Acknowledgments

Credit and appreciation are due publishers and copyright owners for use of the following.

"African Dance" copyright 1926 by Alfred A. Knopf, Inc., renewed 1954 by Langston Hughes. From SELECTED POEMS of Langston Hughes. Reprinted by permission of Alfred A. Knopf, Inc.

"Night" from COLLECTED POEMS by Sara Teasdale. Copyright 1930 by Sara Teasdale Filsinger, renewed 1958 by Guaranty Trust Co. of New York, Executor. Reprinted by permission of Macmillan Publishing Co., Inc.

"The Night Will Never Stay" from ELEANOR FARJEON'S POEMS FOR CHILDREN. Copyright 1951 by Eleanor Farjeon. Renewed 1979 by Gervase Farjeon. By permission of J.B. Lippincott, Publisher and Harold Ober Associates.

"Snatch of Sliphorn Jazz" from GOOD MORNING AMERICA, copyright, 1928, 1956, by Carl Sandburg. Reprinted by permission of Harcourt Brace Jovanovich, Inc.

Picture Credits

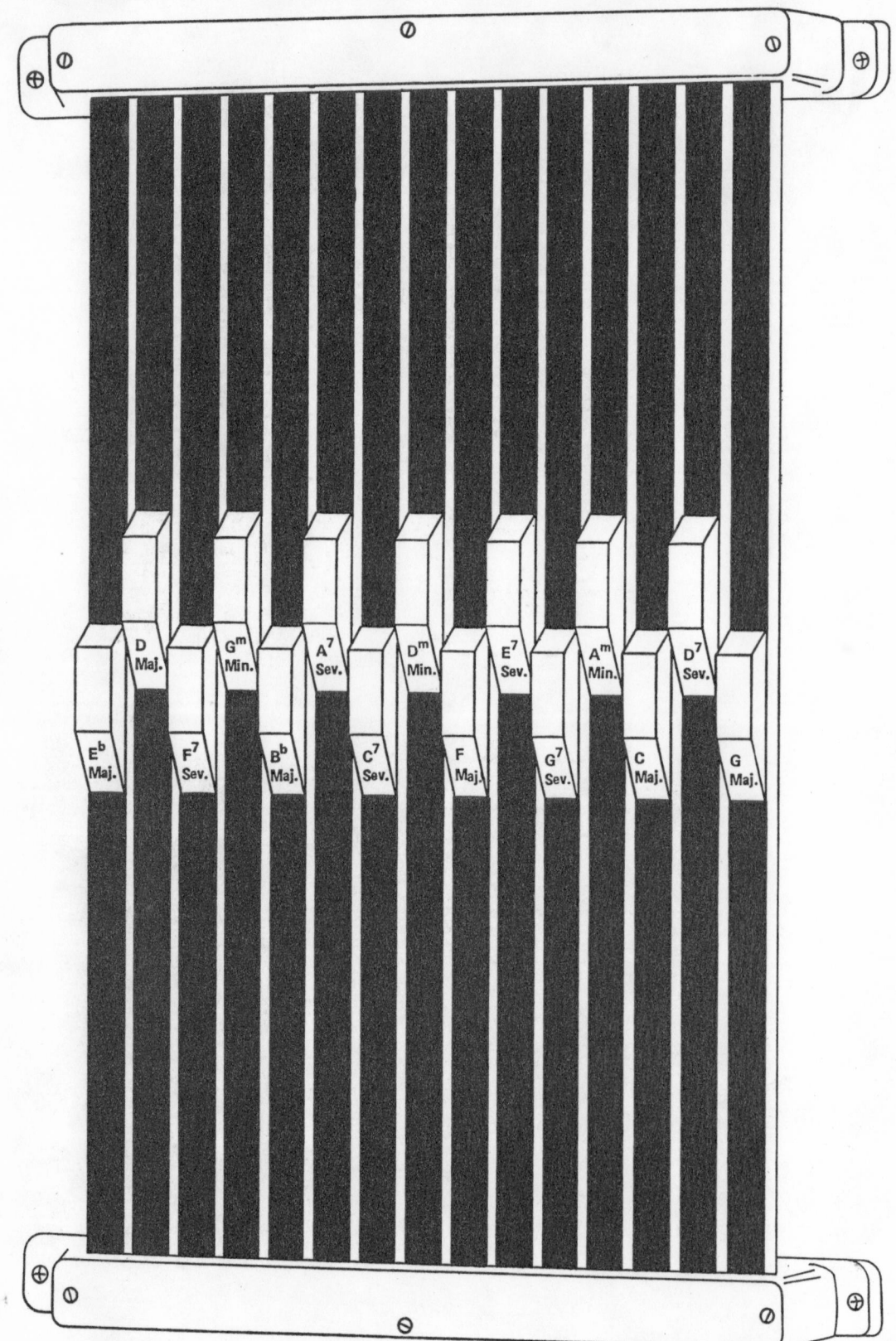